Praise for

THE RECKONINGS

"Looking for literature that will help you process the injustices and frustrations of today? Listen to Lacy M. Johnson, the sage we need. . . . A revelatory must-read."

—Refinery29

"*The Reckonings* is not a book about changing the world. It's philosophy in disguise, equal parts memoir, criticism, and ethics. It has bits of Eula Biss, Leslie Jamison, and Simone Weil, but its patron saint is Grace Paley."

—NPR

"In this searching collection of essays . . . Johnson explores ideas of justice, retribution, and mercy."

—Newsday

"A collection that converses with itself and the reader, asking us to question our beliefs and our roles in a system that perpetuates violence."

—The Millions

"The twelve essays collected in *The Reckonings* form a kind of song cycle on the subject of justice, with recurring motifs and a *basso continuo* of moral urgency. Themes develop, intersect, change key. . . . Johnson dexterously arranges these disparate topics into a larger unity."

—*The Texas Observer*

"[Johnson's] essays on the violence humans inflict on each other and the earth—including racism, misogyny, and a variety of pollutions—challenge our culture's expectations of justice and expose the limits of vengeance and mercy."

—*Ms. Magazine*

"*The Reckonings* is a beautiful and complicated collection of essays. . . . A gorgeous combination of personal narrative and investigative journalism, these essays ask more questions than they answer—in the best possible way."

—*Book Riot*

"Johnson writes with palpable compassion and brilliance, illuminating her deep humanity, while imbuing it in equal measure in the people she writes about and quotes."

—*Literary Hub*

"This essay collection, which deals with bleeding-edge issues like sexual violence, social justice, and the misuse of power, feels like a necessary read for our times."

—*Electric Literature*

"In *The Reckonings*, Lacy M. Johnson reflects on justice and retribution and raises difficult questions, all while using her own personal experiences with violence and injustice, as well as examples that affect the masses."

—*Bustle*

"These essays attempt to parcel out several knotted problems and suggest forms of meaningful justice. . . . Johnson's questions and answers are hard but necessary."

—*Booklist*, starred review

"Johnson excels at providing critical analysis of social justice and uses a variety of works, including mythology and film, to make the case for forging ahead with mercy and compassion."

—*Library Journal*

"[Johnson] makes a plea for activism, art, and . . . common decency . . . [in this] thoughtful and probing collection."

—*Kirkus Reviews*

"As ever, Lacy M. Johnson's work here is ambitious and brave, and with *The Reckonings* she has written an essential book about what it means to emerge from darkness, bounding step by bounding step."

—Wendy S. Walters, author of
Multiply/Divide and *Troy, Michigan*

THE RECKONINGS

ESSAYS ON JUSTICE FOR THE TWENTY-FIRST CENTURY

LACY M. JOHNSON

SCRIBNER

NEW YORK LONDON TORONTO SYDNEY NEW DELHI

Scribner

An Imprint of Simon & Schuster, Inc.

1230 Avenue of the Americas

New York, NY 10020

First Scribner trade paperback edition June 2019

SCRIBNER and design are registered trademarks of The Gale Group, Inc.,
used under license by Simon & Schuster, Inc., the publisher of this work.

For information about special discounts for bulk purchases,
please contact Simon & Schuster Special Sales at 1-866-506-1949
or business@simonandschuster.com.

The Simon & Schuster Speakers Bureau can bring authors to your live event.
For more information or to book an event, contact the Simon & Schuster Speakers
Bureau at 1-866-248-3049 or visit our website at www.simonspeakers.com.

Interior design by Kyle Kabel

Manufactured in the United States of America

3   5   7   9   10   8   6   4   2

Library of Congress Control Number: 2018038664

ISBN 978-1-5011-5900-8
ISBN 978-1-5011-5901-5 (pbk)
ISBN 978-1-5011-5902-2 (ebook)

Certain names and identifying details have been changed.

"On Mercy," "The Fallout," and a portion of "Speak Truth to Power"
(as "Trigger") originally appeared in *Guernica*, and "Trigger" also appeared in
The Kiss: Intimacies from Writers. A slightly different version of "Art in the Age of
Apocalypses" was published online by *Tin House*. "Girlhood in a Semibarbarous
Age" appeared in a very different form (as "I Don't Want to Be a Girl") at *Dame*.

Excerpt from "The Snowfall Is So Silent" by Miguel de Unamuno
from *Roots & Wings*, ed. Hardie St. Martin, © 1976, 2005 by Hardie St. Martin.
Used by permission of White Pine Press.

for you, with love

The unendurable is the beginning of the curve of joy.

—Djuna Barnes, *Nightwood*

CONTENTS

THE RECKONINGS

THE RECKONINGS

Usually it is a woman who asks the question—always the same question. She is sitting near the door in the last row of the auditorium, having spent the last hour listening to me talk about what it means to have once been kidnapped and raped by a man I loved, a man with whom I lived, a man who even before the kidnapping had already violated me in every way you might imagine possible, especially if you were a man like him. Someone else in the audience asks what happened to the man, and I explain how he got away, how he is a fugitive living in Venezuela, raising a new family. This is not the ending anyone expects.

Now the woman has a question. She raises her hand, and when I call on her, always last, she stands and speaks in a clear, assertive voice: "What do you want to have happen to him, to the man who did this to you?" By "this" I know she means not only the actual crime the man committed but also all of the therapy, the nightmares and panic attacks, the prescribed medication and self-medication, the healing and self-harm. "I mean, you probably want him dead, right?"

No, I think. "No," I say out loud. Her expression crumples; she looks confused. Everyone in the audience looks confused. This isn't supposed to be how the story ends; it's not the ending they want for themselves, for me.

The women at the book club don't want this ending either. They are sitting around a long oak dining table in the home of our gracious host, who brings food out in many courses, during each of which the wine flows freely. They ask questions, mostly bookish ones, but eventually the conversation turns to the man I lived with, to how he got away.

"I'd kill him for you," one says.

"I'd kill him on the spot," says another.

They carry guns in their purses, they have told me. Maybe they are angry enough to use them.

One brings up a story she heard earlier in the day: a local man has been convicted of a boy's murder. The boy was seven when the local man raped him; he turned eight on the day the local man burned him alive. The boy survived long enough to implicate the man, who was charged with capital murder after the boy died. He was tried, convicted, and sentenced to forty years in prison.

"Justice has been served," one of the women in the book club says.

"How is this justice?" asks another. "He's going to spend the next forty years living off our taxes."

"He should be burned alive," the host says, "the same way he tried to kill that boy."

She has been quiet the entire evening, in and out of the kitchen, up and down from her chair. Now she is seated at the head of the table, looking at her hands, which twist and untwist an ironed napkin over the middle of her plate. "What do *you* want to have happen to him?" she asks me.

This woman, like every other woman who asks the question, sits with her back to the wall, like I do when I have the choice, or near the door in the last row of every auditorium. Sometimes she is my mother's age, or my age: she wears oversized sweaters, little makeup, pulls back her hair in a simple bun. She does not want attention. She has children, like I do, and like I do, she sometimes struggles to love them well. She will tell me this after I have finished answering questions, when I am sitting at a little table signing books. She has a story that is similar to mine "in ways," and she doesn't even know what to feel about it anymore.

Sometimes the woman sitting near the door, or against the wall, is an old woman with crepe paper hands. Sometimes she is not a woman but a man—an old man my father's age in a ten-gallon hat, who tells me he was raped by an uncle when he was the age of my son. Or the person who asks the question is a man young enough to be my son if I had started much earlier, who tells me the question is for himself, or for his girlfriend. They both have a story like mine, he says, and they have not yet found an ending to it. I am surprised at how the people sitting near the door in the last row of the auditorium always have a story like mine.

I carry these stories with me because I don't know what else to do with them. The details may differ. If it is not the story of an abusive lover, perhaps it is a mother, or a father, or an uncle; or it is the story of a friend who has been killed by a stranger while trying to do the right thing, or a woman who is shot in the back of the head while asking for help; it might be a story about the abuse of power, or authority, of the slow violence of bureaucracy, of the way some people are born immune from punishment and others spend whole lifetimes being punished in ways they did nothing to deserve.

In my story, there was a man I once loved very much, and because of the self-destructive way in which I loved him, I didn't want to leave him when he abused me first with his words and then with his fists. I told myself I could fix him. That this wasn't who he was, not really. I let him keep showing me who he really was until I finally believed him and left.

I had already lived a few lives by that time, I thought—a farm girl from Missouri, a door-to-door steak salesperson, a sex worker, a model in New York, a survivor of domestic violence and sexual assault—but I was afraid none of these lives had sufficiently prepared me to live the one I wanted more than anything else. I had only just begun thinking of myself as a writer around that time, but I told myself I had probably not read enough books, had not visited enough continents, was not smart enough or wise enough, didn't have anything to say, and no one would want to hear it if I did. I thought there had been a mistake in the cosmic register. Somewhere there was another Lacy Johnson who could keep straight when to use *lay* instead of *lie*, who actually belonged in all the places I began finding myself, who deserved all the good things that suddenly seemed to be happening to me.

This is all to say that the worst violence that man committed was not against my body but against the story I told about the person I believed myself to be.

I was twenty-one when that man kidnapped and raped me and tried, but failed, to kill me. The man got away, and I got away; he is a fugitive living in Venezuela, and I am a writer of books. The last one I wrote was about him, about the day he meant to kill me but I lived. It was not easy, not the writing and not the living—not until I often found myself standing in front of strangers telling them there is justice for me in standing here, in this room, alive and breathing and telling my story with my own voice.

It is not the ending to the story anyone expects—not even the one they want, because they want a return, a redemption, a retrieval of all I had lost for my part in the story; they want suffering for him. They want blood, guts, gore.

Now that *would be justice,* they think.

My mom tells me she wants him dead. She has just read the book—even though I told her not to, even though she told me she wouldn't. She, like the woman sitting at the head of the table in the book club and like the woman sitting near the door in the last row of the auditorium, feels unsatisfied by the story I have told about my life, because it cannot be reconciled to all she has been told about how these things should end: that the man who did the terrible thing should suffer as much as I have suffered, and as much as she has suffered, if not more. In all of the movies she has seen, this is how it goes: the person who has done a terrible thing falls from a very tall building, or is incinerated in a ball of white-hot flames, or is shot in the dark by police, or at the very least is led away in handcuffs. She wants an ending like that for herself, for me.

I also watch these movies on occasion, and I admit there is a certain satisfaction when Uma Thurman's Beatrix Kiddo finally kills Bill on the patio of his villa with the five-point exploding heart technique. He knows what he has done, why she has come; he does not even try to stop her. I take pleasure watching Noomi Rapace as Lisbeth Salander condemn her rapist by tattooing that word into his chest. She violates him in the same ways he violated her, and a few more for good measure. When Sophie Turner's Sansa Stark allows Ramsay's own dogs to eat him alive, she smiles a little, and there is something in me that smiles also. These men deserve this punishment, the stories tell us, and it feels good to see someone get what he deserves.

I know this is spectacle, entertainment, not actual life, though life also has its share of spectacles. I would be horrified, find I often am, to see anyone actually murdered, much less tortured, out of some thirst for revenge. The spectacle reinforces over and over a story I want to believe about the world even though I have never yet witnessed it for myself: that everything will come out right in the end, that bad things eventually happen to bad people, that good people eventually receive all the blessings they deserve. *Everyone gets their just desserts*, the story tells me so I can go on.

But what if that doesn't happen? What if, as in my story, the person who does the terrible thing more or less gets away with it? Does that mean there is no justice to be had or made or found? What does justice look like in a situation where the crime is not intimate and personal but massive and public, and there is no one person to blame? What if the wrong person is blamed? What if we punish the right person but in the course of doing so cause unnecessary pain? What if we ourselves feel pain by performing this duty of punishing person after person, day after day? How could we not? What does justice look like in these situations? Is justice even a "real" thing that any of us can achieve at all?

There is a story we have each heard from birth that when someone does something bad, something bad should happen to that person in return and that this turnabout is justice. This story is a very old one, I've learned, older even than the law of an eye for an eye we find in the Old Testament, traceable back to the pre-Babylonian period, to the Code of Hammurabi, the oldest surviving record of ancient law:

> If a man has put out the eye of a free man, put out his eye.
> If he breaks the bone of a free man, break his bone.
> If he puts out the eye of a serf, or breaks the bone of a
>   serf, he shall pay one mina of silver.

This is the *lex talionis*—the law of retaliation—written more than five thousand years ago when vengeance ran amok, when a man might steal his neighbor's cow, for instance, and the neighbor would respond by murdering that neighbor's entire family. As we tell it now, the lex talionis is mandate — you *must* put out his eye — but the law was in fact meant to put a limit on vengeful action, to curb what humans understood to be our baser instincts.

Then, as now, we want to transform our suffering: to take a pain we experience and change it into the satisfaction of causing pain for someone else. We watch Clint Eastwood as Josey Wales turn his grief into hatred in order to pick up a gun, and watch Ving Rhames as Marsellus Wallace turn his terror and near annihilation into the promise of "going medieval" on his rapists, and us as his audience into accessories to all the suffering this promise might mean.

"To see another suffer is pleasant," Nietzsche writes; "to make another suffer is still more pleasant." He's thinking in particular of how tempting it is to imagine punishment as a kind of redemption for guilt — the German word *shuld* means both "guilt" and "debt," and one primary meaning of the word *redemption* was to buy that debt back — a trick of the mind that tells us that every injury has some equivalent of pain or sacrifice. There is, as Nietzsche points out, a strange accounting in this: a crime creates a debt; the criminal becomes a debtor, the victim his creditor, whose compensation is the particular pleasure of bearing witness to a cruel and exacting punishment.

———

Is that justice? Would I cheer, and cry, and jump up and down if the man who kidnapped and raped me were kidnapped and raped, and beaten, if I could grind him down with my rage until there was almost nothing left of him? If I could watch him suffer in all the ways he made me suffer or, better yet, cause that suffering myself? The story tells me to imagine it would feel satisfying: a release of adrenaline or perhaps the relief from it. *Catharsis: a cleansing.* To be honest, I'm not sure what justice is supposed to feel like. There is a shut place I carry inside me. If I caused him to suffer, would that go away?

I have found photographs of him on the Internet that suggest he is living with a woman who has given birth to two of his children, both girls. In the photos, he is as unhappy in his new life as he ever was in the one he lived with me. On vacation, he grows sullen because the trip isn't going his way, and when the family joins him in the ocean he frowns and looks away from the camera, afraid of being recognized, of what the photograph will reveal. The older daughter, who is the same age as my son, sits on her mother's lap, the mother who is love and safety, who makes a wall with her body between the daughter and him. Does he notice she does this? He holds the baby a little above his lap and away from his body. At a party, he dances back and forth in front of the children, and also their parents who are watching, because he has an audience, and in public he performs a version of himself who is charming, who is fun to be around, who is everything anyone ever wanted a person to be. Behind closed doors, he is angry and irritable, a man so fragile and insecure that he rages at anyone who does not reflect back the version of himself he wants to see. This is why his wife and daughters look, in the photographs, a little hollowed out inside. I can see everything he is doing to them. Everything he has already done.

You probably want him dead, strangers tell me.

"If we know in what way society is unbalanced, we must do what we can to add weight to the lighter scale," Simone Weil once wrote. In the years since I left that man, I have fallen in love many times, made a father out of a man I met on the Internet. I have created life, written whole worlds, outlined entire moral geographies for two barely domesticated children, and have learned to welcome the strangers who arrive at the doorstep of my soul. I've called myself a writer now more than half of my life, and during all this time, I have learned that sometimes the hardest and most important work I've done has meant turning a story I couldn't tell into one that I can—and that this practice on its own is one not only of discovery but of healing.

Is justice a story about healing? Justice is blind, we are told; it is served, maybe like a severed head on a plate. It is a destination, the path to which is long and sometimes crooked and bent. The Roman emperor Nero called it justice when he threw Christians to the beasts in the Colosseum. For some, justice means sticking to the laws, or enforcing them. For others, it means helping friends and harming enemies. Aristotle observed that justice, like language, is a "special characteristic" of humans. Plato suggested that justice is "an inward grace."

"Might is right" is another enduring view—*might* meaning violence, of course, and violence being the opposite of grace.

More than anything else, what I want is a reckoning. Not only for myself, not only for him. I want it for everyone who asks the question: the woman with the crepe paper hands, the man in the ten-gallon hat, the boy who burned and his mother who must have barely lived. I want a reckoning for the woman shot in the back of the head and the man killed while running away—for the children who survive him. I want a reckoning for the person who believes he deserves to take life, and for the person who has been sentenced to offer his. I want a reckoning for all the wars politicians ask our children to fight on their behalf, and for all the children those wars fail to protect. I want a long line of reckonings. I want the truth told back to us. I want the lies laid bare.

"No," I say to the woman who has asked the question from the back of the room, or from against the wall, or sitting at the head of the table. "I don't want him dead. I want him to admit all the things he did, to my face, in public, and then to spend the rest of his life in service to other people's joy." She is struck silent and leans back in her seat.

This is the ending I want. I don't want him dead. I don't even want him to suffer. More pain creates more sorrow, sometimes generations of sorrow, and it amplifies injustice rather than cancels it out. I want to let go of my anger and fear and pain. I want to let go of the hatred and enmity and spite. I want that shut place to open. The ending I want is inside.

GIRLHOOD IN A SEMIBARBAROUS AGE

In my dream I hear the dog barking. I'm rushing down a hill through the forest and looking over my shoulder. I'm running and hiding and afraid for my life, and all the while the dog is barking. He barks as I open my eyes and adjust to the darkness in my bedroom, and barks as I rise from the bed, and barks as I shuffle to the other side of the house, where I find the dog with his slick black nose inches from the door leading from the kitchen to the garage. My husband is out of town, and the dog has heard a noise outside in the driveway, and now his bark is a deep, frantic alarm. I place my hand on his head, rub his ears. I tell him, "It's okay, buddy. Go back to bed." I rub my thumb through the soft hair on his temples and speak to him in a whisper even though I know he doesn't understand a word I say. The dog barks and growls, his hair standing up on end. I rub the underside of his ears and say, "It's okay, buddy. It's okay."

Back in the bedroom, the documentary I was watching before I fell asleep has continued to play. Werner Herzog is leading his camera crew down a ladder into the limestone cave of Chauvet-Pont-d'Arc, in the Ardèche region of southern France, where a group of spelunkers has discovered the oldest cave paintings in the world. Herzog and his crew make their way through the cave single file. They are instructed not to touch anything, not even to step off the two-foot-wide metal path. In the last and deepest chamber of the cave, the camera focuses briefly on a hanging stone outcrop, on a triangle etched in black charcoal. It's supposed to be a female body, the oldest painting ever found.

Standing in the very back of the farthest, deepest chamber of the cave, the scientist explains that on the other side of the outcrop, the black triangle of the Venus is joined by a second figure, The Sorcerer: a bear-man or mammoth-man who appears to be crossing over the female, consuming her, taking her body for his own.

"And here we are," says the scientist, "some thirty thousand years later, with the myth that has endured until our days." Female and bull. Woman and beast.

I wake up when a hand grabs my nightgown and pulls. My son is climbing into bed next to me, insinuating himself under the covers, laying his head down on my arm. It's bright outside the window already, and we nearly drift back to sleep before I sit straight up, note the time, and then we are all racing to eat and dress and tumble out the door. We drive too fast to school while my son sings a song he has learned and my daughter talks over him about the lessons she will have today.

A talk show plays on the radio: "It's not so much the attacks on the villages but specifically the abductions of girls that is telling them that they should not be going to school. They say girls are supposed to be married and in the home," the guest says before I turn off the radio. My daughter stops talking to listen, then says, "Wait. What happened to the girls?"

I change the subject back to her lessons, to geometry and multiplication and plot maps, to the research she has been doing on the world's smallest island nation, the Republic of Nauru. As she begins telling me about pandan cake, we pull into the parking lot of her school.

She likes to walk to her classroom alone, so I hug her at the gate and watch her go. Today she is wearing leopard-print leggings under floral-printed jean shorts with high-tops and black socks pulled up to her knees. She hasn't brushed her hair in days, and it forms a kind of ratted halo at the back of her head. She tucks one strand of matted hair behind her ear, hikes her backpack over her shoulders, and walks toward her classroom in long, confident strides. She never waves to me, never even looks back.

My son likes to have his hand held, his backpack removed, to thumb-wrestle and win, and then to give me an elaborate high five with one and a half turns, three kisses, and two hugs before he will allow me to leave him with his most beloved teacher in the classroom. By the time I return to the car, the radio segment is over, so I search on my phone for the video that has apparently surfaced. It is fuzzy, out of focus. A man stands in the center of the frame, a machine gun slung over his shoulder. He is flanked by two armed soldiers, both wearing balaclava, both standing still as stone. There's an armored vehicle in the background. The man is laughing and scratching his head. Subtitles scroll at the bottom of the screen while news anchors provide commentary: what the Nigerian government is and isn't doing, the ways the Nigerian military is and isn't corrupt, the role the US government does and doesn't play in all of this. The man in the fuzzy video laughs and gestures and scratches his head while he says: "I repeat, I took the girls! And I will sell them off! In this world there is a market for selling girls!"

No one is in the office when I arrive. I unlock the door, turn on the lights, and put on a pot of coffee. I leave the lights off in the room where my desk is so I can see anyone who comes in before that person sees me. It's one in a set of self-protective habits I have, all of which I do without thinking. There are scissors in a cup near my monitor; I keep them visible and sharp.

I drink a cup of coffee while reading the news and learn there is some controversy surrounding an upcoming retrospective in Japan of the now-deceased Polish-French painter Balthus. Throughout the many decades of his controversial career, Balthus's paintings reflected an ongoing, even obsessive infatuation with prepubescent girls. In one painting, the young girl has her eyes closed, her fingers locked above her head; she raises one foot on the stool in front of her, revealing her white underwear. In another, a partially dressed adult woman holds the undressed school girl across her lap, pulling her hair with one hand, strumming her genitals with the other. The child appears nearly catatonic except that with one hand, she reaches up to pinch the adult woman's right nipple.

Over three years, the painter made ten portraits of this girl, the adolescent daughter of his neighbor; over his career, he painted dozens of portraits of girls around her age, always in some state of vulnerability and undress. He famously claimed a quality of sacredness for his "angels"—that's what he called these girls he painted—rejecting all accusations of eroticism as a perversion in the mind of his viewer. In each painting, the girl closes her eyes, or looks away from the painter's gaze. The violence is insinuated but not explicit. It is art, after all, and art must be, above all other things, beautiful.

I admit: I do not understand what about these paintings is supposed to be beautiful. There is violence here, a brutality that annihilates, that destroys. They give me the same hunted-animal feeling as that painting at the back of the farthest, deepest chamber of the Chauvet cave. The cave was discovered by spelunkers in 1994, when I was sixteen. That same year, Nicole Brown Simpson was found murdered just inside the front door of her Brentwood home. I remember coming home from my after-school job each day to see a recap of the televised murder trial. The chief suspect was her ex-husband, the former football star and actor OJ Simpson.

At the time, I knew very little about Nicole Brown Simpson. I learned from the trial that she had been beautiful, a former model, the mother to OJ's two young children. She had been crowned homecoming queen by her high school football team, had met OJ when she was a girl herself, barely eighteen and just out of high school, working as a waitress in Beverly Hills. After they married, she was a dutiful mother, her friends told reporters, waiting for her children in the car pool lane, shuttling her son to karate and her daughter to dance. "You beat the holy hell out of me & we lied at the X-ray lab & said I fell off a bike," she wrote in a letter to OJ before their divorce.

Photographs from the crime scene appeared on the cover of nearly every tabloid at the supermarket where I worked: photos of the bloody footprints on the floorboards of the white Bronco OJ had driven through Los Angeles in a low-speed chase. Photos of Nicole Brown Simpson's bloody legs sprawled across the sidewalk. The men in my checkout line would gaze—blankly? longingly?—at these photographs while they waited for one another to pay. As one walked out the door, the next approached and turned his gaze to me.

According to the prosecutors' version of events, the murderer knocked Nicole Brown Simpson unconscious, placed his foot on her back, pulled her head up by her hair, and slit her throat, a wound so deep that her severed larynx could be seen through the opening. I remember the day OJ tried on the leather glove found at the murder scene, how he stood from his seat behind the wooden table and tried to pull the leather glove over a white latex glove he wore to protect the evidence. He smirked when he realized it couldn't be done.

I remember how he held his partially gloved hand up for the jury, the cameras. *See? See?*

My students don't see the brutal connection between the Balthus and the Venus painting in the Chauvet cave. I have gotten off topic. Today we are talking about the evolution of feminist art in the second half of the twentieth century, particularly about the history of women painting naked, dancing naked, fighting naked men, rolling on the floor naked covered in raw meat. I am showing clips of Marina Abramović's early performance work; in this video, she is smashing her naked body into the gallery walls. It is upsetting one of my male students. "How is this not pornography?" he asks. He's almost had it with this class, and especially with me, with the "weird sex art" I keep showing them, the "uncomfortable conversations" I keep asking them to have.

"It's rage," I tell my student. "Or perhaps the symptom of it." He's unconvinced, just as frustrated by *Expansion in Space* as he is by Yoko Ono's *Cut Piece*, in which she allows audience members to use a pair of scissors to cut away her clothing. A recording of one performance in 1965 begins with women from the audience climbing onto the stage to snip a portion of Ono's sleeve, a button, a square inch of her collar. They are not practiced in reducing one another in this way. Soon men also join in, one at a time, and cut off long strips of her skirt, her sweater; one cuts off a whole sleeve, and another in the audience cheers him on. One cuts off the front of her sweater, exposing the slip she wears underneath;

he is applauded by other men. Throughout all of this, Ono's face is expressionless, and remains expressionless until a man cuts her slip along the line of her cleavage, revealing her bra, and goes on cutting. She moves her hand slightly to cover her body, an instinct toward modesty. He cuts her bra straps, and she moves her hands up to keep herself covered. He is still cutting when the recording stops.

I watch this performance now, fifty years later, and I can't help grinding my teeth. Here is the lesson all women must learn beginning in girlhood: how to accept the brutality others are willing to commit. Girls are taught that to show anger, to yell, or to fight back is "unladylike." To curse or shout is to be "vulgar," and unattractive and undesirable; and if we are undesirable, we have no value or worth. At all times every day, we are saturated with an ideal of the woman we are all supposed to become: a woman who is soft and pliable, who is round and supple, who is easily overcome, is penetrable, vulnerable—someone who is small and powerless and weak. Each day we see this ideal projected at us from movies; it is sold to us on billboards and in magazines; it arrives as fact each day in the headlines and is reinforced by the mythology of our most ancient art.

There is nothing more sacred in our culture than precisely this: that a woman's body belongs more easily to any man than it does to herself; that every man is allowed to be not only a full and complete person but also, whenever he wants, a total beast.

My student doesn't like *Cut Piece*, and he doesn't like Marina Abramović either: how she yells and curses naked, fights her male collaborator naked, and dances naked to the point of exhaustion, to the point where her nudity doesn't even seem like nudity anymore.

"Why do they always have to be naked?" my male student wants to know.

I ask whether he has this same objection to any of the many traditions of European art by men for other men that take the nude female form as their primary subject. "Think, for example, of *The Birth of Venus*," I say. The nude goddess emerges from the ocean, freshly born and fully mature, covering her body with her hands. Or the *Sleeping Venus*, in which the nude goddess reclines on a pile of blankets on a hillside, one hand behind her head, the other covering her genitalia. Or the *Venus of Urbino*, which depicts a naked woman reclining coyly on an ornate couch, one hand curling inside herself, the other around a cluster of flowers. She looks directly at the viewer, meets his gaze with what we are to understand is a blush of shame or desire. Or both, in turns.

"The artists we are talking about today intervene in the myth of that tradition," I tell my student. He shakes his head. "I just don't get it," he says.

He is being intentionally difficult, I think, because he has been allowed, all his life, to be however he wants. It isn't that he is scandalized by what he sees but by what he refuses to. Earlier this semester, after one of our first classes, he approached me and asked whether I would be interested in "hanging out." Whatever possessed him to proposition me—his professor, a woman nearly old enough to be his mother—it wasn't any idea he has of the woman I am, but his idea of the person, as a woman, I could not possibly be.

I tune into the radio show while I am driving to my children's school and hear the guests agree that there likely won't be justice for the girls. Boko Haram has split them—the nearly three hundred of them—into dozens of groups of maybe five or six. One suggests that many of the girls, if not all of them, have now been smuggled across the border from Nigeria into Cameroon, Chad, or even farther. Another video has apparently surfaced in which the girls recite the first chapter of the Quran. They are dressed head to toe in gray and black veils, eyes down, palms up, their lips barely moving. The leader of Boko Haram is joyous and exultant: "These girls you occupy yourselves with . . . we have already liberated them!"

Boko Haram might use the girls as ransom, the guests say, asking for tens of thousands, if not hundreds of thousands, of dollars in exchange for the girls' return, and if anyone pays it, chances are they will use the money to kidnap more girls, whom they will also ransom. Meanwhile, the kidnapped schoolgirls serve Boko Haram as human shields, preventing the Nigerian Air Force from attacking Boko Haram camps.

The guests on the cable news show agree that as days turn to weeks, which turn to months, and then into years perhaps, the greater the likelihood is that the girls will be used as a form of twisted compensation for new recruits. The leader of Boko Haram has threatened to sell them into marriage "in the market." The guests do not say, but we all know, that a time will come for that final brutality: when we cease to refer to them as girls.

My son runs into my arms as soon as I turn the corner and his embrace nearly knocks me down. I gather his lunch box, and school supplies, and the worksheets he has completed and stuff them into his backpack. The two of us walk hand in hand across the playground in search of my daughter, who likes to hug me only after we are out of sight of all of her friends. She has had an "interesting" day at school, she says.

On the way home, she wants to know what sex is. It's not the first time she has asked. She's in a mixed-age classroom, and her older friends have begun to develop breasts and body odor, moving toward a border she hasn't fathomed yet. I try to deflect the question. I say, "We talked about that the other day, remember? Dad and I said that sex is a way we describe our bodies." She says that isn't what the older boys in her class say. I want to know what these boys say. She looks out the window, furrows her brow, and says, "Something else."

I hear the dog barking even before I open the door. He is barking and barking up to the moment the door is open, and then his tail is wagging, and he is so relieved that he rubs his muzzle over every inch of my legs, and all over my children's faces and in their armpits as they drop their backpacks by the door.

While my son gets a snack from the kitchen, my daughter goes into her room to play with her dolls. She sits on the floor with her long legs folded under her while she changes their shoes and brushes their hair and moves them through a tiny beautiful house. In the tiny kitchen, the dolls decide what kind of tiny cake to eat. In the tiny bathroom, they apply makeup and look in the tiny mirror. *This is how it begins,* I think, *playing along at the game of being beautiful, captive, small.*

I read the mail and water the plants in the garden and put the children's dirty lunch kits in the dishwasher while my son crawls between my legs taking bites of his food and growling like an animal. There's a torn piece of construction paper folded at the bottom of his backpack. Inside is a crude sort of drawing: a wide cloud of black scribbles next to a stick figure that looks vaguely like a dog, or maybe a small bear. He says, "It's you and me, Mommy," his smiling mouth full of apple and string cheese.

Female and bull. Woman and beast. That myth I am supposed to believe haunts my past, and present, and also my future—a threat, or maybe a promise, that is fulfilled in all our days. What kind of man does this myth ask my son to become?

My daughter cries out, "Help!" and I rush to her room, to find that only the dolls are in danger. She has tied the tiny beautiful feet together with rubber bands, the tiny beautiful hands with long pieces of ribbon. She has put all the tiny beautiful dolls together into a box and placed it on a very high shelf.

They call out with my daughter's voice: "Help! Help!"

At night, the dog shuffles with me toward the back of the house where my son sleeps soundly in his room, one hand around his blanket, the other under his cheek. My daughter hears me passing her doorway and asks for a glass of water with ice in it. When I hand her the green plastic cup, she asks what a terrorist is, a word I am at first surprised to learn she has heard. "A person who does terrible things to make other people feel afraid," I say.

"So he's a bad guy," she says with her mouth to the rim of the green plastic cup.

"Yes," I say, thinking it is better, just now, to keep things simple. "A terrorist is a bad guy."

"Sometimes bad guys take girls," she says, the tiny lift of a question mark at the end, to show me she wants to understand the terrible story about the kidnapped school girls we have heard on the news.

"Yes," I say, sitting down on the edge of her bed. "Sometimes bad guys take girls." And I do not say this out loud to her, but this is what keeps me up at night checking all the locks on the doors. I sleep with one eye open because of a danger that I know is real. I do not go running in the dark of early morning without the dog I have trained to protect me because I have been told since birth that I am not strong enough to protect myself. It's why I do not take my eyes off her when she walks away from me, except to see who else might have their eyes on her. It is a lesson I want, very much, to unlearn.

In the darkness of her tiny room, I can see her eyebrows fold together as she hands me the empty cup.

"I don't want to be a girl."

The barking begins while the dog is lying right beside me on the bed and grows louder and louder as he races through the house, sliding toward the door, sounding his frantic alarm. Outside, a man walks his dog in the darkness past our house. Tomorrow, it will be the man who comes to install the washing machine, or to paint the walls, or to deliver a package; the man who delivers pizzas, or flowers, or offers to update our security system; the man who wants to bring us into the fold with his pamphlets and his skinny black tie. The dog growls, his nose to the window, his hair standing up on end. He listens for the threat he believes may be outside.

I stand beside him, my hand on his back, listening also.

THE PRECARIOUS

My father kept two guns in the house where I lived as a child: a shotgun for hunting quail and a rifle that had been his father's, which is what he used to hunt deer. One winter, he showed me how to hold the gun against my shoulder, where the safety was, how to pull the trigger, when to brace for the kick. He emphasized, in his solemn, intimidating way, that shooting even one bullet has an effect that you can't take back. He tossed clay pigeons toward the forest while I fired bullets after them. Each clay pigeon exploded into dozens of pieces once I got the hang of it. He made me learn how to load the rifle—bullets as long and slender as my fingers—and how to load the shotgun, each round a casing that held tiny metal pebbles that would spray in a wide stream, like so many seeds on the wind.

On quail-hunting days, I woke early to dress in my warm-est clothes, ate breakfast quietly in the kitchen, and then went into the garage to put on someone else's coveralls, a kelly green John Deere ski cap, and gloves stiff with someone else's sweat. I slipped into someone's tall boots, left sitting by the back door for all the months and years of my memory.

My father opened the garage door, and as the cold blew in toward us, he gave me a look that contained all the gravity of the moment and held out the shotgun to me.

My father and I walked through the frozen pasture down to the creek bottom while the dog ran ahead, listening, smelling, rooting out the birds. The Earth is so quiet in the winter, the sound turned down, and the color turned down, and also the temperature. I could hear my feet crunching the ground between the frozen turned-down cornstalks, and my breath in the scarf over my face, and my father's feet and the quiet grunts he made getting over a hill. The dog stopped and pointed into a bush. My father gave the signal for me to turn the safety off, to raise the gun and get ready. He reminded me with his eyes to be careful, not to shoot the dog or him or myself accidentally, and gave the command to the dog to flush the birds. My heart raced. The dog followed its nose into the bush. The birds exploded in every direction into the sky. I raised the gun and looked down the end of my barrel, my finger on the trigger.

The words *autopsy* and *atrocity* share an ancient root, I recently learned, a single proto-Indo-European syllable from which we derive dozens of words about seeing—words like *biopsy*, *binocular*, and *optics*, as well as *panopticon*, a device like a telescope once used to "see everything" and also a prison where the warden can see everyone else but remain unseen.

I stumbled across this little fact while looking for a word that might describe all the violence I find myself seeing lately.

It seems that not very long ago, I saw a photograph in the newspaper of three people, shot dead, lying side by side in an empty lot littered with plastic cups and water bottles and bits of trash. I will never forget this photograph and wish I had a word to describe its effect. In the background, there are more people, out of focus. People take cover behind a fence. Emergency responders perform CPR. Right there in the newspaper, next to headlines about the stock market and on the same page as an ad for toothpaste.

What kind of seeing is required to take a photograph like this? What kind of seeing is required to look at it? I learn from the story accompanying this photograph that half an hour earlier, these people were dancing and singing and having a great time. From his hotel room window, the shooter saw thousands of people in the crowd below. From that distance, they were anonymous, meaningless, vulnerable to harm. *More vulnerable than me*, the shooter must have thought, while he spread an arsenal of semiautomatic weapons at his feet.

I was eleven when I went quail hunting with my father for the first and last time. Later that same year, my great-grandmother died of natural causes. She was eighty-nine. I'd never been to a funeral before, but my mother told me I should put on tights and a dress. I rode in the back of a car and sat with my cousins in pews at the church. We passed notes and poked one another in the ribs until the time came to approach the casket. I stood in line, head bowed, until my turn came. I almost didn't recognize her: hands crossed and eyes closed under the too-thick makeup, the too-poofed hair. I couldn't hold back the tears that came and came. I hadn't known her very well, and I wasn't even very sad. But there she was, dead, and before that she had been alive, sitting in a wheelchair in the sunroom of a smelly nursing home and calling us all by the wrong names. In my memory, the light in that sunroom seems to come from everywhere.

Something changed when I saw my great-grandmother's dead body. Something in me broke a little, and then it broke again when a friend crashed her motorcycle in the forest and snapped her neck. There was a wake for her in the middle school gym, all of us looking at the photos of her propped on easels next to her coffin. We held hands, leaned our heads together, passed tissues back and forth down the rows of seats. A year later, one friend drove his truck head-first into another truck on the way home from a football game. I already knew by then what to expect, how to prepare. Another was missing for days before they found him in the barn, a gun still in his mouth, his finger still on the trigger. I stood in the line, looked, one last time, into a face that no longer looked like a person I knew. I feel much older in this memory than the date, 1993, tells me I actually am.

Suddenly I noticed that there was always someone on the bus or at my lunch table talking about a movie a friend or cousin had seen that was rumored to show real footage of people dying—of being killed in executions, suicides, and particularly gruesome road accidents. *Traces of Death*, it was called. I never wanted to watch that movie, but I've since grown so numb to images of extreme violence that it isn't even particularly disturbing to watch it. In the footage of Pennsylvania state treasurer R. Budd Dwyer's live televised suicide, for instance, Dwyer reads a long prepared statement before passing sealed envelopes to his staff. A final brown envelope in his open briefcase on the table contains a .357 Magnum. He pulls it out, waves it around carelessly while people in the audience begin screaming. He holds out his hands, telling them to stop, "or someone is going to get hurt." They go on screaming. He puts the gun in his mouth, pulls the trigger, and slumps to the floor. I barely even flinch.

Both *autopsy* and *atrocity* require a witness—someone who survives, who sees for herself, with her own eyes. But the violence changes the person who looks. I remember seeing a set of photographs of atomic bomb explosions in a required textbook in college: the first three milliseconds of the Trinity test in July 1945. In the first photograph, there is a flash of light; in the second, a warbled, wrinkled, uneven quantum marble, then a larger one, and then a round orb of brilliant light that consumes itself, rolling inward and inward, up and up into the atmosphere. The photographs were taken by Harold Edgerton, an engineer at MIT who invented a device that allowed him to capture images of stopped time: photographs of birds in flight, of gymnasts somersaulting in midair, of a bullet shooting through an apple, exploding from both sides; a bullet shooting through a lemon, a banana, a balloon, a bullet through shattering glass.

The photographs of the Trinity test were in the same textbook as photographs of the carnage of the war that bomb eventually ended, if wars ever in fact end. Right there in our textbooks: a violence that didn't announce itself as violence but as history—piles of bodies in mass graves, arms and legs and shoeless feet, too many bodies to even understand as bodies, as people who had once been.

I met the man who would later kidnap and rape me around that time. He also kept guns in the home where we lived together: one, a rifle for hunting, he said, the other an assault rifle for I knew not what. It was a gun that was illegal to acquire in the state where we lived, though I didn't know that then. I didn't know much of anything then.

One weekend near the end, we took a trip to his stepfather's cabin in the southern part of the state. There was snow on the ground already, and no one had thought to turn the heat on in the cabin or to stock it with firewood so early in the season. His much-younger brother was sitting on the porch when we arrived, a beer in his hand. I got along well with his brother; we were closer in age, and in many ways we had more in common. That night his brother and I were talking about music, maybe, while the man I lived with made dinner, until he came into the room and suggested that if I wasn't planning to fuck him, I should go to bed. I was humiliated but not surprised. It was not the first time he had said something to embarrass me, or more likely to shame me, when he felt like I was getting too relaxed, having too much fun, behaving in a way that was too free. The two of them stayed up late drinking, smoking pot, playing backgammon or chess, while I listened from the bed in the other room, watching my breath billow like a cloud in front of my face, wishing I had a lamp so I could read. I woke up hours later with him pulling my pants to my knees.

The next morning, dressed in the warm clothes I'd brought with me, I put on a pair of hiking boots and a ski cap and Day-Glo vest and followed him to a rickety tree stand, where we sat for hours watching for antlers, listening for the rustling of leaves. We didn't say much to each other, didn't have much to say. We couldn't talk while hunting anyway since it scares away the deer. I watched birds flit from branch to branch, watched light play on the feathers of their wings. We walked through the trees, across the road, down to the bottoms, the gray-brown mud nearly frozen already, the crops long since harvested or plowed back under the earth. We saw no deer the entire day: no buck, no doe, not even a fawn—only a rafter of turkeys, but it wasn't their season. I felt relieved, since I didn't really want to shoot anything anyway. We climbed back through the woods, back toward the cabin, where we spotted his brother's buck hanging from a tree, antlers grazing the ground, the red gash of its belly gaping open, a noose around its hind feet. I gasped, I think.

A fat brown squirrel scurried across the forest floor. The man I lived with told me to shoot it. I didn't want to shoot it, but I knew the danger it would mean to refuse. He and his brother treed the squirrel, kept telling me to shoot it. I missed and missed and missed as the light went on fading. Finally, he came over to where I stood, put his hand on the back of my neck in a way that was not encouraging, not tender. "Aim the gun and shoot it," he said into my ear, a command that contained within it all the violence to which I had already become accustomed. I raised the gun to my shoulder, looked down the barrel at the squirrel looking back at me, fixed my eye on where it clung to the tree.

Violence changes the person who survives to see it, sometimes by making us more capable of violence ourselves. Seven months before I went hunting with the man I lived with, two seventeen-year-old boys killed eleven classmates and one teacher, and then themselves, using a pistol, a machine gun, and a sawed-off shotgun that one boy's eighteen-year-old girlfriend had purchased on their behalf at a gun show. Weeks before, they had filmed themselves practicing with the guns they would use in the massacre. In the footage, they stand on a wooded mountainside, snow still heaped in piles. They take aim at bowling pins and the surrounding cedars, laughing as they examine the slugs buried deep in the bark of the tree. "Imagine that in someone's fucking brain," one says.

After the shooting, footage of children running from the school building played in a loop on the news. I watched from the apartment where I lived with the man who would later try to kill me. I'd never seen anything like it, had no words to describe its effect. The children were a few years younger than me. People blamed the parents, blamed video games, blamed Marilyn Manson, blamed themselves. People examined the photographs from the crime scene for some explanation of how these two boys could have done something like this: the boys lay sprawled together on the floor of the library, blood pooling from their heads, guns under their bodies or at the tips of their fingers. *The explanation is right there*, I thought at the time. When violence becomes easy to see, it becomes so much easier to look.

That rifle, the one I used to kill the squirrel, is the same one the man threatened to shoot me with after I left him, when he kidnapped me from the parking lot of the magazine where I worked and held me captive for five hours. It leaned against the wall outside the soundproof room he had built, where he planned to kill me but failed.

After I escaped, I went to hide at my sister's apartment in a city two hours away. She had a handgun when I got there: a revolver, small and silver, much heavier than it looked. She loaded it and put it in my hand before she left for work. I didn't want to hold it—not the weight of it, not the responsibility of it—and left it sitting on the coffee table right in front of me all night. I tried to imagine myself shooting it, shooting him—I would shoot his kneecaps off, I imagined—but I kept imagining accidentally shooting myself, in the foot, in the leg, accidentally putting it to my temple and pulling the trigger. I never imagined shooting him in a way that might kill him, never in the heart, in the head, in the face. How could I destroy someone I had once loved?

"What allows a life to be visible in its precariousness," Judith Butler asks, "and what is it that keeps us from seeing or understanding certain lives in this way?" I once had a student, a combat veteran, who had been shot in the head in Iraq. He was in a rush, he told me during one of our first meetings, because he was going blind as a result of his injuries. There wasn't any way to stop it, he told me, and he didn't say much more than that about it. He was writing about the war, and in a way about his own role in it, and he needed to finish faster than either of us believed was humanly possible before he lost his sight, couldn't type, could no longer see what he had written, couldn't even look at himself in the mirror.

During this time he was my student, I traveled to a conference to talk about teaching writing and sat on the plane next to another soldier; this one was being deployed for the first time. He sat by the window, his hair shaved nearly off, his face still pocked with acne. He held a piece of folded paper printed with his deployment orders: where and when and to whom to report, how to get there, when to leave, what flight to take, when to arrive. He kept rolling each end of the folded piece of paper together like a scroll, unrolling it and reading again the same few lines, rolling it, unrolling, reading, and rolling, over and over, as if maybe the message might change, as if his future might yet be undetermined. I remembered myself at that age, how wrecked my life was after I had come so close to losing it. I cried the whole flight, wanted to tell him: run, escape, do not lose yourself, stay alive.

"When we are afraid, we shoot," Susan Sontag wrote in *On Photography*. "But when we are nostalgic, we take pictures." I am afraid almost all of the time, but I am not afraid of my own fear, which is why I do not own a gun and never will, but I have shot millions of pictures, which perhaps means I am at least as nostalgic as I am afraid. Pictures of myself in the good blue light of my office, pictures of my husband wrestling with our children, pictures of our children when they wake from sleep with messy hair, pictures of my children on their first days of school. In one photograph of my two children when they are six and two, they balance on a narrow ledge in front of a brick wall. We were on a walk, already twenty minutes in, and had made it only a few yards from our house. My daughter has her back to the camera, her arms extended as she is balancing on the ledge; my son drinks chocolate milk from a box. That was a Thursday. It was a clear, cool afternoon. We went to the park and they played on the jungle gym; both got mulch in their shoes. We walked home and I made dinner, gave them baths, and put them to bed. On Friday, I dropped them off at school in the morning, and by afternoon, I heard that a man had shot and killed his mother, two teachers, a teacher's aide, a principal, a school psychologist, and twenty children the same age as my daughter, before shooting himself in the head. Perhaps you also saw this footage on the news: the children—the ones who survived—being led from the school in lines, each child with her hands on the shoulders of the child in front of her, each child held by the one behind: a drill they have learned for sticking together. There is safety in trusting, and being trusted by, one another.

Thoughts and prayers: that is what people offer. Prayers, and nothing more. *Prayer* is a word that comes to us from Old French, for "petition, request," but it also has roots in Medieval Latin, *precaria,* from which we get "precarious," a very different word that makes us think of a state of uncertainty, unpredictability, or risk, but which also means a state of being dependent on the will of another. "The function of prayer is not to influence God," Søren Kierkegaard writes, "but rather to change the nature of the one who prays."

Not a single day passes that I don't think of my own children being shot at their school or imagine having to go to the morgue to identify their bodies. Every day I pray that they come home safe. A man killed twelve people in a movie theater, and now each time we go to see a movie, I plan our escape while my children eat popcorn, plan how I will use my body to shield them and how we will all die anyway. Each time I fly across the country, I remember how a man shot five people in an airport baggage claim. Five months later, a man entered a church during an evening Bible study and killed nine of the men and women gathered there while they bowed their heads to pray. A man killed forty-nine people in a nightclub, and we called it an atrocity. A month after the shooter in Las Vegas killed fifty-eight concert-goers and injured hundreds, a man in Texas entered a church and killed twenty-six people. Witnesses say he walked up and down the aisles, looking for the crying babies. These men prey on the ways we offer our vulnerability to one another because they cannot face the vulnerability in themselves.

Just yesterday a man entered a high school and killed fourteen children and three of their teachers in Florida. In one photograph, two girls embrace, both sobbing, both covering their open mouths. One has braces; the other has painted her fingernails sky blue. They'll never see the world the same again.

On that day I went quail hunting with my father, the dog rushed in, and the birds exploded in every direction, their wings frantic against the winter air. Faster and faster, their wings carried them away from the harm I intended, away from the barrel of my gun and toward survival, toward safety. I never went hunting with my father again, never even saw the two guns I had learned to shoot sort of well, not until I returned to my new apartment after having been kidnapped and raped by the man I had loved. My father met me there, the shotgun in his outstretched hand. I didn't want it, didn't want to be responsible for it. Guns weren't even allowed on the property, were against the terms of the lease, and I was terrified of being evicted and having nowhere to go. He wouldn't take no for an answer. He said I wouldn't even have to shoot it; if someone came to my door, all I would have to do is pump the barrel—make that unmistakable sound—and that would tell anyone on the other side of the door that I am armed. He brought it inside and gave me a box of ammunition. I put the gun in my closet, zippered into its brown leather case. It made me feel weaker, not stronger. More vulnerable, not less. I couldn't sleep with it there, with all the ways it made me feel afraid. Two weeks later, my father returned, and I handed the gun back.

The memory of that moment returned to me when I was running on the trail near my house recently. A few days earlier, a man had pulled an assault rifle out of a duffel bag at a gas station up the street from my house and began shooting at random: he shot the gas station attendant and his wife; he shot cars and the people inside them; he shot retaining walls and houses across the street. He was eventually killed in a standoff with police. He was a combat veteran, had been deployed multiple times to war, and each time he came back changed, more and more like a weapon, less and less like himself.

The street was closed, and when it reopened I ran with my dog along that street and entered the trail near my house. It was late in the morning, and the trail was mostly empty. I turned a corner and saw a man approaching. He reached across his chest into the inner pocket of his jacket. *He has a gun,* I thought, and my blood ran ice cold. There is only one kind of terror, and it feels like a terrible loneliness. But not as lonely as the man who fails to recognize the humanity of others, who believes his life is the only one that matters.

His hand reeemerged from his jacket, empty. He walked past me along the trail.

I ran home: faster and faster. That shut place inside me taking flight.

ON MERCY

Nothing can make injustice just but mercy.
—Robert Frost, *A Masque of Mercy*

The sight of the children rattles me every time. They sit around a tiny table in a too-small classroom, the walls stacked high with textbooks and technologies they will never use. The frailest ones wear hospital blankets draped over their shoulders. IV trolleys trail and beep behind them. Chest catheters peek out from under their clothes. One of the older girls wears a loose hijab. Her eyes are dark and bruised, her skin faintly gray. She lives in this hospital, in a private room down the hall. The healthy-looking children tend to live in nearby apartments and attend this hospital-school because they are just beginning their treatments and must be hooked to an IV trolley too often to attend a traditional school in the district. They are bright-eyed and rosy-cheeked, dressed in the fresh first-day clothes any healthy child might choose for herself. One girl wears platform sandals and a bright neon wig.

My teaching partner, a ten-year veteran of this placement, spreads supplies on the table—construction paper and markers—and together we all begin to draw and to chat, to tell jokes and ask silly questions. Soon the children leave their seats and crowd together. They write or scribble or dictate to one another or to us. Torn paper and marker caps are strewn on the table, the chairs, and the floor. The girl in the neon wig asks to sit on my lap and doesn't wait for me to answer before climbing aboard. I'm uncomfortable with this. I dislike being touched by anyone, most of all strangers, and have not forgotten the prohibition against physical contact with children who are not my own. But the child on my lap leans over the table. Her right hand holds down the paper while she scribbles furiously with her left. I place my hand on her back. A tumor bulges on her shoulder underneath her shirt. Within the year, the cancer in this tumor will spread: into her bones, her blood, her lungs, and head. In the end, she'll be in so much pain that whatever kills her is a mercy.

"To have great pain is to have certainty," philosopher Elaine Scarry writes. "To hear that another person has pain is to have doubt." Scarry must mean a different kind of pain from the one I witness in the pediatric cancer ward. Here pain is sometimes experienced as fear, or bewilderment, or the ghost of future grief, depending on whether the pain is your own or that of a child who sits on your lap, only briefly; who enters your life, only briefly. What makes pain subject to doubt, Scarry suggests, is the difficulty of expressing it: "Physical pain does not simply resist language but actively destroys it." It is telling, I think, that the word *pain* finds its root in the Latin *poena*, or "punishment, penalty, retribution." To bestow pain on another is cruelty. To relieve it is mercy. Even those sentenced to death by execution have a constitutional right to an instantaneous and painless death, though their constitutional rights extend to little else.

"The act of verbally expressing pain," Scarry continues, "is a necessary prelude to the collective task of diminishing pain." I have no illusions that teaching dying children to write poetry will cure them, but that's not to say the task isn't, in so many small ways, profoundly healing.

I meet my teaching partner at the coffee shop to ride together in the elevator to the seventh floor. As she opens the door to the classroom, she tells me that one of her students has died. She heard just this morning. She turns and walks into the classroom, leaving this news with me in the hall. The boy was never my student; he was too ill to write with us in class long before I arrived.

With the young writers at the hospital, we cut or tear paper into tiny little squares and look up synonyms for all the colors: *azure, cobalt, sapphire, olive, emerald, virescent.* We arrange the scraps on sheets of white paper. Some collages are made entirely of variations on a single color—arranging them is a tranquil, meditative act—and others burst and explode with patterns that do not cohere. We hang them on the walls with strips of tape.

Back in the car, I ask my teaching partner about the student who has died. She tells me about the kind of boy he was by recalling the tiny details of his manner with the other children, a metaphor in a poem he wrote one day during the many years she knew him. There is a pause during which I can think of nothing useful to say. We're sitting at the stoplight waiting for the passengers to board the light-rail.

I've never been good at compassion, which might be one reason I'm here. I teach writing in a pediatric cancer ward because I get paid to do it and because compassion challenges me in ways I wish I could rise to meet. When my friend's brother fell ill from brain cancer years ago, I fell out of touch with her. I never knew what to say when she described his deteriorating health, or the conversations they had while she sat at his bedside, or her decision to move back to her mother's house. Her pain was not my pain, and I wasn't eager to take it on. I didn't mean to be cruel. Probably I told myself that my silence was a form of self-preservation. I was, after all, suffering from pain of my own. When I heard years later that my friend's brother had died, I thought often of writing or calling but didn't. We haven't spoken since. I wouldn't know what to say if we did.

When the light changes, I ask my teaching partner, "How do you do it? What do you do with the grief?" She takes a long time to answer. She takes a breath. "Some lives are very long," she says. "Some are very short. And when a person knows they're going to die and chooses to spend any moment of the remaining time with you, you take it as a gift. Life is a gift."

We ride back to the coffee shop in silence: past men blowing leaves into the street, past people in their cars talking on their hands-free cell phones, past an old woman clutching her grocery trolley while waiting for the bus. I gather my things, say, "See you next week," and reach for the door. "Actually," she says, "you won't." She says she meant to tell me earlier, but then she got the news about the boy's death. It's been ten years of this for her, teaching writing to children who will die. She needs time. She needs space. She needs a break. I hug her once, hard. It's the only thing I have to give.

We tend to associate mercy with alleviating pain and suffering, but also with reducing punishments and relieving our guilt. During the year I teach writing in the pediatric cancer ward, thirteen men are executed in Texas, the state where I live. One of them is Lawrence Russell Brewer, who was sentenced to death in 1999 for the murder of James Byrd Jr. On the night of June 7, 1998, Brewer and John William King, both self-identified white supremacists, rode as passengers in a truck driven by Shawn Berry. Sometime after midnight, the three white men encountered Byrd walking home from a party. In the morning, a mutilated human torso was found in the road in front of a historic African American cemetery.

Police followed a gruesome trail back to the scene of a struggle, where they found Byrd's wallet, keys, and dentures, as well as a cigarette lighter engraved with the words "Possum" and "KKK"; a wrench engraved with the name "Berry"; empty beer bottles, a pack of cigarettes, and three cigarette butts. That evening, police stopped Berry in his 1982 Ford pickup for a traffic violation. Behind the seat, police discovered a set of tools matching the wrench discovered

LACY M. JOHNSON

at the fight scene. At his apartment, which he shared with King and Brewer, they discovered blood-stained clothing and piles of white supremacist propaganda. DNA tests on the three cigarette butts matched Brewer, Berry, and King.

During Brewer's sentencing, a prosecuting attorney read from one of Brewer's letters to another jailhouse inmate, introduced as evidence into the proceedings: "Well, I did it. And no longer am I a virgin. It was a rush, and I'm still licking my lips for more." The prosecution hinges on this: that this was to be the first of many murders he would commit as part of his initiation into a white-supremacist gang affiliated with the KKK offshoot Confederate Knights of America, which he joined in the Beto I Prison Unit in Texas. There he met William King, who was serving an eight-year sentence for a violation of his probation for a burglary he had committed at age seventeen. Over his prison term, King covered his body with racist tattoos and vowed to kidnap and kill a black man when he got free as part of a "blood tie." Prosecutors said Brewer murdered James Byrd Jr. to attract attention and recruits to a racist group he planned to start in Jasper. They argued that people like Brewer, who can kill with no remorse, are the reason for the death penalty.

By all accounts, even in the final moments before the execution, Brewer showed no contrition for his part in the murder of James Byrd Jr.: "As far as any regrets, no. I have no regrets," he said during an interview earlier that week. "No, I would do it all over again, to tell you the truth."

———

In his remorselessness, Brewer is unlike other prisoners on death row, many of whom spend their last breaths expressing sorrow and regret. They affirm their love for their mothers and children; they beg for mercy—not for a stay of execution, mind you, but for forgiveness; not from God, but from the families of their victims.

"I hope you find comfort in my execution," says Jermarr Arnold, executed by lethal injection in Texas in 2002 for the 1983 murder of a jewelry store clerk.

"I pray that you find closure and strength," says Timothy Titsworth at his 2006 execution in Texas.

"I just ask that my death bring you peace and solace. If my death brings you that, then I will gladly give it," says Jeffery Tucker to the widow of his 1988 murder victim. He recites the Lord's Prayer as the chemicals begin entering his bloodstream. He and the victim's son together say, "Amen."

Consider, by way of contrast, the last words of Troy Davis, executed in Georgia, and at the same time, on the same day, as James Russell Brewer: "I am innocent," Davis proclaims. Sentenced to death for the 1989 murder of white police officer Mark MacPhail, Davis never ceased proclaiming his innocence, and the justice system never ceased pronouncing his guilt: four times the governor signed Davis's death warrant, and four times Davis's lawyers appealed for clemency. Despite serious doubts about Davis's guilt, about the rigor of the trial, about the racial biases of the trial judge and jury, and the racist sentencing practices of the state of Georgia; despite recantations by seven of the nine original witnesses; despite no physical evidence linking Davis to the shooting; despite more than 1 million signatures on petitions asking for clemency; despite the protests of former President Jimmy Carter, Archbishop Desmond Tutu, fifty-one members of Congress, Amnesty International, the NAACP, and numerous world leaders, the Supreme Court reviewed but failed to act on an appeal to stay Davis's sentence, and allowed the execution to proceed.

"I ask my family and friends that you all continue to pray, that you all continue to forgive. Continue to fight this fight," Davis says, as he is strapped to the gurney, looking straight into the faces of the witnesses. "For those about to take my life, may God have mercy on all of your souls."

It is winter when I meet my new teaching partner at the Starbucks counter near the hospital's entrance and we ride together in the elevator to the classroom on the seventh floor. Only a few of the youngest writers are here today, and the classroom teacher lets us know that one of our writers, the teenage girl who sometimes wears a hijab, has been too sick to come to class this week. She hopes someone will come to visit her. As a group, we decide to make snowflakes for her room. It is winter, after all. The writers—one from West Texas, another from the United Arab Emirates, another from Ecuador—have never seen snow and have never made snowflakes out of paper. It's hard to work the scissors, which are made to be safe for use by healthy children, not for children who are weak from chemo. We watch YouTube videos of snow falling in a blizzard, of icicles forming on eaves, of a dog hopping joyfully through drifts. We choose the best snowflakes for the sick teenager's room. We write poems in which we are all snowflakes on a harrowing adventure from the clouds to the ground below. We tromp toward her private room and pile in around her bed. She leans back on her pillow, smiling, too weak to sit up or cover her head. While my teaching partner and I tape the snowflakes to the windows, the writers take turns reading their poems to the girl, who listens with her eyes closed, grimacing in pain. A nurse comes in to fiddle with her IV trolley, which promises relief but does not deliver it. The children are hungry for their lunch, so we climb off the bed and head quietly toward the door. "Stay," she calls after us. My teaching partner leads the children back to the classroom to meet their parents; I stay to read one more poem, Miguel de Unamuno's "The Snowfall Is So Silent." "The flakes are skyflowers," I say:

> pale lilies from the clouds,
> that wither on earth.
> They come down blossoming
> but then so quickly
> they are gone . . .

Her eyes loll in their sockets as I read, the morphine at last reaching its mark. Her mouth goes slack. The teenage girl becomes a child like any other child. She sighs and falls asleep.

———

People tend to associate mercy with forgiveness—with compassion offered by those in a position to instead impose cruelty. But I associate mercy with a tiny classroom on the second floor of the First Baptist Church in my hometown, with shoes I notice are scuffed, tights I notice are torn, and a dress I notice is smudged as I sit with other scuff-shoed children on the floor while one of the deacons' wives holds a picture book open on her lap. She is part of one long memory in which we learn about the Flood because it is March and raining, or about the crucifixion because it is Easter, or the trials of Job because it is summer and there is a terrible drought. We learn about the Garden of Eden when it is fall and our fathers, who art in the fields, are harvesting the crops. *Hallowed be thy name.* When we, who have until now sat on the floor together, are separated—boys in one room, girls in another—the stories become warnings. Lot's wife, who disobeyed the angels, is turned into a pillar of salt. Eve disobeys a direct order from God, and every woman everywhere for all eternity is punished for it. Pain is what humanity inherits from her curiosity. It is only through God's mercy that any of us is granted a reprieve.

This notion of mercy—the one of compassionate clemency, of divine forgiveness—requires that we believe people deserve to be punished. The deacons' wives, with their loose navy dresses, taught me and all the other girls that we deserved whatever pain was unique to our experience as punishment for the sins we'd committed, or those we hadn't committed yet but might commit later, or any sins committed by others on our behalf. It didn't really matter how pious a life we led because we could expect pain, that great equalizer, to arrive at any moment to punish us for the sin of being born.

"Tonight the state of Georgia legally lynched an innocent man," one of Troy Davis's defense attorneys tells the media. Hundreds of protesters have gathered outside the prison, quieted by the pronouncement of Davis's death, chanting and singing as they face an army of sheriff's deputies, state police, and baton-wielding prison guards in full riot gear: *We shall overcome someday.* Only members of the slain officer's family, resolute in their certainty of Davis's guilt, express relief about his death, having consistently fought his efforts for clemency. They leave the chamber with smiles on their faces. Anneliese MacPhail, mother of the victim, tells an interviewer outside her home that, yes, Davis's execution has brought her relief: "Twenty-two years we've been going through this, and he is gone now." To her, Davis's execution is a victory.

But six months later, MacPhail admits that some of her hatred for Davis might have been fueled by resentment that his story—the story of racial injustice in the justice system—became the prevailing narrative of the case. "It was always poor Troy Davis," MacPhail says. "There was never anything about Mark, his wife, and the babies he left behind." Ultimately, Davis's execution doesn't fill the hole left by her son's murder, and now MacPhail is blamed for the execution of an innocent man. She receives hate mail from

Davis's supporters, who also continue to call her house. "I didn't sentence him to die," MacPhail says. "He was found guilty and that was the state—not me."

"The contention that violence is inevitable is one of the great unexamined assumptions of society," write Bible scholars Stephen P. Wink and Walter Wink, who argue that every myth of creation requires a story of destruction, and this cosmology, in which violence is redemptive, legitimates systems of domination and oppression. Consider the words of Justice Potter Stewart, writing the majority opinion in *Gregg v. Georgia*, the 1976 Supreme Court case that re-legalized the death penalty: "Capital punishment is an expression of society's moral outrage at particularly offensive conduct. This function may be unappealing to many, but it is essential in an ordered society." Gary Gilmore was the first death row inmate to be executed after this decision—in Utah, by firing squad. Three years later, John Spenkelink would be executed in Florida, by electrocution. He often signed his letters, "Capital punishment means those without capital get the punishment."

Spenkelink's words point to a disturbing truth about the administration of capital punishment in the United States. Time and again, studies show that an overwhelming majority of defendants charged with capital crimes cannot afford their own attorneys to represent them. As a result, they are much more likely to be represented by public defenders and to be convicted of the crimes with which they are charged. Clear evidence shows that the harshest sentences are often reserved for the poor and for people of color, who are less likely to be offered probation, more likely to be sentenced to prison, more likely to be sentenced to longer prison terms, and more likely to serve a greater portion of their original sentence. In murder cases, they are more likely to be sentenced to death.

In 1987 Warren McCleskey, an African American convicted of murdering a white police officer in Georgia, appealed his death sentence to the Supreme Court, arguing that his sentence should be nullified because his race and the race of his victim had played an unconstitutionally significant role. He based these claims on what has become known as the Baldus study—a comparative review of more than two thousand murder cases in Georgia—which concluded that the single most reliable predictor of whether someone will be sentenced to death is the race of the victim. Despite this evidence of racial bias in the administration of justice, the Supreme Court upheld the death sentence for McCleskey, arguing that "apparent disparities in sentencing are an inevitable part of our criminal justice system." Before McCleskey was executed by electrocution, he told the room of witnesses: "I pray that one day this country, supposedly a civilized society, will abolish barbaric acts such as the death penalty."

Soon after, states across the nation would abandon electrocution in favor of lethal injection as the preferred method for maintaining an "ordered society," because at that time, it was considered the most humane of all the variously gruesome ways we execute our condemned, and, if not humane, at least the most painless. Painless because it relies on a combination of three drugs: an anesthetic that sends the prisoner into a deep coma; a paralytic, which prevents the prisoner from involuntary movement; and finally, a dose of potassium chloride sufficient enough to stop the prisoner's heart.

This manner of dying—a heart attack in one's sleep—is what the historian Suetonius might call a "good death," describing how the emperor Augustus died quickly and without suffering—in the Greek, *euthanasia*, from *eu*, "good," and *thanatos*, "death." The word first appears, in this "good death" sense, in the writings of Francis Bacon, who described medically induced death as "a kindly and pleasant sleep." Bacon argued that a doctor's role was "not only to restore health, but to mitigate pain and dolours; and not only when such mitigation may conduce to recovery, but when it may serve to make a fair and easy passage."

He meant pain in the physical sense: chronic pain, acute pain, physical pain—pain that "destroys language," but for which we do in fact have words. We have hundreds of pain words—words like *burning, searing, penetrating, radiating, punishing, suffocating*—that doctors use to classify and alleviate pain and, whenever possible, offer mercy.

"I'm ready to be released. Release me," says Kenneth Allen McDuff at his execution in Texas in 1998.

"I feel my whole body burning," says Michael Lee Wilson, one of the first death row inmates to be executed by lethal injection after the drug company Hospira refused to continue manufacturing sodium thiopental, a barbiturate and anesthetic, because it was being used for lethal injections. Prisons, so desperate to execute their condemned, have turned to other anesthetics: to pentobarbital, and then, after European manufacturers refused to sell pentobarbital to the United States for executions, midazolam; to drugs manufactured under lax regulations, to drugs imported from overseas, to drugs bought with petty cash by prison officials and smuggled into the country illegally.

"Man," says Clayton Lockett in 2014, in Oklahoma, as he writhes in agony on the gurney. The IV has been placed incorrectly; his vein has ruptured; the midazolam has entered his tissue rather than his bloodstream; he is pronounced unconscious; he is injected with vecuronium bromide to paralyze his body and potassium chloride to stop his heart; and yet he wakes up, raises his head, and tries to rise from the gurney. A pool of fluid bulges under his skin. He twitches and convulses and tries to speak but cannot. He dies of cardiac arrest ten minutes after the warden halts the execution.

"Blessed are they who mourn, for they will be comforted," says Larry Donnell Davis, executed in Texas in 2008. He is quoting from the Beatitudes, the eight blessings in Christ's Sermon on the Mount. The sermon, recounted in the Gospel of Matthew, continues:

> Blessed are the meek, for they shall inherit the earth.
> Blessed are those who hunger and thirst for righteousness,
>   for they shall be satisfied.
> Blessed are the merciful, for they will be shown mercy.

———

Today I learn that the girl who wears a bright neon wig has had surgery to remove the tumor from her back. When I knock on the door to her room, the nurses are trying to move her in the bed and she cries out in pain. No words: only a single, involuntary wail. She is skeletal, bald, sobbing while they lift her on a white sheet and move her only slightly. I don't understand why they are moving her at all. I ask if I should come back later. "No no no," her father says. "Please don't go." I say, "I'll just go get a book and come right back." When I return minutes later, the girl is a little more comfortable. She realizes I'm in the room this time and smiles. She is so happy to see me. I ask if she'd like me to read her a book. "Let's read it together," she says. As we're reading, her older brother and younger sister come into the room and climb onto the bed with us. I'm hamming it up as best I can. It's a silly book, and the kids laugh, even the very sick girl. We write the most ridiculous story we can think of, in which we fill the top floor of the hospital with water in order to give everyone on the lower floors a shower. An elephant comes into the room and tries to talk to us, but elephants don't speak English and it's all very frustrating, especially for the elephant, who has something important to say. The children's mother comes into the room with their grandmother and grandfather. When they ask who I am, the mother calls me a tutor. The error couldn't matter less.

———

We hear reports of the children's health mostly through rumor. The classroom teacher tells us that the teenage girl who sometimes wears a hijab has checked out of the hospital, which seems like good news. But the following week, I see her being wheeled through the hospital by her mother and another woman. The girl slouches in the wheelchair, her body folded over onto itself, her eyes looking at nothing in particular. She doesn't recognize me. She doesn't even see me. And then we hear that she has been admitted to the ICU. And then that she has stopped eating. "Nauseated by the chemo," the teachers say. She is thirteen or fourteen years old. They say, "It is only a matter of time."

When the girl in the neon wig comes back to class, she does not feel like writing the story everyone else is writing. She doesn't feel well and swivels in her chair with her head on the table while the rest of us are writing. Suddenly she bolts upright—*an idea!* She retrieves a piece of white paper from the pile at the center. She writes: "Thank you, Mom, for taking care of me, for cooking good food for me, for hugging and kissing me. Thank you for your love." It's the last line that sends me to the window to collect myself, where I remember this child is not my child. Her mother's grief is not my grief.

My teaching partner and I don't ask the children to write about their pain. Unlike the doctors and nurses who visit them every weekday to check their catheters, to poke and prod them with frightening-looking instruments, or to inject them with toxic chemicals that make them suffer in order to make them well, we don't treat what ails their bodies. Asking children to write about pain does nothing to alleviate it, so instead we write about islands of our own invention, the imaginary landscapes of our brains, or the future economies of child rocket transportation. We pull board games from the shelves and throw out the rules. We become way too excited and make far too much noise. Official-looking adults in scrubs keep opening the door to investigate our commotion. We clap and cheer. In our games, everyone wins.

At lunchtime, when the mothers and fathers come to pick up their children, they speak to us with tears in their eyes. They thank us very sincerely for the poems and stories: artifacts of a life that has not yet extinguished. I do not want their teary thank-yous. The children are right here, smiling and waving good-bye.

I think there are different kinds of mercy: big Mercy and little mercy. Big Mercy is so big because it is made out of suffering and ultimatums, out of saviors and omnipotence, and out of stories that are brutal and where almost nobody wins. It's big Mercy that annihilates the many to redeem the few: a whole world purified by fire, rinsed by flood, and made perfect and shiny and new. Big Mercy decides who lives and dies and how. It cleaves humanity in two: the few chosen to be powerful, the many they render powerless. Big Mercy teaches us the first lesson of righteousness: that other people are not as human as we are. No one deserves to receive big Mercy, and no one deserves to offer it either.

But maybe there's another kind of mercy—mercy so little that it costs almost nothing. So little most of us never notice it. The kind that arrives as a child sitting briefly on your lap, as a poem, a letter, a loving hand on your hand, a piece of paper cut with tiny scissors, held by strips of tape to a wall or window. Little mercy teaches a lesson too: that everyone is human, just as we are. There's no one—*no one*—who doesn't deserve that kind of mercy.

It's mercy, a little one, that I want for the girl in the bright neon wig, who is now not expected to live, who checks out of this hospital and is moved to another hospital in a faraway state, where she will undergo an experimental treatment that requires her to be in quarantine for thirty days. I'm furious with her parents for choosing this when the odds of saving her are so slim, though I know it's unjust of me to judge them for making a choice I could not. This child is not my child. Every day her mother posts pictures of the girl on Facebook: without her wig, wearing only a hospital gown, lying in a hospital bed. In these pictures, which I visit often, she is completely alone, perfectly preserved behind a window, staying exactly the same: bald, pale, skeletal. Her younger brother has outgrown her. In one photo she's pressing a hand to the glass of the quarantine room; outside, her younger sisters stand together—their blond ponytails, their T-shirts and leggings and mismatched socks, their hands on the glass—pressing back.

_____

On James Russell Brewer's last day, he speaks to his friends and family by phone in a booth no bigger than a water heater closet, separated from the people he loves by a pane of glass, by armed guards, by a sentence that is coming to an end. For his last meal, he has asked for two chicken-fried steaks, a triple-meat bacon cheeseburger, fried okra with a side of ketchup, a pound of Texas barbecue (meat unspecified), three fajitas, a Pizza Hut Meat Lover's pizza, a pint of Blue Bell Homemade Vanilla ice cream, and a slab of peanut butter fudge with crushed peanuts. He eats none of it, claiming he has lost his appetite.

Around 6:00 p.m., Brewer is taken to the execution chamber: a tiny room with turquoise walls, made tinier by its emptiness. The only thing inside the room is the gurney, to which he is quickly strapped by thick leather belts buckled across his arms, legs, and torso. Two windows look into the chamber from opposite sides of the room: one for the family of James Byrd Jr. and the other for his own family, where his father, mother, and brother, and two friends look on. He offers them a little smile.

After the execution, one of James Byrd's sisters addresses the media, saying, "It didn't bring me any sense of peace or relief." Another sister stands behind her, nodding, looking down. "It's just a matter of saying that this one chapter in the book was now closed, and we can move on." Noticeably absent from the crowd gathered outside the prison is the victim's only son, Ross Byrd, who opposes the execution, telling interviewers that Brewer's death is simply another expression of the hate shown toward his father on that June night in 1998. "Like Gandhi said, an eye for an eye, and the whole world will go blind." He wishes the state would have shown his father's killer mercy.

Mercy often coincides w/ remorse?

The girl who no longer wears a neon wig has one last wish: to go to Disneyland. The experimental treatments have failed; the cancer has spread: to her bones, her blood, her head. In the photographs of her final days, she looks peaceful: a wide smile spreading across the pale mask of her face as Disney princesses kneel and smile beside her. She reclines in a three-wheel stroller, her head propped up on pillows, her hands resting on blankets tucked around her lap. Her family crowds around her: always a hand placed on her arm, her leg, her cheek. I don't know anything about her final moments—whether there was a gasp, or a sigh, or the last gift of an injection—only that they come during the third night. Her mother writes, "Our girl has found peace."

"Life becomes death," writes Paul Auster in *The Invention of Solitude*, "and it is as if this death has owned this life all along."

In the comfort of my own home, I cook dinner for my healthy children. I sing to them as they drift off to sleep. I plan lessons to teach in the pediatric cancer ward: little poems and drawings for the families to keep after their children are gone.

"Poetry has its uses for despair," writes the poet Christian Wiman of his own battle with cancer. "It can carve a shape in which a pain can seem to be; it can give one's loss a form and dimension so that it might be loss and not simply a hopeless haunting."

My husband says time heals all wounds. I nod my head. But deep down I know this isn't really true. The wounds change shape, change forms. Pain appears as a gash, then a cut, then a scab, then a scar—all near-synonyms extending on and on along the signifying chain.

On the last day of school, only one child comes. She is nervous and tall—in that angular way of all adolescent girls—and keeps touching the thin cloud of her hair. My teaching partner has brought cookies and lemonade and has printed the booklets we've made, plenty for every writer we've worked with at the hospital, every teacher in the classroom, and lots and lots of extras. So many children are absent today—they are too ill, or too tired, or they have gone home to spend their remaining days in the company of those they love. We take turns reading aloud. I read a poem written by the girl who used to wear a neon wig: "I remember the shape of the mountains," she begins:

> The color, which was mostly green
> (like Christmas trees) and gray
> (like pencil lead). And the water, so
> beautiful, even though it was too cold
> for swimming. My whole family was there.
> They would never leave me.

The tall girl reads her own page in the booklet, though reading her own writing makes her even more nervous. Her mother comes to pick her up: early, as usual. We all shake hands; I tell the girl to take care of herself, to take an extra cookie or two or, okay, three. My partner and I turn off the lights and ride the elevator to the bottom floor, then walk out of the hospital into the street. We won't be back next year. The sun warms our hair and shoulders, arriving as a little mercy.

SPEAK TRUTH TO POWER

The first time I admit in public to having been kidnapped and raped by a man I used to live with, I am at a nonfiction reading at the university where I work. I've given enough readings now that I'm usually no longer nervous, but as I sit in the front row at this reading, waiting for my turn to approach the podium, I feel profoundly ill. Because I was, some time ago, a graduate student at this same university, audience members include my former professors and mentors — people I now consider colleagues and friends. Also in the audience are former students, current students, future students, as well as people I've never met before, and for all I know will never meet again. One reader goes before me, but I don't hear a word he says. My hands shake as I hold the book I will read from — still only a galley copy then. My legs nearly buckle underneath me as I stand from my chair. My armpits swim. Bile burns the base of my esophagus. The blood rising to my face tells me that what I am about to do is shameful, embarrassing, wrong. But for fourteen years, I have kept a silence. Today I want to break it.

———

The story of Philomela seems relevant here—that ancient cautionary tale against speaking about rape, which is in many ways about the impossibility of speaking about rape. In Ovid's *Metamorphoses*, Philomela is considered a minor character—a princess from Athens who is raped by a somewhat less minor character, who happens to be her sister's husband, King Tereus, a tyrant from a war-waged kingdom across the sea from Philomela's home in Greece. After the rape—after she has torn her hair and scratched and beat her arms—she curses Tereus and vows to tell everyone what he has done. Half out of fear, half out of rage, Tereus draws his sword. But instead of killing her, as she hopes he will do, he cuts out her tongue to prevent her from speaking.

It seems impossible to speak about rape precisely because this threat of violent retribution is real, whether explicit or implicit, but also because of the widespread belief in our culture that rape is an aberration: a violence so unthinkable, so unfathomable, so taboo as to render it unspeakable. It is unspeakable, we are told, because respect for the sanctity and integrity of a woman's body is the norm. This is, of course, not the way most women have experienced their own bodies throughout history. For most women, rape has been the norm and respect the exception.

I learn first from social media that, in the early-morning hours of August 12, 2011, a sixteen-year-old girl in Steubenville, Ohio, woke up in her front yard, still a little drunk, unsure how she got there. She learned by checking Instagram, Twitter, and Tumblr what happened the night before. She got drunk at a party, where she was very possibly drugged, before a group of high school football players also at the party taunted her, urinated on her, carried her unconscious by her wrists and ankles from that party to another party, and to another, while they fingered her in public, in the back seat of a car, on the sidewalk as she vomited into the street. They flashed her breasts to anyone wishing to see, stripped off her clothes, and took turns slapping her with flaccid penises.

When her parents took her to the police station two days later to file charges, the pictures and tweets and videos bystanders recorded of "the incident" had mostly been removed. "My daughter learned about what had happened to her that night by reading the story about it in the local newspaper," the girl's mother tells the press. In a video recorded that night, one of the party-goers, Ohio State football player Michael Nodianos, jokes about men raping and urinating on a dead girl. Between each line, each riff, each variation on the joke, he and the person recording the video laugh hysterically.

"She's deader than Obi-Wan," Michael Nodianos sputters in the twelve-and-a-half-minute video to his own hysterical laughter.

She's deader than Andy Reed's son.
She's deader than Chris Henry.
She's deader than OJ's wife.

They raped her harder than that cop raped Marsellus
  Wallace in *Pulp Fiction*.
They raped her quicker than Mike Tyson raped that one
  girl.
They raped her more than the Duke lacrosse team.
She is so raped right now, she is just a dead body.

During the rape trial in Ohio, it emerges that the person who recorded the twelve-and-a-half-minute video in which Nodianos jokes about the rape is the same person who recorded a video of one of the defendants molesting the victim in the back of a car. He's a witness for the prosecution and has been given immunity for his testimony. Although he admits later deleting the video because he realized "it was wrong," he says he recorded it because he thought the girl should know what had happened to her. It's something he wanted her to see: how she was naked, molested, exposed. The witness admits it was his basement where the twelve-and-a-half-minute video is filmed. It's his laughter we hear. It's his hand trying to steady the camera. In another room of that same basement, maybe even while he is filming the video, another boy takes pictures of the sixteen-year-old girl: naked, unconscious, lying facedown on the floor.

Two boys, both juveniles, are found "delinquent" (the juvenile equivalent of guilty) in the case. "Such promising futures," one anchor says on network television. At the reading of the verdict, one of the boys breaks down in tears in the courtroom, sobbing like a child: "My life is over. No one is going to want me now."

The girl remains anonymous in all of this, though a few reports have carelessly revealed her identity and then quickly redacted it. It doesn't matter; most of the people in the town already know who she is. She receives death threats. She is ostracized, abandoned by her friends. In the comments section of any of the articles about the case, she might be called a slur I won't repeat. Her attorney speaks for the girl, says she feels relieved: "She just wants to get back to her normal life." He's nodding as he says this, as if this were not already "normal life" for many girls.

Each day, women and girls come forward to voice accusations against men who are famous or unknown, who are powerful or paupers. They voice accusations against Harvey Weinstein, Bill Cosby, Woody Allen, Dustin Hoffman, Matt Lauer, and Peyton Manning; against men whose names we haven't heard before at colleges and prep schools and high schools and middle schools, in hospitals and universities and prisons, in the military, in law offices, even in the White House. We are told that these accusations are the exception, or that this is an affliction particular to our present moment, or that these women are lying or trying to get even or get attention or extort money.

"The finest trick of the devil," writes Baudelaire, "is to persuade you that he does not exist."

———

In Houston, where I live, a sixteen-year-old girl known simply as "Jada" comes forward to publicly accuse two men of drugging her at a party, gang-raping her, and posting pictures on social media of her unconscious body, one arm tucked behind her back, legs akimbo, naked from the waist down. That these men post these pictures without fear of the consequences is only proof they have no reason to believe there will be consequences. Jada was not the only girl at the party assaulted in this way. These same men, along with other adult men, drugged other girls, raped them, recorded video of themselves raping them, and posted these photos and videos to social media, where they are shared and shared and shared.

After her assault goes viral, Jada appears on MSNBC to speak with Ronan Farrow, who draws connections between her story and the story of his own family's history of violence and abuse. That February, Ronan's sister, Dylan Farrow, had penned an open letter about her experience of sexual abuse at the hands of her famous and powerful father, Woody Allen. The *New York Times* published Farrow's 936-word letter in an online column; six days later, the *Times* gave Allen 1,800 words in the print edition to respond, a retaliatory account in which he denies the accusations, calls them "ludicrous," their malevolence "obvious." According to Allen, the whole thing is a long-enduring revenge plot by Mia Farrow, Dylan's mother, who was, he says, hysterical and vindictive that he had an affair with her adopted daughter Soon-Yi Previn, herself a teenage girl when their affair began. In his account, Mia can't be believed because of her own history of dating much older men, because of her spite at being spurned, because perhaps she lied about the paternity of her son Ronan—that Dylan's experience is a fiction created by her mother, that he couldn't have committed this crime because of his fear of enclosed spaces, that in fact the accusation is a crime and he is its victim.

When two men—Clinton Onyeahialam, who is an adult, as well as an unnamed juvenile—are arrested in December, Jada returns to MSNBC to speak with Ronan Farrow again. As before, she appears with a family friend, a self-described activist named Quanell X, who is her advocate, her spokesperson, helping to call out the police for dragging their feet and to draw media attention to the case. This seems to be Quanell X's main skill. In 2011 he held a rally in Cleveland, Texas, in support of a group of twenty-one men who were later convicted of gang-raping an eleven-year-old girl. At that rally, he blamed the girl's parents for the men's violence, blamed the girl, pointed to her social media profiles as evidence she had already been sexually active with adult men, accused the police of letting the investigation be run by the KKK—all of this in spite of the crime having been caught on video, which had gone viral by the time the girl went to the police. The excerpts of the video that could be shown over and over on the news were extremely graphic, though not as graphic as the portions that were not shown. All twenty-one men were convicted, but only because they had pled guilty to lesser crimes, some receiving sentences as minor as seven years of probation.

Quanell X is sitting beside Jada when Farrow asks how she feels about these two men being arrested, what she wants to see happen to them. There is a long pause. She blinks several times, then says, "I would like to see justice. That's it."

All across the country this situation is replicated with slight variations: a woman reports rape, is told that boys will be boys; a woman reports rape, is not believed. She is shamed. She is ostracized, traumatized, and retraumatized. At best, the woman's life is forever and irrevocably changed. At worst, she self-destructs. Men, however, seem to thrive in a culture in which they can rape women with near impunity.

I know, I know. Not all men.

One man—a white professor in Georgia—learns his memoir has been rejected by a publisher YET AGAIN, around the same time that I give that reading at the university where I work. "What do I have to do to sell a memoir in this country?" he laments to his female colleague. "Get kidnapped and raped?" His female colleague thinks first of ignoring him, of saying nothing at all, but instead asks him if he is talking specifically about me, about my book. He says yes and makes some kind of James Frey reference, maybe accusing me of making the whole thing up to get attention and a publication. Months later, the female colleague resigns her job—I don't know if the two things are related—and much later she tells me this story while standing in the kitchen of my house.

———

Susan B. Anthony, writing in 1900, twenty years before women earned the right to vote, offers this: "No advanced step taken by women has been so bitterly contested as that of speaking in public. For nothing which they have attempted, not even to secure the suffrage, have they been so abused, condemned and antagonized."

I am on the phone with an editor at a women's magazine known more for its sex advice than for its coverage of contemporary literature. The editor has a British accent—I think it is British anyway—and she is asking thoughtful, sensitive questions about my book and my life, about what connections I see between BDSM and sexual violence, if any, and about my advice to women who have survived sexual assault and domestic violence. It does not feel strange or uncomfortable to tell her about being raped. I cannot, after all, see her face.

After we hang up the phone, I don't hear from her or anyone else at her magazine again until weeks later, just before the issue is scheduled to go to press, when the lawyer for the parent company of this magazine asks to see the police reports from my case, claiming they need to do due diligence to protect themselves against a defamation lawsuit from the man I accuse of kidnapping and raping me.

Keep in mind: I do not name this person—not in the book, and not in the interview. I give no identifying information about where the assault took place—not the city, not the state, not even the region. The man is an international fugitive, wanted on the same charges I recount in my book. Nevertheless, the lawyer for the parent company for the women's sex advice magazine is concerned this international fugitive might bring a defamation lawsuit against them, so he asks me to provide copies of the police reports from my case. This makes me very uncomfortable. But after gnashing over the idea for a couple of days, I agree to send the reports.

Hours later, the lawyer responds by saying that these reports are insufficient to satisfy their burden of proof. I might have forged the reports, the lawyer says; there's nothing preventing me. Now he needs the police reports to come directly from the police department itself. I offer a contact name and number. The lawyer calls and the sergeant from the records department informs him that though, yes, she can confirm that there is indeed a warrant for the man's arrest, and though, yes, she can confirm the exact charges, she cannot send him the records because the state has laws to preserve a victim's confidentiality rights, which prevent the police department from releasing any information about the case. The lawyer then asks me to waive my confidentiality rights and ask the police department to send the files from my case directly to him. He alone will determine their veracity.

I learn at this moment that there are some people who will believe I am lying about what men have done to my body no matter what evidence I present to the contrary. I also learn it is not my responsibility to convince them.

———

Jon Krakauer points out in *Missoula* that, unlike murder, which results, very convincingly, in a dead body; or a kidnapping, which results in the clear absence of one; or even a violent physical attack, which results in medically verifiable wounds or contusions; rape is the only violent crime with a victim who is subject, and subjected, to doubt.

We find expressions of this doubt in our long and troublesome history of men deciding what rape is and what it is not. Several years ago, Representative Todd Akin of Missouri waxed ignorant on the phenomenon of so-called legitimate rape, wherein he opined that pregnancy never results from "legitimate rape" because a woman apparently "has ways of shutting that whole thing down." Although this claim shows appalling ignorance about human biology, the choice to distinguish "legitimate rape" from other supposedly lesser crimes is not without precedent in the law. Many states, following the Model Penal Code created by the American Law Institute in 1962 to influence and standardize criminal lawmaking, still require prosecutors to prove that a man used force in order to find him guilty of raping an adult woman, and in every state, there is a distinction between the rape of an adult woman and the statutory rape of a girl, which, surprisingly, is a fairly recent development. For most of the history of this country, statutory rape existed only as a crime of "seduction," punishable not by imprisonment but by fines.

Critics of harsher punishments claimed young girls should be held responsible for protecting themselves or for failing to:

"In point of fact, the white girl of twelve anywhere throughout the civilized world, unless she is degenerate and imbecile,
is abundantly qualified, so far as intellect is concerned, to
protect her virginity if she so desires," wrote Representative
A. C. Tomkins of Kentucky in 1895. He opposed raising the
age of consent since "sexual desire belongs equally to the
male and female human being, and the law-makers of this
state were then, and are now, unwilling to inflict the heaviest
penalty of the law on the male when there is a possibility
that the female is also to blame." He goes on to make his
case further against raising the age of consent from twelve
by drawing on "science"—specifically the "scientific" fact
that "negro girls" go through puberty earlier than white girls,
become sexually active earlier than white girls, and are more
"naturally sensual" than white girls—a "fact" he cites as proof
that it is impossible to rape a woman of color.

I refer to this abominable text only because this "science"
still survives today. We see evidence of it in our justice system,
our literature, our television shows and movies. It survives
as attitudes, as biases, as stereotypes, as bigotry.

In *I Know Why the Caged Bird Sings* Maya Angelou writes how,
at seven years old, she is raped repeatedly by her mother's
boyfriend, who threatens to murder her brother if she speaks
about what they've done. *What we've done?* she wonders. When
the man's crime is finally discovered, far too late, and when
young Maya, then called Marguerite, is hospitalized with injuries and the man is finally arrested for his crimes, Marguerite

testifies against him. The lawyer asks her if it was just the one time or if it was many times, and Marguerite feels herself caught in a trap: if she tells the truth and says *yes, it was many times*, the lawyer will use it as proof of her "natural sensuality," that she in fact could not have been raped by this adult man; and yet if she lies and says *no, it was just the one time*, she fails to convey the full force of his crimes against her. *No* is what she feels everyone in the courtroom expects her to say, even wants her to say. The lie enters her mouth and she lets it escape.

Her rapist is sentenced to a year and a day in prison, though his lawyer arranges his release later that afternoon. That night, he is found beaten to death, likely by Marguerite's brothers and uncles, seeking justice where the courts failed to deliver it. She is struck mute with guilt about his death and does not speak for the next six years.

When an institution like a court, or a police department, or a district attorney's office, or a university, or a family does not listen to a woman who speaks about her sexual assault, they betray an attitude that women's speech does not matter—not when we give testimony, not when we make appeals, not when we report the violent crimes committed against us, not even when we say, very clearly, no.

Perhaps the lesson isn't, then, that the violation of women's bodies is unthinkable, but that men wield immense power when they think about, plan, and perform an act that we are told is forbidden. To be sure, one can often find pleasure in doing things that are expressly forbidden. We can each, no doubt, think of examples from our own youth. And yet I do not believe that the exclusive reason men rape is because they find pleasure in breaking a taboo. There are also taboos against cannibalism, but we hear of people eating other people almost never. But men rape women every day.

Part of the problem seems to be the myth that is perpetuated about the sort of person a rapist is and the sort of person he is not. "The man I know would never do this," say the people who protect and defend these men. Perhaps these people truly believe these men are incapable of the things they have been accused of doing. Or perhaps they believe these men *are* capable of those things—even believe they are guilty of the crimes of which they are accused—and yet they love these men anyway and cannot reconcile that.

We are told that rape is something only "monsters" do, undeterred by the accumulation of the suffering it inflicts. A rapist is a man in a mask who jumps out of the bushes with a knife—a man who cannot control his baser instincts, whose physical impulses get the best of him—as if rape is a natural temptation some men simply fail to resist. In reality, most rapists are men who have been taught from an early age that to be feminine means to be weak, and to be masculine means to overcome all weakness to prove that they are manly and strong. The insults boys learn teach them that a weak man is always a feminine one. The result is a culture of men who hate women because they have learned to hate the feminine in themselves.

Not all men, to be sure, but there are, without a doubt, some men for whom this mandate toward virility and strength is so strong, holds such sway on their minds and their actions, that the possibility of any culpability, or any violence, or aggression, or wrongdoing, simply cannot also exist. A man like this has been taught to understand that women are not people, not in the same way as men are. Resistance to his advances are seen as an invitation to advance more aggressively. Lack of resistance is also seen as an invitation to advance more aggressively. In either scenario, overcoming all resistance is a mark of virility for the man, but it doesn't mean anything at all for the woman because she is seen as meaningless.

"I don't hear her say anything," Bill Cosby tells a team of lawyers during his deposition in the Andrea Constand civil suit. "And so I continue and I go into the area that is somewhere between permission and rejection. I am not stopped." Cosby's euphemisms and innuendoes call to mind an image of the violence without the language of violence. To speak frankly, to admit drugging and raping this woman, would produce horror and revulsion, because drugging a woman in order to rape her is supposedly an unthinkable act. Cosby's language is playful, as if the woman—what she says, what she does, what she might want for herself, the goals she might have set for her life—are entirely beside the point. It's as if the fact of his eventual conquest has the power to remove his culpability for committing a crime, to remove the crime from history, to remove it even from the realm of possibility.

This trick, in which a man disappears himself (or is disappeared) from his actions, isn't magic. We perform it on behalf of men whenever we talk about this violence that is supposedly unthinkable. We talk about the number of women and girls who are raped—in high school, in college, in marriages, in an attic, on a Tuesday—but not the number of men who rape women and girls. We talk of the women and girls who are murdered, kidnapped, found decapitated or frozen or barely alive in the front yard, or on the porch, or tossed on the side of the road, but not the number of men who murder, or kidnap, or maim, or destroy them. Nicole Brown Simpson was a "battered woman" before she was a dead one, but the man who beat her, and very possibly murdered her, escapes our sentences. We call Andrea Constand an "accuser," a label we apply also to each of the dozens of women, individually and as a group, who have come forward to demand justice for being drugged and raped by Bill Cosby. Our language shields him, disappears him from the scene of the crime, transforms his crime into an allegation, a suggestion, a rumor.

The lawyers for Owen Labrie—a student at a private preparatory school in New Hampshire—disappeared him in exactly this way from accusations that he had raped a fifteen-year-old classmate. The girl's testimony was harrowing: Labrie took her to a locked mechanical room, where he took off her pants and removed her underwear, where he kissed and bit her breasts as she was crying and telling him, "No, no, no," where he scraped inside her vagina with his fingers, and held her hands above her head, and penetrated her with what she believed to be his penis. On the stand, Labrie denied this version of events, telling jurors, "I thought she was having a great time." He denied penetrating her, denied that she had said no—although, when pressed by his lawyer about whether he had perhaps kissed the girl's breasts too aggressively, he acknowledged that he "may have been a little carried away."

If getting "carried away" is intelligible as any part of a defense, it is because some part of us believes that all men have this inside them—an instinct to which he had simply succumbed. And in the end, that defense succeeded. The prosecutors could not prove "beyond a reasonable doubt" to the jury—made up of nine men and three women—that the sex was "nonconsensual," so they acquitted him on the charge of felony rape. But they could prove that he used a computer to lure a minor for sexual activity, a felony, and that he endangered a child, a misdemeanor, and these are the crimes for which he was convicted, along with three misdemeanor charges of sexual assault. He wept as the verdict was read, even though his defense had prevailed in what it set out to prove: that he was, in fact, just a "normal" young man.

"One in five women who goes to college will be assaulted," Vice President Joe Biden says in a press conference. The year is 2014. A presidential task force has just released the results of a study on sexual assault on college campuses. I know these numbers are inaccurately low, since estimates predict that only 13 percent of women who are raped report the assault to authorities. The rest keep silent out of fear they'll be shamed, fear of retribution, fear of invasive, inappropriate, and insensitive questions. "It's a parent's worst fear when you drop your daughter off at college," the vice president says to his audience. "You say a little prayer for one thing: that your daughter will be safe. You pray that your daughter will be safe."

The White House's 1 Is 2 Many campaign launches with a PSA that stars Benicio del Toro, who is seated in a black leather wing chair in front of a fireplace in a wood-paneled room. "We have a big problem," he begins, "and we need your help." The problem, we are told by an A-list roster of celebrities like Dulé Hill, Seth Meyers, Daniel Craig, and Steve Carell, is sexual assault. The PSA encourages men to speak up, to act, to become part of the solution to the problem only they can name.

The message is important and necessary, although it may be somewhat undermined by its spokespeople. Daniel Craig, for instance, is best known for reprising the role of James Bond, a character whose reputation for seducing women is topped only by his reputation for disposing of them. "If I saw it happening," Daniel Craig says in the PSA, tilting his head to one side, "I'd never blame her. I'd help her."

Del Toro continues: "If I saw it happening, I'd speak up." It's uncanny, really, because his characters don't show this same moral fiber. In *Fear and Loathing in Las Vegas*, for instance, it's Johnny Depp's Raoul Duke who speaks up, who acts, who intervenes when he finds his lawyer, Dr. Gonzo, sequestered in a hotel room with an underage "religious freak," having plied her with LSD on the plane in order to more easily pressure her into sex once they reach the hotel. In the PSA, del Toro looks directly into the camera: "If she doesn't consent, or if she can't consent, it's rape. It's assault."

Which is the real message? The franchise or the PSA? The paycheck or the community service? If our role models tell us they in fact have high respect for women and we all should too, how should we understand the roles they play that reinforce the opposite message: that a man's value is determined by his virility, by the number of women he's slept with, by his disregard for a woman's body, her autonomy, her age? Do they mean it when they say that women matter? Do we matter or do we not?

I was fourteen the first time a man raped me. It was February, Valentine's Day, and he wore a baseball cap, stood with one hand plunged deep into his jean pocket; the other held out a bottle, offering a drink. We stood in a liquor store parking lot beside the highway. Where did I tell my parents I would be? He was a few years older than me. *Tall, like a man*, I remember thinking. What did I know? He was on the basketball team, over six feet tall. His mustache and chest hair appeared in earnest patches. He took a drag of his cigarette, blowing the smoke over one shoulder. He never took his eyes off me. What did he see? I lifted the bottle to my lips, tipped it back, and took a drink.

In the morning, my thighs were purpled with bruises from his sharp pelvic bones, a rust-colored stain on the sheet beneath me. My arm was sore at the shoulder, my lips swollen, full and smashed-looking in the mirror. I bent over the toilet while the night returned to me in heaves and waves: our lips met once, and then again, and then he was clawing and desperate. I wanted to move away from him, from what was approaching and unstoppable, and let a "no" fall from my mouth—then a string of them dripping like pearls. Afterward he dressed and slipped out the door. The bile in my stomach surged, acid and cinnamon and sweet.

When people heard what had happened they explained it back to me: "Slut," they said. "Liar." "Whore."

That was ages ago, and very little about our situation has evolved. Then, as now, people will ask questions: What was that girl doing there in the first place? What clothes did she wear? To whom did she talk? At which jokes did she laugh? How did she hold her hand while she was laughing? Did she touch her tongue to her teeth? Did she cross or uncross her legs? What else had she done with her body that day? What about the previous day? What about the weeks or months or years before? What messages did she send, because he must have gotten the wrong ones. He was behaving as boys do, as men do. Men have needs. What did she expect? Then, as now, a community will coalesce to protect him—a chorus of accomplices, of friends, of parents and mentors and law enforcement officers, of district attorneys and judges, of lawmakers and teachers and neighbors, of celebrities and colleagues and football coaches and babysitters—who validate and corroborate and shield the man from the reach of the terrible consequences we might inflict. They have so much more at stake than only him.

Twenty-one years later, a few months after that first reading in the library at the university where I work, I am standing at the bottom of an outdoor amphitheater in Portland, Oregon, where the seats are filled with people. I feel certain the man who kidnapped and raped me when I was twenty-one is among them. I am planning, after all these years, to tell everyone what he has done. *He's here*, I think. *He has come to shoot me with a gun.* But nothing, not even that, will prevent me from speaking.

And here I am, alive, still speaking.

"Maybe none of this is about control," Margaret Atwood writes in *The Handmaid's Tale.* "Maybe it isn't really about who can own whom, who can do what to whom and get away with it, even as far as death. Maybe it isn't about who can sit and who has to kneel or stand or lie down, legs spread open. Maybe it's about who can do what to whom and be forgiven for it."

"Power," says Foucault, "is a set of relations between two persons."

———

"Power," says Voltaire, "consists in making others act as I choose."

"Power," says Hannah Arendt, "belongs to a group and remains in existence only so long as the group keeps together."

We all know that men have power as a group, but I want to be clear about something: women as a group do too.

Before Elliot Rodger murdered six people and injured fourteen others in Isla Vista, California, he had a long history of expressing hatred and violence toward women. He planned the crimes, and his premeditation is documented in YouTube videos he posted days and hours before the shootings, citing rejection by women as one of his motivations for the slaughter. In one of the videos he says, "I don't know why you girls have never been attracted to me, but I will punish you all for it."

When women on Twitter begin pointing out that these attitudes of sexual entitlement are consistent with a broader, misogynistic, sexually aggressive culture, men on Twitter get defensive and assert that "not all men" are misogynistic or aggressive or homicidal. One woman—I wish I knew her name—begins tagging her tweets #YesAllWomen in response to the "not all men" argument, to make clear that, no, not all men are homicidal maniacs, but, yes, all women live in fear of those who are. Within days, millions of women everywhere in the world are tweeting their experiences of fear, intimidation, and harassment. At one point, there are as many as fifty thousand tweets a minute, each sharing an experience of everyday misogyny.

The backlash against #YesAllWomen is harsh, with women being trolled, harassed, insulted, and threatened. It happens again, years later, with #metoo, as women reveal they have been blacklisted, fired, sued. The threats and punishments are intended to silence us. In this, they must fail.

The phrase "speak truth to power" applies here. Often considered an eighteenth-century Quakerism, a form of pacifist resistance against King George I of Britain, the phrase actually first appears in a letter from civil rights activist Bayard Rustin, who was in fact a Quaker and who wrote a letter in August 1942 to the Quaker leadership urging them against providing spiritual support to troops being deployed in World War II. "The primary social function of a religious society," Rustin writes, "is to 'speak the truth to power.' The truth is that war is wrong. It is then our duty to make war impossible first in us and then in society."

As I see it, to speak truth to power means to struggle against various silences: the official silencing of a criminal justice system that claims to protect us but instead renders us mute; a cultural silence that seeks to discredit us before we even open our mouths; and the smaller, private silences we have sometimes imposed on ourselves. It is this last kind of silence I have found to be the most dangerous.

In Ovid's *Metamorphoses*, the story of Philomela does not end with Tereus cutting out her tongue. For a year, she remains imprisoned, weaving a tapestry that depicts the crime she suffered at this war-king's hands—threads of deep purple on a white background. When the tapestry is finished, Philomela gives it to a servant, communicating to him through gestures to deliver it to her sister, the Queen. The servant obeys, not knowing what message the tapestry contains. The Queen understands the message, rescues her sister, and takes her back to the castle in secret. The two sisters conspire together to kill Tereus's son, Itys, and serve him as dinner to the King. While feasting away, Tereus asks after his son. At this climactic moment, Philomela reveals herself, disheveled, disfigured, smeared in blood, and throws Itys's head into Tereus's lap. As he begins to understand what has happened to his only son, he flies into a rage and chases the two women out of the castle, through the woods, and into a field before the gods finally intervene and turn them all into birds.

In some translations, Philomela becomes a nightingale, doomed to sing her attacker's name for all eternity: *tereu, tereu*. In others, her sister becomes the nightingale and Philomela is turned into a swallow, a bird that has no song at all.

———

Two things interest me about this story. The first is Philomela's metamorphosis at the end, which is either justice or a further injustice, depending on your interpretation. The second, and more important, is her tapestry, an act of courageous speech that is not speech, this way of speaking out despite the impossibility of speaking. There is much to be learned from this.

Perhaps it is useful here to return to those famous lines by Muriel Rukeyser: "What would happen if one woman told the truth about her life? / The world would split open." It is a powerful image. But though I have turned to these lines often, I think what she is saying has proved only partially true. Many women have told the truth about their lives, however impossible that may seem at the time, and the world has gone on pretty much as before.

As you must have realized by now, the world does not shatter after I admit publicly to being kidnapped and raped. My mentors hug me, and offer kind words of praise and admiration. Yes, I have a few very awkward conversations in which it becomes clear that others find the subject of my rape a more uncomfortable topic than I do. I now realize this has little, if anything, to do with me and have stopped considering myself responsible for other people's feelings about that. And though I felt compelled to protect my family all these years from the painful story I carried, my mother and I had the most honest conversation of our lives after she read my book. My husband, whose opinion matters to me more than that of any other person on this Earth, said if anything, he loved and admired me more. Though my fear was that this secret would come to define me as "that woman who got raped," that I would be shamed, ostracized, shunned, what occurs with far more frequency is that a woman approaches me, soaking wet with her own tears. She says nothing, which communicates a story for which she has not yet found the words.

In the 1960s, Betty Friedan called domestic oppression "the problem that has no name." We might now call the epidemic of sexual violence against women the problem that has no language.

If we are going to do the difficult work of grappling with these failures, it is not enough that we speak our truth to one another in private or behind closed doors, though this is an important and necessary step. I understand the fear of breaking a long-held silence. It is a fear that holds tremendous power. But if there is any hope for justice, we must speak truth to that power. We must tell anyone and everyone who will listen. And those who will not listen must be made to hear.

WHAT WE PAY

"Someone has to pay," the woman in the white skirt tells my students. She's sitting across from me, in a wonky circle we've made with the metal folding chairs we found stacked in a corner of the classroom. Her hands are on her thighs, and she's leaning forward in her chair. She's one of many guests I've invited to my class this week. In addition to my students, there are three environmental activists, and three activist artists, and, of course, the woman in the white skirt. I expected her to talk about her work as a community organizer, but she is instead talking about the BP oil spill, how BP has destroyed the lives and livelihoods of so many people all along the Gulf Coast. People have lost their jobs, their homes. Some have lost their lives.

"BP won't pay the claims but they have no trouble paying to make those stupid ads," says the woman in the white skirt, standing up out of her chair. She raises her voice, points her finger, but I'm not sure at whom. My students watch, motionless in their chairs circled around her, maybe, like me, surprised to be feeling accused.

One of the artists asks us to stand, to join the woman in

the white skirt, to push our chairs toward the wall and out of the way. The artist asks us to imagine a spectrum of our relationship to the oil industry. "If your livelihood is very dependent on the oil industry, stand on this side," the artist says. Then she gestures the other way. "And if your livelihood is not at all dependent on the oil industry, stand on that side."

Many of my students stand with the woman in the white skirt on that side, on the Not at All Side. I want to stand there too. But I remind my students that in Houston, everything is tied to the oil industry, even, and especially, art. The major renovation of the Museum of Fine Arts is funded by money from oil; most of the major collectors in town became rich from oil; even the person who donated money to the university to found the art center where I work made his fortune because he invented fracking.

My students hang their heads as they shuffle toward me on this side, on the Very Dependent Side.

To be perfectly honest, before oil began washing up on our beaches, I'd never given it much thought. Years ago, when news that the *Deepwater Horizon* had exploded in the Gulf of Mexico reached us, my daughter, then only three, was home sick and I was newly pregnant with a second baby, nauseated by everything: my daughter's illness, the smell of the sweat-dank blanket she insisted on lying under while watching hour after hour of *Dora the Explorer*, the dog hair in every crevice of the couch, the taste of my own breath. I sat in a chair across from my sick child and watched the footage of the oil gushing from the ocean floor on my laptop. I watched in total horror. But eventually I had to close my laptop and continue on with my day.

Since then I've learned a lot about oil. It is a clear to tar-black mixture of hydrocarbons and comes in many forms: crude oil is subcategorized as heavy if it is very dense, light if it has low density, sweet if it is low in sulfur, or sour if the sulfur content is high. Light crude produces more gasoline, while sweet crude requires less refining and produces fewer environmental hazards. Bitumen, another form of oil, is associated with oil sands, tar sands, and natural asphalts. Shale is a fine-grained sedimentary rock from which petroleum can be extracted. Although the technology for doing this is relatively new, the word *petroleum*—Latin for "rock oil"—is quite old, appearing in 1546 in a work by German mineralogist Georg Bauer, who was the first to document the production, refining, and classification of the Earth's "solidified juices."

Thankfully, our understanding of geology has improved in the last 470 years. We know now that petroleum, like other fossil fuels, dates from an unfathomably earlier period of Earth's development—so much earlier that Earth might as well have been another planet, and, in fact, it was. When the world's petroleum reservoirs were created, Earth was mostly swamp and vegetation, and the only land mass above water was the supercontinent of Pangea. Now, reservoirs have been found on every continent except Antarctica. The largest of these are in Venezuela, which recently surpassed Saudi Arabia as the holder of the largest-known oil reserves in the world.

What I find fascinating is that these reservoirs were created almost entirely by chance, when dead organisms, mostly zooplankton and algae (not dead dinosaurs, as some would have us believe), collected on the seabed in vast quantities over tens of thousands of years, a relatively short period in Earth time. Slowly, layer upon layer of sediment accumulated on top of that rich layer of decaying organic matter, creating warmth and pressure that transformed it first into a waxy material known as kerogen and then, ever so slowly, into liquid and gaseous forms of hydrocarbon. This is not to say that all decayed prehistoric organic matter has been transformed into fossil fuels. On the contrary, the creation of the world's reserves of petroleum all those ages ago was dependent on a perfect set of conditions: the layer of massive quantities of decaying organic matter needed layers and layers of rock at a sufficient depth to create enough pressure and heat to cook it for millions of years inside a reservoir rock porous and permeable enough to allow it to accumulate underneath a cap rock dense enough to trap it from escaping to the surface. The hydrocarbons collected by accident in these traps formed oil reservoirs, from which we now extract petroleum very intentionally by drilling and pumping and flushing and squeezing, and a variety of other processes that can be completed only at great danger to the people executing them.

The United States imports oil from these giant reserves—mostly from Venezuela, but also from Mexico, Canada, the Persian Gulf, and Nigeria—and it is pumped through giant pipelines thousands of miles long, or shipped on giant oil tankers across the ocean through the shallow waters of the Caribbean, into the Gulf of Mexico, navigating the eddies spiraling off the Gulf Loop current until it at last arrives at the Houston Ship Channel, where hydrocarbons are separated from one another by type and distilled from crude into any of the myriad forms petroleum can take: forms like fertilizers, dry cleaning chemicals, solvents and adhesives, pesticides, and plastics, which we use to make everything from our streetlights to our cooking utensils. The keys on which I am typing right now are plastic. We even use petroleum to make fabric. The pants I am wearing contain polyester, a man-made, petroleum-based fiber. Elastic is petroleum based, as is most of the ink we use to print our money. Crayons are made in part from paraffin, a derivative of petroleum. The PVC pipes carrying water through my house are made from petroleum. The wires bringing power from the wall to this laptop rely on petroleum-based coating for insulation. Even the so-called clean power generated by wind farms in West Texas require petroleum, since the turbines must be carried individually by enormous gas-guzzling tractor trailers before they are assembled as windmills across the state. Petroleum drives our politics, our society, our technology, and our economy. And the fact is: it has driven us mad with an insatiable thirst.

"Holy shit," mumbles one of my students, crowded, like the others, around my laptop open on the desk in our unlit classroom. This week we're watching the archived footage of the spill. They're seeing it for the first time: oil gushes at the bottom of the ocean in rust-colored plumes. An eruption keeps erupting in a place that looks so unlike Earth it might as well be the surface of the moon. The camera pans out and out, then stops so suddenly the camera jars, wobbles: a loose precarious thing. Robot arms maneuver in and out of the plumes, sawing the riser pipe free, now falling out of the frame.

Years ago, when the rig exploded 250 miles southeast of where we now sit, most of my students were still in high school, and, like most other high school students, they did not grasp the consequences of every story on the news. Now at twenty and twenty-one, they are bombarded each day with grim news about gentrification, terrorism, and climate change. They open their Facebook feed to stomach-churning video of a boy shot for carrying a toy gun on a playground, of girls gang-raped for getting drunk and being fifteen. The world they've inherited is not the one we promised them. We promised them the American Dream, the land of opportunity, a house in the suburbs with a white picket fence. But that dream, as my students keep pointing out to me this semester, is broken, and besides, it was never really their dream in the first place.

"Holy shit," the student says again, shaking his head. He's a man of few words, a bearded hipster—a stoner, I suspect. He reminds me of how white Christians must imagine Jesus. Another student, a Latina, "first generation," majoring in photography, stands to turn the lights back on. The rest lean back in their chairs.

"Do you know what the most fucked-up thing is?" asks one student as she closes my laptop. She's my favorite student this semester. One of my favorite students ever probably: a self-proclaimed mixed-race queer femme New Orleanian who could teach this class if I got out of her way. "So the fishermen couldn't fish because of all the oil, right? So then BP hired them to take their boats out and spray dispersant into the ocean." "Vessels of Opportunity," BP called it. "The fishermen couldn't say no because what choice did they have? But BP wouldn't let them wear protective gear because they didn't want the public to know they were putting poison in the ocean. They were more concerned with the optics than with doing the right thing."

She's right, of course. Oil itself is toxic enough, but BP arguably made the disaster far worse by applying 1.8 million gallons of the controversial dispersant Corexit to the oil gushing from the well in order to break it up into trillions of tiny droplets and potentially keeping it from floating to the surface, reaching the shore, and making apparent the full scope of the damage it had caused. Five years after the spill, the Gulf is still devastated: oyster beds have been destroyed along the coast; fish continue to wash on shore dead or dying; dolphins in the Gulf are dying at rates four times higher than before the explosion. People who helped with the cleanup are sick, unable to work; people on the coast are sick, getting sicker. BP doesn't have much to say on the matter: "The environmental catastrophe that so many feared, perhaps understandably at the time, did not come to pass, and ... the Gulf is recovering faster than expected," a public relations expert for the oil company writes. The depleted oyster beds? The dead baby dolphins? The fishermen bleeding from their ears and noses? That could be caused by anything.

Anyway, my turn is over. The student who reminds me of white Jesus holds up a photograph he's taken of a half-demolished building. "This is what gentrification is doing to queer culture," he says. The assignment was to document a problem that most people don't see. The next student holds up his phone and shows us a photo of a Jeff Koons sculpture, one of the balloon animals, which has just sold for about a zillion dollars at auction, he tells us. We all agree it's total bullshit. The next says he's going to describe some graffiti that got removed in the neighborhood. "Describe?" I ask. "Yeah, sorry," he says. "I forgot my visuals." My favorite student, the one pulling her blue hair up into a bun, uses her cell phone to play Pitbull and Ne-Yo's "Time of Our Lives." I raise an eyebrow. She holds up a hand to stop me from objecting and explains that the song is about the struggle to make ends meet and always failing, and that constant failure is why people give up and just go party instead. "We all have so many problems," she says, "and because we can't even solve our personal problems, like how to pay our rent, how can we even think about, much less solve, the big problems we all have in common?"

I'm still thinking about these questions on the drive home, about the "big problems" we watch unfolding in slow motion or, worse, the ones we can't even see. Many of my students live near campus, in Houston's Second Ward, which is home to the Houston Ship Channel, the second-largest petrochemical complex in the world. The Houston Ship Channel is where the oil industry's dirty work is done: not only the refinement and distribution of petroleum itself, but also its vast network of ancillary industries, which each year release hundreds of millions of pounds of a number of dangerous chemicals into the air in service of the oil industry. These chemicals have been linked over and over again to rare forms of leukemia and other aggressive cancers. One study conducted in 2006 by the University of Texas Health Science Center at Houston showed that the likelihood of developing a rare cancer is 56 percent greater for anyone who lives within two miles of the Houston Ship Channel than for people who live anywhere else.

In fact, the Houston Ship Channel is what some might call a "sacrifice zone," a term government officials coined during the Cold War to describe areas that had been hopelessly contaminated by the mining and processing of uranium into nuclear weapons. More recently, the term *sacrifice zone* has been applied more broadly to include low-income semi-industrial communities, often populated by African Americans, Latinos, Native Americans, and poor whites, whose disproportionate exposure to toxic substances forces them to sacrifice their health and safety in ways that more affluent people do not.

Although *sacrifice zone* is a term that is increasingly applied to the entire Gulf Coast region as a result of the primary and ancillary operations of the oil industry, it's not a term that I think of as I pull in to my own neighborhood, on the west side of Houston, far from the polluting smokestacks and refineries of the ship channel. Houston calls itself the "energy capital of the world" because it is home to four of the world's seven super-major oil and gas companies, and all of them are headquartered in midrise glass-plated office buildings perched on wide green lawns on the west side of town, near where I live. Most of my neighbors work in the oil and gas industry. They wave from their yards as I walk my dog. From a distance, they seem like nice enough people.

Would they still seem nice if an oil company built a refinery in our neighborhood? If the waterways in the park down the street were choked with toxic waste? If our children were breathing toxic fumes while they slept in their beds? If it were us dying of rare cancers? And, more importantly, if we can't imagine being okay with that for our own neighborhood, our own health, our own children, why are we okay with it for anyone else?

There are no comfortable answers to these questions, but we need to keep asking them anyway. In fact, one reason we have decided as a class to join the woman in the white skirt in a protest at BP headquarters is to question the seemingly widely held idea that some lives—any lives, for that matter—are worth their sacrifice.

"IT'S TIME," shouts the woman in the white skirt, and the crowd falls into line: youngish hippies, tribal elders, faith leaders, musicians, actors, artists, a group of Vietnamese fishermen, community organizers, my students and me. We're gathered in a parking lot along Terry Hershey Park on Memorial Drive, in the Energy Corridor, less than a mile from the headquarters of BP America and about four miles from my house. We each have our duties. Those in the front hold signs with slogans like "The Gulf can't wait any longer for restoration," and "ENVIRONMENTAL JUSTICE STARTS @ THE SOURCE." A couple of my students lift to their shoulders a model of a shrimp boat, in which there is a petition with more than a hundred thousand signatures demanding restoration for the Gulf Coast. I'm standing near the end of the line, holding a sign that says, simply, "JUSTICE."

"It's time for BP to pay!" shouts the woman in the white skirt as we begin marching out of the parking lot. Another woman jogs toward our line, waving to a group of people she knows. I recognize her from somewhere. She's wearing a white shirt, white pants, a loose blue cardigan buttoned at the waist. She doesn't see me; she smiles and reaches out to embrace a woman who approaches her. They lock arms in the line. We march past mothers who stop pulling jogging strollers from their shiny Chevy Tahoes; past children who play on the playground while their nannies eye us suspiciously; past a line of police officers with their hands resting on their black belts. "Someone has to pay!" the woman in the white skirt shouts as SUVs pass us on the road. The passengers wave and smile as if this is a parade and we are passing out candy.

"I've seen children who are sick," one activist tells the crowd when we reach BP's headquarters. "In the early days we had rashes and respiratory problems, but now it's moved into cancers, very aggressive cancers. In parts of where I live in Louisiana, just south of us in Plaquemines Parish, they say they're burying about a person a week."

We're standing on the sidewalk, in the sun, because the cops won't let us approach the building. The cops stand on the grass, in the shade, between us and the BP compound, which spans several buildings and sits on ten acres of land. Above the main building—I kid you not—actual vultures circle overhead.

The translator for the Vietnamese fishermen raises her voice above the others: "They don't have to answer to us?" she shouts with her hand raised, her finger pointing at the building. "They don't have to follow our laws?" From windows in the floors above us, two white men in bright polo shirts and pleated khakis film our protest with their cell phones. They're smiling and laughing, as if her accusations, her voice, her presence here, are a kind of joke. They wave and point and bend over laughing. The translator steps back into the crowd, shaking, spitting, too angry to cry, as we all now are.

Several of our group try to approach the building to deliver the petition. The cops stop them, turn them around, point them back toward the crowd. One of the fishermen steps up and demands firmly, "Talk to us." The cops look past him too. The tribal elders join in: "Talk to us. Please, talk to us." The youngish hippies join in, and the faith leaders, and the musicians, and my students. I see the woman from the parking lot, the one I recognize, joining in as well, but I still can't remember how I know her. "TALK TO US! TALK TO US!" She and the crowd shout at the cops, at the building, at the two men in bright polos and pleated khaki pants filming us from the windows above.

I raise my voice too, though in truth, I know the executives aren't in the building. They're miles away in downtown Houston at the CERAWeek IHS Energy Conference, billed as "the premier annual international conference for energy industry leaders, experts, government officials and policymakers, leaders from the technology, financial, and industrial communities—and energy technology innovators." This year's theme is "Turning Point: Energy's New World." I imagine them schmoozing and congratulating one another and eating tiny croissants.

A woman comes out of the building to film us on her pink iPad. She's wearing a white pressed blouse tucked into a black pencil skirt, a pair of shiny black heels. She stays behind the row of cops. People drive by in black SUVs. The crowd continues shouting: "TALK TO US! TALK TO US!" The shouting grows louder and louder, though the cops continue standing with their hands on their belts. The musicians join our voices with their drumming; the drumming gives way to music, to singing, which is at once full of rage and something that leads us, inexplicably, to dance, to turn to shake our asses at the cops, at the woman with the pink iPad, who watches the protest unfolding right in front of her on the tiny screen.

The vultures are still circling overhead when we finally dance away from BP headquarters, down the street, and back to the park where we've all left our cars. The woman in the white skirt passes out plastic bottles of water and snacks, hugs and high-fives, and invites us all to a crawfish boil at her nonprofit's headquarters across town in the Second Ward, the neighborhood that runs adjacent to the Houston Ship Channel.

My students and I drive away from the Energy Corridor in two cars, watching as sprawling subdivisions give way to townhouses packed six to a lot, to historically protected neighborhoods where all the houses have picture windows and wide porches, and then to taquerias and washaterias, leaning buildings where flowers sprout from planters on the stoop. Sidewalks buckle and crack, when there are sidewalks at all. One student in the car with me—the Latina, "first generation"—points out landmarks from her childhood. She grew up here, she tells us. She still lives just down the street.

We enter the nonprofit headquarters—a maze of protest signs, brochures, books, staple guns, and hammers piled on every surface. An elder leans forward in her chair, a pile of sewing in her lap. She motions us to the back of the building without looking up. We walk through a door and out to the back patio, where we discover the entire crowd of protesters sitting cross-legged on the floor, midway through a Mayan prayer ceremony.

My students look at one another, at me, as if to say, *Really?*

I shrug my shoulders in response. *Sure. Really*.

We sit on a table outside the circle and lean back against the cool brick of the building. The Mayan elder tends a small fire while speaking to the group through her interpreter. Those in the circle around her place small bundles of herbs and grass into the flames. "It is a trade," the interpreter says. "You offer before you ask in return." The musicians and artists are there, and each places a bundle into the fire. One says she offers art in exchange for healing. Another offers her voice in exchange for strength. The fire goes out very suddenly, and the Mayan elder shakes her head. Her interpreter says, "You give too little and ask for too much."

When the fire is burning again, the woman in the white skirt puts a bundle into it and begins to speak. She is tired, she says, her voice low and full of grief. It's uncomfortable to see her like this, after all of her shouting, her finger pointing, her bluster and bravado. "So much effort," she says, "and so little progress." All these years and the Gulf is still devastated: the dead marsh grasses, the dead baby dolphins, the dead fish, and dead fishermen, the children who are dead or dying. One of the artists wraps an arm around her shoulder, whispers encouragement in her ear. The Mayan elder stirs the fire. She's humming, her song and the smoke billowing upward together in a single plume. The woman in the white skirt leans her head back. "Someone has to pay," she says, long and low—to the roof, to the smoke, maybe to us all.

I look around the circle: artists and organizers and youngish hippies all sit, heads bowed, cross-legged on the floor. My students watch carefully, their eyebrows furrowed, their faces so earnest and eager and intent. The student who reminds me of Jesus has tears in his eyes. The one with blue hair— the queer femme from New Orleans, my favorite student ever—has one hand to her mouth, the other hand clutches her elbow.

And then it hits me: they are already paying for this, and maybe have been all along. At the end of the day, they'll come home to this neighborhood. They will settle into bed breathing air that may one day kill them. And the fishermen and tribal elders sitting around the circle with their heads against their knees will return to their homes along the Gulf Coast. Or maybe their homes are already gone. I'll drive across town, to where I've bought a house in a suburban neighborhood—probably with money I didn't even fairly earn—where I grow vegetables in my garden and my children play in the green manicured yard. At night I go to sleep dreaming the American Dream. My students are paying for every benefit I reap. And the injustice of that is staring me right in the face.

Just as I'm about to leave, I notice that the woman I recognize from the protest is here too. She sits cross-legged on the floor, like the others, a bundle in her lap. "I'd give it all back," she begins. Suddenly I know her: a student of mine from years ago, from a community writing workshop I once taught. On the first day of class, she introduced herself as a geologist working in the oil industry. She submitted her writing to the group only once: three short little essays, one about yoga, one about childhood abuse, and one about despair. "We do so little," she wrote. She had been watching the news and saw only disaster. She stood in the oil fields and felt the planet crumbling under her feet. She started riding her bike to work and eating healthy, but she knew it wasn't enough. She ended her last essay: "Someone should do something."

By the end of that workshop, she had quit her job, talked of selling all of her possessions. She said she didn't exactly have a plan but that she was thinking of walking across the country, maybe riding her bike. Whatever path she followed, it led her back here, years later: to this protest, to this fire, to the fishermen and the tribal elders, to the woman in the white skirt, sitting across from her. "I want nothing in return," she says, tears streaming down her cheeks. When she was in my workshop all those years ago, I thought she was having a nervous breakdown, but now I see it clearly: more than anything else, she wants to be redeemed.

I motion to my students that it's time to leave. We pick our way around the fire and walk toward the alley behind the building. The woman in the white dress follows us out, her eyes puffy and red, carrying an armload of foil-wrapped tacos. She puts one into my hands, hugs me, though I almost can't take it. She smiles, holds it out, insists. "You can't start a revolution on an empty stomach," she says.

My students and I leave the alleyway, the street, the neighborhood. We keep walking: now two miles, now three. We pass under the interstate. We pass buses with no passengers. We pass through a park where a hundred of Houston's homeless veterans used to sleep. They've all been evacuated. A sign posted at the entrance reads: "NO TRESPASSING / PARK UNDER RENOVATION / UNTIL FURTHER NOTICE." There are no construction crews; the only evidence of renovation is that the park is now no longer safe for people to sleep. We pass the county jail, where prisoners play basketball in tiny outdoor pens, where mothers with their children wait outside the back door for their loved ones to be released. We pass under a highway, leaving the Second Ward, and enter a manicured park, the renovation of which was paid for by a large donation from the Kinder Foundation, the charitable arm of Kinder Morgan, that company whose pipelines wrap the world—and now we can't even enjoy the park because we've seen how much it costs. A white couple pushes a jogging stroller while their white baby fiddles with the white blanket on her lap. The path before them is straight and safe and flat.

At the end of the day, hours later, my students and I pile around a picnic table at an outdoor bar—"Ice Houses," we call them in Houston. We eat tacos and drink cold beer. Some of the artists and the musicians from the protest meet us here, and my students tell them about their perspective on the day. The protest, the prayer ceremony, the walk from there to here. Such a simple activity, they say, placing one foot in front of the other. They plan the work they'll undertake now: a photo essay, a performance, a guerrilla installation. I won't lie: sending them on this path offers me some small measure of relief.

In July 2015, three months after the fifth anniversary of the spill, BP agreed to pay a record $18.7 billion in fines over eighteen years to settle its federal legal disputes, bringing BP's portion of the cost of the spill up to $54 billion, including what it has paid so far in economic claims, its disaster response efforts, fines to various government entities, and cleanup and restoration programs. Of that, $4 billion will go to settle a federal criminal probe and effectively nullifies all criminal charges against them. "They ought to feel that," says Keith Jones, father of one of the men killed in the explosion that night on the *Deepwater Horizon*. "They ought to feel something," he says. "Sometimes somebody ought to feel something other than greed."

The question of whether it feels anything is a good one, because its actions show no remorse. BP, along with Shell and several of the super-major oil and gas companies, continues to purchase lease rights in ever more delicate ecosystems. For most people, it takes a traumatic event to change their behavior, but it seems the oil spill changed nothing. People still say it's the worst ecological disaster in history, as if that means it was an isolated incident. Experts estimate that after eighty-seven days, roughly 210 million gallons of crude was spilled into the Gulf. Devastating as this was for delicate Gulf ecosystems, this crude would have been refined into enough gasoline to cover about a fourth of what we Americans consume in our automobiles in a single day. And gasoline doesn't burn perfectly. For each gallon of gasoline we burn in our cars, we release five to six pounds of carbon into the air—as much as 2 billion pounds in a single year. If carbon were a solid, this would be like throwing a bag of flour out the window for every gallon of gas each of us consumes. But carbon isn't a solid; it's an invisible gas, and if we don't see it, we can pretend it just isn't there.

Now we hear news that the polar ice caps are melting, that Exxon knew that climate change was coming and covered it up. Scientists tell us that carbon levels in the atmosphere have taken us beyond the point of no return.

"Gifts from the earth or from each other establish a particular relationship, an obligation of sorts to give, to receive, and to reciprocate," Robin Wall Kimmerer writes. I cannot count all the gifts I have received from the Earth and from others, but I know that money would be a poor expression of all the things I owe in return. I want BP to pay for the oil they've spilled in the ocean. I want to punish the bonuses and profits, the laughing midlevel executives in their bright polo shirts, the woman in the pointy black heels filming us on her stupid pink iPad. I want them to see the consequences, large and small, of their apathy and greed. But the crime is not only theirs, the harm isn't even only the damage we can see. There is no sum of money the rest of us could exchange for a clear conscience for our part in how we got to this moment. Guilt itself is useless and is worth nothing.

But the relationships we have and make with one another, the obligation we might recognize that we have toward the Earth—that is a gift that could redeem us. To give at least as much as we take, to repair all that we've harmed.

Even now, the present rushes across continents and stirs our future like a stone.

AGAINST WHITENESS

Years ago when I was in graduate school, I took a workshop led by a poet I admired. The class was all women, only three of whom, including the poet I admired, were women of color. One day a fellow student asked the group about a book of poems recently published by one of the tenured faculty members in the program, a white man. She wondered how the rest of us read the poems, some of which seemed to my classmate "a little racist."

The following week we discussed the poems, which seemed to all of us "yes, definitely racist," and the week after that, the white tenured poet visited our class. He began with macho bravura: "Hey there, ladies—so I hear you have some questions about my book?" And my classmate began, "Yes, well, we were hoping you could clarify how race is working in these particular poems . . ." And then the tenured poet began shouting and did not stop until he left the room.

At one point he told one of my classmates to "SHUT UP," and at another, he told the poet I admired, a woman who was his junior colleague, that it didn't matter if the poems made her uncomfortable because the poems were not written for her. "They were written for white people," he said.

I watched the whole exchange and said nothing, though I was floored, flabbergasted—even though I knew what I was witnessing was deeply and profoundly wrong. I said nothing because I was afraid of being yelled at by the white tenured poet, and also because I had never known what to say when watching a man explode under the pressure of his own narcissism, not even when he is attacking the people I love.

I said nothing. Eventually he left. In the silence that followed him out the door, my friend, one of the three women of color in the room, called me out. "Where the fuck were you?" she asked. I didn't have an answer to that question, and none of the other white women in the room had an answer either. It was wrong to say nothing, and I knew it. We all knew it.

I have thought of that moment often over the years: the choice I made to say nothing, how it was a choice I had spent a whole lifetime not fully realizing I was making. A year earlier, I had sat in a different class with the poet I admired. We had all read Audre Lorde's "The Master's Tools Will Never Dismantle the Master's House" and were discussing it in class. Toward the end of the essay, Lorde asks, "If white American feminist theory need not deal with the differences between us, and the resulting difference in our oppressions, then how do you deal with the fact that the women who clean your houses and tend your children while you attend conferences on feminist theory are, for the most part, poor women and women of Color?"

I bristled when I read that question because, on the surface, it appeared to include me in a group to which I didn't feel I belonged. Yes, I have blond hair and pale skin and blue eyes, *but I'm not white like affluent white women are white,* I thought. I put myself through college by working at Walmart and, for one summer, in a strip club, where I scraped together enough money for tuition and rent by taking off my clothes. I brought home furniture I found in a secondhand store, or in the dumpster, or on the street. "White trash" felt more comfortable and familiar as a racial category for me. I was almost white, not quite white, so close to the edge of whiteness I might fall off.

In class I said, "Lorde is saying 'white women,' which is a term that describes me, but she's not actually talking about me, or about any of the women I know," and the poet I admired said, "Well, since no one is talking about that, maybe you should be talking about that."

I think of that moment especially now as I am confronted each day with violences, large and small, that I am asked to accept, how my power and privilege depend on this acceptance, and also on the condition that I keep silent about it all my life. What does "whiteness" even mean? It's not as if being "white" actually refers to my skin, or to anything biological or natural or real. Whiteness isn't even cultural since people who call themselves white do not necessarily share a culture. There is no "white community" that extends from the mansions of Beverly Hills all the way to the farm where I grew up in rural Missouri, though "whiteness," as an idea, wants me to believe that there is and that this community is large and welcoming enough to include even me.

But in reality, at no point in the history of the "white race" has whiteness been large and welcoming. Whiteness scholar Noel Ignatiev has argued that one condition of being white is policing who is not, that whiteness itself exists only in relation to the privileges it bestows and their constant threat of revocation. Whiteness pushes poor whites to the margins, threatens them with terms like *white trash* or its more euphemistic equivalent, *working class*, demands that they demonstrate their allegiance to whiteness by violently protecting its boundaries against the advancements of people of color. Whiteness is in no way inextricable from affluence, autonomy, and the capitalistic promise of accumulated wealth.

"No one was white before he/she came to America," James Baldwin writes. "It took generations, and a vast amount of coercion, before this became a white country." My own ancestors, for instance, gave up being Irish and Scottish and Welsh, and hid being Polish and Greek and African, in order to become intelligible to others, and to one another, as "white." Generations later, I still feel those effects: whiteness has made me a "desirable candidate" for student loans, housing, jobs; it allowed me to become upwardly mobile, to go to graduate school and transform myself from someone who is "not quite white" into one who is affluently white. In exchange, whiteness has demanded all this time that I buy into a system of racial hierarchy that keeps a very few white men wealthy and in power and very many people poor and disenfranchised. It demands that when this hierarchy is enforced with violence, I look the other way, that I accept it or ignore it, that I say nothing at all.

In truth, whiteness did not exist in my imagination until I was twelve years old, when my sister became estranged from our family because she was "living in sin" with a black man. I was twelve when she moved out of our house and into this man's house, and felt somewhat confused by people's reaction. Race had never been a thing that was discussed—not the idea of it or the real, lived consequences of that idea. Only after our family name was exchanged for a racial slur and I found myself unfriendable, always sitting alone at the lunch table, unable to ask questions in class without being sent to the principal, did I understand what people believed the sin to have actually been.

During this time, each of the three television stations in my hometown in Missouri had been running nightly footage of four police officers trying to kill Rodney King on the side of the road—trying to bash his skull in, trying to break his bones. I remember noticing that there were several more officers who did not participate in the violence but stood to the side, letting it happen, their hands on their guns or near them, looking on.

Rodney King suffered a fractured cheekbone, eleven broken bones at the base of his skull, and a broken leg at the hands of those four police officers. They were eventually charged with use of excessive force, though the jury ultimately acquitted them of these charges—a verdict that sparked six days of intense protests throughout Los Angeles that Representative Maxine Waters called a "rebellion," an "insurrection," and that authorities treated like a war.

Each evening the footage ran almost continuously on the news: the protesters attacking motorists, burning buildings, throwing rocks, smashing windshields, overturning cars and setting them on fire, breaking through windows and ransacking stores, exchanging gunfire with police and with store owners trying to fend off looters, burning down entire city blocks. As the Los Angeles Police Department, the Los Angeles County Sheriff's Department, the California Highway Patrol, the fire departments of neighboring cities, the Seventh Infantry Division of the US Army, the First Marine Division, and nearly six thousand National Guardsmen prepared to move in to "restore order," Rodney King made a tearful statement to a crowd of reporters, pleading to the police, to the protesters, to anyone who would listen: "Can we all get along?"

That question arrived in the living room of my home, where I noticed, for the first time, that I was supposed to be part of an intangible something that called itself "white"—like the police officers who beat Rodney King were supposed to be white, like most of the jury who acquitted those officers were white. The mayor of my hometown was white, I realized, and the city council members were white, and also all of the judges and police officers. All of the people who were so upset about my sister's relationship were white: not only my parents, but also their parents, our church leaders, people we ran into at the grocery store, bank tellers, the pharmacist, our neighbor down the road. There were one hundred students in my year, and ninety-five of them were white. The five black students, I suddenly realized, lived very separate lives. Their houses were on the other side of town from mine, across the railroad tracks. There was a church on that side of town, the Second Baptist Church; the Baptist church my family attended, an entirely white congregation, called itself "First."

I wish that I could say that during this time I understood the responsibility I had to destroy a system I knew even at that moment to be profoundly wrong, but in fact I had only a few conversations about it—mostly with my parents about the way they were treating my sister—and those were inadequate and mostly calm. I had no more power to change people's minds, I soon told myself, than I did to stop the police with their swinging black batons in Los Angeles. It was a thing that had already happened, it seemed, a reality with which whiteness demanded I go along.

Most people—aspiring to whiteness—sign on to this social contract without any inkling of guilt or remorse, maybe without realizing they are doing it, maybe without consideration for how the inequality whiteness produces is itself profoundly unjust, or without even thinking about how much of ourselves or others it requires we give away. "If you can convince the lowest white man he's better than the best colored man," President Johnson famously said, "he won't notice you're picking his pocket. Hell, give him somebody to look down on, and he'll empty his pockets for you."

In her unwillingness to accept the terms of this arrangement, Rachel Dolezal notoriously decided to reject whiteness and instead become black. "Nothing about being white describes who I am," she told an interviewer after her parents outed her as "Caucasian," though nothing about the origin of that term in the Caucasus region of Eastern Europe describes her either. Her discomfort with whiteness might more accurately be called a conscience, though having a conscience doesn't give any white woman the moral authority to become a black woman instead.

Whiteness is a claim to this authority, to righteousness, to power, to full protection under the law—a claim to a neutral existence at the invisible, unraced center of an otherwise racialized world. It's a collective fantasy that also leads white Christians to believe Jesus is white and Mary is white, despite the fact that they were Middle Eastern Jews. It is why Santa is white on nearly every Christmas card and why the Tooth Fairy is white in nearly every cartoon. The pathological fantasy of white supremacists is a return to the former greatness of a purely white ethnostate, even though there has never been such a thing in history. Most white people haven't even always been white. They just learned to look the part and to say nothing about it at all.

———

This is all to say that whiteness is not a monolith, is neither fixed nor stable. Whiteness is, in fact, a fairly modern fiction, dating at its earliest to the period of European colonialism and imperialism, when "race" became justification for capturing and selling humans as slaves. There has been no point in history when all "white people" have experienced white privilege in the same way. Even now, Donald J. Trump is white in a different way from how Honey Boo Boo is white. This is not a denial of racism or the real and devastating effects of white supremacy on the lives of people of color, but rather an acknowledgment that whiteness is constructed, and its construction has everything to do with power and very little to do with skin color.

The resistance of poor whites in particular to ideas about white privilege hinges on this distinction: that white privilege at the margins of whiteness doesn't work the same way it does at the center, that whiteness oppresses in ways that poor whites also feel—that power is real and feels just beyond our reach. Poor whites point to statistics that we are also shot by police, are targeted by police, are assumed to be breaking the law, are arrested and detained unlawfully by police. Not at the same rates as people of color, to be sure, but when occupied with alleviating one's own suffering, the comparative suffering of others can sometimes seem a long way off.

So when a term like *white privilege* arrives to suggest that any success we do enjoy is not fully our own doing but a kind of racial cheating—cashing in an unearned advantage because of the color of our skin—and that any prosperity we find

I'd have to disagree, for white people still have that accessibility of power and whiteness is not our own, well, for some people it's too much to take in. And if we cannot take it in, there is no way to admit or acknowledge that the little power we do have comes with the condition that we deny it to someone else. It is much easier for the ego to reject all responsibility, to deny all blame. White people might say, "Well, I have never discriminated against anyone personally." Or, "My ancestors never owned slaves." And yet if we did not in some way already understand that we reap even very small benefits from the systemic oppression of people of color, there would be nothing about which to deny our individual guilt.

"We do not know the history / Of ourselves in this nation," writes poet Jericho Brown. Or we do know our history but deny our responsibility for what is happening in the right here and now. I learned only after moving away from Missouri that it is the type of place where the man my sister loved and with whom she lived could have wound up dead in his own neighborhood; where, in some counties, even in the northern part of the state where I lived, a set of sundown laws at one time prohibited African Americans from remaining in a given county after dark; and where between 1880 and 1940, white mobs lynched at least sixty black men and women in public acts of racial terror (mostly for alleged crimes against white women) and faced virtually no consequences for their actions—the second most of any state outside the Deep South.

We think of it as a dark exception in our history when black men in particular were routinely lynched for using disrespectful language, for insubordination, for laughing at the wrong time or for a prolonged silence, for refusing to tip one's hat to a white person, for failing to yield sufficient space to them on the sidewalk, for resisting a beating by a white man, for writing a letter to a white woman, or simply for looking at her, for political activities, for union organizing, for discussing the lynching of someone they knew, for being in debt, for refusing an offer of employment, for displaying one's wealth or property, for refusing to give up one's wealth or property, and, most egregious, for acting in a way that was offensive for being *too white*.

Less frequently, these same mobs also lynched people who might be described as "white" under any other circumstances; their crime, more often than not, was being *not white enough*. Both cases prove what one southern critic observed: that men are most likely to lynch when the victim offends their sense of "racial superiority."

Whiteness demands this violence: that we either commit it or accept it, and if we refuse we are in danger of becoming its victims ourselves. This is not some relic of our remote past, but rather the current moment on a never-ending time line of seemingly inviolable power. In St. Louis, two hours east of where I grew up, a police officer, believing himself to be white, shot and killed Michael Brown in his own neighborhood in broad daylight after he refused to comply with an order to get out of the empty street. In New York City, a white police officer choked Eric Garner to death on the sidewalk while arresting him for selling cigarettes. In South Carolina, a white police officer shot Walter Scott in the back for running away.

A white police officer shot and killed Tamir Rice, a twelve-year-old boy, on a playground in Ohio, within thirty seconds of arriving on the scene. In Minnesota, a police officer, aspiring to whiteness, shot and killed a beloved cafeteria worker in the chest with his wife and young daughter in the car.

Each time, the officer faces no consequences because he has killed to protect whiteness, and whiteness in turn protects him. Each time, rage swells and carries people out of their homes and into the streets of St. Louis, Oakland, Los Angeles, Seattle, Philadelphia, New York City, Minneapolis, Chicago, Washington, DC —places that are not so different from the Deep South, despite what their white residents like to think. The rage is not pathological. Racism is. Whiteness is. Denying the evidence of our eyes and ears is pathological. Silence is pathological. Apathy is pathological. And yet each time police arrive in riot gear and in armored vehicles, they wear gas masks and launch tear-gas grenades into the crowds of protesters, who raise their hands in peaceful surrender. At home, people who call themselves white watch the violence on television. They shake their heads and change the channel. It is pathological to see this injustice and do nothing about it at all.

"I urge each one of us here to reach down into that deep place of knowledge inside herself and touch that terror and loathing of any difference that lives there," Audre Lorde writes in "The Master's Tools." "See whose face it wears." For most of my life, I didn't know enough to recognize that the face of difference I most feared was my own. When I was twelve, and twenty-seven, and all the ages in between, I had no sense of perspective, of my own power or purpose—or I did have a sense but refused to acknowledge it for reasons I am now ashamed to admit. I wanted to deny my responsibility and blame for the difficulty others experienced because I had also experienced difficulty. I didn't think I should be held accountable for a history of racist violence because I had also been a victim of violence. When I had gotten stuck on the only line in Audre Lorde's essay that seemed to prove my exception from her critique of white feminism, it was, in effect, a failure to see the most important thing about it, which is how it also, and maybe especially, applied to me.

When I watched a white man yell at a woman I admired in front of her class and said nothing, that was a failure too: a failure to reckon with the fact that my struggle was not the only one that mattered, that my experience was not the only one that had meaning, that I would never be the only person in any room who had something I was afraid to lose. It wasn't that she needed me; she was then, and still is now, quite capable of holding her own. It's that I stood by and let whiteness work in the way it has always worked, watched how it can assert itself as almost anything: as poetry, as superiority, as the loudest voice in a tiny room, as a violence that demands I watch and do nothing at all.

At the end of that academic year, the poet I admired left the university where, to my knowledge, the white tenured poet faced exactly zero consequences for yelling at his junior colleague in front of her class. That's the protection whiteness gave him and, for all I know, gives him still. There's no reason to expect that anything has changed in that regard, and if we continue to do nothing, it never will.

Whiteness is a moral choice: if it is learned, we must unlearn it. If it is a transaction, we must refuse to buy in. If whiteness is a structure, it is vulnerable at its margins, like all built things, and we have a responsibility to burn it to the ground.

GOLIATH

I am sitting in my car at a stoplight in a small midwestern city. It is a bright, cloudless Tuesday in that tiny wedge of time between late summer and early fall when each day begins with a chill that evaporates just after sunrise. Today I am driving from the suburb where I live in my sister's basement to an office building downtown, where I have a job interview scheduled for 8:00 a.m. The radio DJ who is normally so coarse and insulting is saying they don't know what has happened exactly, only that there has been an explosion in New York. The other DJ, who normally laughs at everything the coarse DJ says, isn't laughing. There are no answers, only questions and more questions. I know only that it is my birthday and just last night I was saying to my older sister that it is probably lucky to have an interview on my birthday.

Outside the office building downtown, I sit in the parking lot and listen to the radio. Newscasters are describing the scene in faraway Manhattan: smoke and fire and everyone running for cover. I take the elevator to the sixteenth floor, introduce myself to the receptionist, and sit down on a couch in the waiting room. There is a television on the wall.

Journalists are interviewing onlookers about what they have seen, microphones in their faces, cameras and eyes on the burning tower, as a plane crashes into the second tower, and the newscasters each say, "Oh my God." A woman calls me into her office to interview me for a job that just this morning I was desperate to have, but if she asks me any questions, I do not hear them, and if I give any answers, they do not sound like human speech.

Back at my older sister's house in the suburbs, she and I are watching the news, where they keep playing footage of the planes crashing, over and over; footage of the towers crumbling, over and over; footage of people jumping out of the buildings and falling, their clothes blown loose and flapping. We watch stone-faced journalists break down in tears. We hold hands, sit close together on the couch. My younger sister calls to wish me happy birthday but instead says, "Oh God," and I say, "Oh my God," even though I have just decided once and for all that I do not believe there is one.

"Tonight I ask for your prayers for all those who grieve," President Bush tells us from the Resolute Desk in the Oval Office, "for the children whose worlds have been shattered, for all whose sense of safety and security has been threatened." My sister and I watch this address from the couch in her living room, where we have been sitting all day, a bottle of whiskey between us. We are afraid to move, afraid to leave the house, afraid to look away from the flickering spectacle that is President Bush and his steel-gray tie. "I pray they will be comforted by a Power greater than any of us, spoken through the ages in Psalm 23: 'Even though I walk through the valley of the shadow of death, I fear no evil, for you are with me.'"

The next morning I shuffle to the kitchen to make coffee while my sister lights two cigarettes, hands one to me. We have not slept all night, or if we have slept at all, it is only in fits on the couch. The front page of the *New York Times* has announced "U.S. ATTACKED; President Vows to Exact Punishment for 'Evil,'" and pins responsibility for the "thousands" of deaths on Osama bin Laden, a name most of us have never heard before. We learn throughout the day that he is a Saudi prince, the leader of a terrorist group called al-Qaeda, that he wears his beard long and his head wrapped, and that, with this attack, he has declared war on the United States. Our mother calls to tell us that our aunt, who works in the Pentagon, is safe and accounted for. She recently had foot surgery and had struggled to walk on crutches, but when it came time to escape she found that she could run.

All day we watch reports about Osama bin Laden, and each time the newscasters talk about al-Qaeda and the Taliban, they show video of a call to prayer. Slurs have been graffitied on the wall of the mosque in town, though that is not reported on the news. Instead, there are reports that the group of men who managed to crash the flight destined for Capitol Hill called their wives and mothers from the plane before rushing the cockpit. They are heroes, we are told. This scene—of the men rushing the cockpit and crashing the plane in a field in Pennsylvania—joins the others that play on a loop over and over while I am in the shower, or shopping for groceries for the first time in days, or filling my car up with gas: the second plane hitting the tower, the firemen rushing up into the tower, the man jumping and falling from the tower, his white shirt fluttering like wings.

The attorney general appears on television claiming that he knows the identities of the eighteen hijackers but gives almost no information about their names or their nationalities—only that they were "Middle Eastern." Envelopes dusted with anthrax begin arriving in the mailboxes of journalists and politicians in Washington and New York. Now there are estimates that more than three thousand people died in the attacks. There are reports that a seventy-six-year-old man in South Huntington, New York, tried to run a Pakistani woman down with his car; that two teenagers have thrown a Molotov cocktail onto the roof of a convenience store owned by Arab Americans in Somerset, California; and that in Phoenix, a Sikh-American gas station owner, who wears a beard and a turban in accordance with his faith, was shot five times while planting flowers outside his Chevron station. When the shooter is arrested, he declares to police, "I am a patriot! I stand for America all the way!" In Dallas, a Pakistani immigrant has been shot to death in his convenience store. Middle schoolers in Texas have been charged with making terrorist threats against a schoolmate of Indian descent. My sister and I watch the mailman from behind the blinds. We also watch the delivery man, our neighbors, people driving by the house in their beat-up Toyotas. She keeps the silver revolver in one of her dresser drawers. It is loaded.

A little more than a week after the attacks, President Bush addresses a joint session of Congress to make the case for war: with Osama bin Laden, with al-Qaeda, with the Taliban, in Afghanistan, and in any other nation that provides aid or safe haven to terrorism. "Either you are with us or you are with the terrorists," he says. I can hardly watch with my stomach turning to ice. My sister and I keep the lights off in the house, the bottle of whiskey between us on the couch. "Freedom and fear, justice and cruelty, have always been at war," President Bush tells Congress, "and we know that God is not neutral between them." Later, people will say, *That was the moment he became president.* All I can think about are the people on the planes, in the mailroom, the man in the convenience store, the children who watch bombs fall from the sky, the various ways they might try to hold on to one another, or to themselves.

This is the story I think of now when my son asks me to tell him what I know about evil. He is six, born nearly a decade after the attacks, and though evil has only recently entered his imagination, he has quickly become obsessed. Tonight it will take the form of a long, slinking animal with sharp teeth and slick fur in the dark under his bed—or something that has folded itself flat, like only a shadow can, to fit under the pile of his shirts in the closet. It will curl into baskets on the shelf, into each drawer of his dresser, behind his open door. The evil he believes in does not rest: it keeps vigil when it is sunny or cloudy, summer or winter, morning or night.

My son suffers from no particular affliction beyond one we all share. He is afraid of dying, of the malice of strangers, a fear that he expresses sometimes by crying and sometimes by clinging to my shirt, a fear that surpasses all appeals to logic and reason. My son is six years old and does not believe in logic and reason. This is his life: he eats breakfast, goes to school, learns to read, plays soccer on the playground with his friends, practices tae kwon do, eats dinner, takes a shower, and all the while his fear of being consumed or possessed by some shadowy evil thing keeps him from his own room, from his toys, from the comfort of his bed. He can't go to sleep alone, will not do it, and if he wakes in the middle of the night and finds himself with his fear of the evil in the dark, he leaves his room and comes immediately to mine.

My son is afraid of evil because he believes the stories he has been told on television and in movies. A bedroom door creaks open, and the bogeyman jumps out from behind it as my son also jumps in his seat. A shadow is only a shadow until it becomes something with teeth, a possibility that seems, at least to my son, entirely real. He doesn't know about CGI, doesn't believe me when I explain that these are actors wearing makeup and masks. He hears on the radio that evil men are bringing death and destruction to our hemisphere, and he believes it is only a matter of time before they arrive at our door. Increasingly he is told that he won't recognize evil when he sees it because it can look like any stranger, or like a neighbor, or a friend.

———

I heard my first stories about evil when I was around my son's age while sitting cross-legged on the checkered tile floor of the second story of the First Baptist Church in my hometown, while the deacon's wife read a picture book she held open on her lap. David is a hero, the book told us, but Goliath is a monster: six feet tall or nine feet tall, depending on whom you asked. He wore gilt armor on his shins and forearms and also on his chest; a bronze helmet with a bright red plume rose above his bearded face; he raised a spear above his head, aimed it, prepared to bring it down. He charged, open-mouthed, unafraid of the small boy with delicate European features who faced him with a leather sling in his outstretched hand. This boy was *good*, the deacon's wife told us, because his people were favored by God. Their enemies, the Philistines, were *evil* because of their worship of false idols, their warmongering ways, the ritual sacrifice of their children. "They were so evil," she whispered, "they were barely even human."

The moral of this story was clear to me then, even if she didn't state it explicitly: there are people whose religion is different from ours, and whose language is different from ours, and their food is different from ours, and if they are different in all of these ways, their morals must also be different from ours—all upside down or backward, where good is evil and evil is good. It is morally good to fight them; it is virtuous to win.

In the decades since I sat cross-legged on that checkered tile floor, I've learned how stories work, and so I know now that for every story we tell, there are countless more that are left out, that go untold, and what the deacon's wife's picture book left out in this story of David and Goliath is that the people we call the Philistines were a tribe encompassing perhaps thirty thousand people at its height, that they likely emigrated from Greece, that they made pottery, mourned and buried their dead, planned their towns carefully, and took great pride in their cultivation of olive trees. But that is not what we think of when we think of evil, and the deacon's wife was not known for her nuances. I understand now what I may have only suspected then: that any story that cannot accommodate nuances is not interested in truth, but in obscuring it instead.

Then, as now, the idea of evil creates fear, and people who are afraid are more easily controlled. I turn on the radio in the morning while cooking breakfast and hear that ISIS is waging jihad against the United States. We are told that "radical Islam" represents an evil like the world has never seen before. Terrorists are evil, we are told; so are serial killers, drug dealers, gang members and immigrants, murderers, warmongers, and all those lurking in our prisons. We hear the word *evil* applied to anyone who opposes us, or threatens us, or sometimes simply disagrees with us. Hitler was evil. Osama bin Laden was evil. Saddam Hussein was evil. Fidel Castro was evil, as was Chavez in Venezuela. Putin is evil, except now that he isn't. Kim Jong-Un is evil, as is Bashar al-Assad. We hear this on the radio, see it on television and in movies, read it in newspapers, hear it from the lips of the president of the United States. Increasingly we are told that we won't recognize evil when we see it because it can arrive in the form of the peaceful teachings of whole religions, whose followers harbor secret hatred for us, intend only harm toward us and our way of life, against whom we are fighting a global existential war for all that is good and righteous. And, we are told, we are losing.

"Never react to an evil in such a way as to augment it," Simone Weil wrote in 1933 as she contemplated the various temptations to which she was inclined to succumb, such as the impulse to turn against others when the world falls apart. The world has always been falling apart, it seems, and the idea of evil has always been available to us to describe those who engineer its destruction.

On January 29, 2002, four months after the attacks on the World Trade Center, President Bush delivered his famous "Axis of Evil speech" to Congress, saying that "a terrorist underworld . . . operates in remote jungles and deserts, and hides in the centers of large cities," that, in fact, our "war on terror" would not stop with Afghanistan but might extend to the Philippines, Bosnia, Africa, and Pakistan, places where they kill women and children, where they hold families hostage in their homes, where they think only of poison and weapons; that the nature of certain nations is hostile, murderous, corrupt. No one applauded as these words echoed through the chamber and into my sister's living room, and across the world, where, I learned much later, that twenty-five hundred American troops had already deployed to

Afghanistan, where roughly three thousand Afghani civilians
had already died as a result of our airstrikes, though some
estimates put the number closer to forty-five hundred. Or
twenty thousand. The estimates vary. No one knows for sure.
No one has bothered to keep track.

A year later, in March 2003, President Bush again
addressed the nation on television to warn us about an evil
regime with a history of reckless aggression in the Middle East, "a deep hatred of America," and in possession
of "weapons of mass destruction." Diplomacy was not an
option, he explained, because "when evil men plot chemical,
biological and nuclear terror, a policy of appeasement could
bring destruction of a kind never before seen on this earth."
Three days later, 130,000 US troops invaded Iraq; the government collapsed within three weeks. That December, US
soldiers found the former dictator, Saddam Hussein, hiding
in a six-foot-by-eight-foot bunker outside his hometown of
Tikrit. In December 2006 he was hanged for "crimes against
humanity" for the execution of 148 Iraqi Shiites, though he
has been blamed for hundreds of thousands more. When
asked for comment, President Bush said of the hanging,
"He was given justice. The thousands of people he killed
were not."

The difference between good and evil is "the first idea the
child must acquire," Maria Montessori writes, but as I con-
template how to explain evil to my son, I admit that it is a
difference I still do not fully comprehend.

It's been a decade now since Bush was president, and we are still at war. As I write this, we have more than ten thousand troops in Afghanistan, and in the sixteen years since President Bush sent troops there, nearly forty thousand civilians have died violent, gruesome deaths. In Iraq, more than a hundred thousand Iraqi troops perished while defending themselves against President Bush's crusade against evil, and together those troops and our troops have claimed nearly two hundred thousand additional civilian lives.

Is the world safer now? In the past few months, hate crimes are on the rise again, reaching nearly the same level as right after the attacks. Recently a mosque under construction near Austin, Texas, was burned to the ground, as was a mosque in Victoria, Texas. In Kansas, a man shouted, "Get out of my country!" before shooting two men he believed to be Iranian, killing one and also striking a third man who intervened to protect the others. A Florida man tried to burn down a corner store whose owners he believed to be Muslim in order to "run the Arabs out of our country." A man in Salem, Oregon, called an employee at a Mediterranean restaurant "a terrorist" before attacking him with a metal pipe he referred to as his "horn of Gabriel." This man told the authorities who arrested him that he perpetrated this attack because he is on a "warrior's path." In Washington, a man put on a mask and approached his thirty-nine-year-old Sikh neighbor, telling him, "Go back to your own country," before shooting him in the arm. What is perhaps most shocking about these crimes is that the people who commit them do not believe their actions are harmful or wrong or evil in any way; rather, they believe that what they are doing is in fact righteous and good.

Customs and Border Patrol agents detained a five-year-old American citizen for three hours at Washington's Dulles Airport because his mother was born in Iran. This boy is nearly the same age as my son, and video shows him clinging to his mother when he is released, just as my son might cling to me. She sings "Happy Birthday" to him and showers him with kisses as she carries him to safety. He is wearing a red shirt and buries his face in her neck. What wouldn't we all give to be carried to safety by someone we love? The White House press secretary justified this particular detention in a briefing: "To assume that because of someone's age or gender they don't pose a threat would be misguided and wrong."

Make no mistake: these are acts of fear. Fear of possibility, of unpredictability, of the unknown. These men know nothing about the people they are harming—whether they are Iranian or Indian or Sikh; whether they practice Christianity or Hinduism or the peaceful teachings of Islam. None of us knows what is in another person's mind and heart.

We human beings are not born with prejudices. Always they are made for us by someone who wants something. We are told that we have enemies who hate us, who want to make war with us, that they will come to destroy our way of life, that they are coming to destroy us, that their arrival means we are already destroyed. This is not the full story or even a particularly true one. Even as I write this, the American military is dropping bombs from drones, flying bombs on rockets, planting bombs underground. We drop bigger bombs than have ever been dropped, bombs that can kill people we call our enemies from miles away. We call our bombs "mother." We drop bombs on mothers and their children. The images of their bodies, if we see them at all, do not move us as they should.

I have an opinion on evil that I know is not very popular: I don't really believe it exists. I don't believe that any person arrives in this world predisposed toward another's destruction, which is not to say this isn't something we all learn. We learn to see evil in others because we do not wish to acknowledge a painful truth: none of us is as good as we imagine ourselves to be. This is not to say I don't believe in malice and destruction and moral depravity. I do. I see evidence of it every day. I see how we teach ourselves to hate one another and, in our hatred, to destroy. I believe in the harm that stories can do, but also in their power. If people can tell stories that cast shadows where there are none, perhaps stories can also shed light where there is darkness, and can promote understanding where there is confusion and fear.

My son's fear is cyclical. The evil comes and goes, resurfacing each time he reaches the edge of his moral geography. A classmate bites him on the playground. Would it be evil to retaliate? A friend no longer wants to play together. Does that make them enemies? His sister says she hates him. Does this mean he is unloved? He has an invisible friend named Mr. Nobody, on whom he blames all of his worst misdeeds: a broken vase, greasy handprints on the wall, that time he pulled out my hair by accident or curiosity or mistake.

At night, I hold him by the hand, and we look together under his bed, where we find only his own toys; behind the chair are only the dust bunnies I missed during my last time coming through with the broom. Under the shirts folded in his closet we find only more shirts. I ask him to tell me all about the evil he imagines there. There is a monster made entirely of bombs. "His head is a bomb and his hands are bombs and his feet are also bombs," he tells me.

I understand why this monster would frighten him. Each day we are told our enemies are monsters, that our annihilation is imminent, and it's hard to remember a time when I didn't feel myself living under that shadow. A plane passes overhead and I watch it, expecting to see I know not what. I hear several loud bangs in a row down the street and I freeze, waiting to hear a scream, a siren, or the distant brilliance of a firecracker overhead. A paper bag left on the corner might contain discarded leftovers or a homemade bomb. I don't think I'm alone in imagining the terrible ways each of us might fail in our responsibility for being human.

"What does the monster want?" I ask my son. He tells me the bomb is looking for a place to live. "His own home was exploded by bombs," he explains. I ask, "What should we do?" His brow folds on itself, a sign he is thinking very hard.

"Maybe we should help him find a place to live," he says. I agree, and together we draw a map to this place.

My son will grow out of this particular fear. Already he is made a little braver by the story we have told together. Just now he walked alone into the darkness of his own room. And as perhaps we all should, he turned on the light.

THE FALLOUT

Dawn Chapman first noticed the smell on Halloween in 2012, when she was out trick-or-treating with her three young children in her neighborhood of Maryland Heights, Missouri, a small suburb of St. Louis. By Thanksgiving, it was a stench—a mixture of petroleum fumes, skunk spray, electrical fire, and dead bodies—reaching the airport, the ballpark, the strip mall where Dawn bought her groceries. Dawn could smell the odor every time she got in her car, and then, by Christmas, she couldn't not smell it. In January, the stench hung in the air inside her home when Dawn woke her children for school every morning. "That was the last straw," she told me recently. Dawn made a call to city hall asking about this terrible smell. The woman on the phone told Dawn she needed to call the Missouri Department of Natural Resources, gave her the number, and abruptly hung up. Dawn called the number, left a message, and then went on with her day.

Her youngest son was napping when the phone rang. Dawn was sitting on the top bunk in his bedroom folding laundry. The man on the phone introduced himself as Joe

Trunko from the Missouri Department of Natural Resources. Joe spoke gently, slowly. He told Dawn that a landfill near her home is an Environmental Protection Agency Superfund site contaminated with toxic chemicals. He said there has been an underground fire burning there since 2010. "These things happen sometimes in landfills," he said. "But this one is really not good."

Joe told Dawn that this landfill fire measures six football fields across and more than 150 feet deep; it is in the floodplain of the Missouri River, less than two miles from the water itself, roughly twenty-seven miles upstream from where the Missouri River joins the Mississippi River before flowing south and out to the sea. "But to be honest, it's not even the fire you should be worrying about," Joe continued. "It's the nuclear waste buried less than one thousand feet away."

Joe explained that almost fifty thousand tons of nuclear waste left over from the Manhattan Project were dumped in the landfill illegally in 1973. He explained, so gently, that Dawn should be concerned that the fire and the waste would meet and that there would be some kind of "event."

"Why isn't this in the news?" Dawn asked.

"You know, Mrs. Chapman, that's a really good question."

As soon as she hung up the phone, Dawn picked it up again and called her husband. He thought someone must be making a mistake. "Dawn, this is the United States of America," he said. "The government doesn't just leave radioactive waste lying around."

Dawn agreed: there must be some mistake. "They wouldn't do that. Our government would never do that."

She called the regional office of the Environmental Protection Agency (EPA) to ask about the status of this Superfund site, and when staff there returned her call days later, they knew surprisingly little about the fire, Dawn thought. In fact, they wouldn't even call it a fire, but kept using the term "subsurface smoldering event" and shared almost no information about what they called the "radiologically impacted material." They told Dawn it wasn't dangerous, that the landfill wasn't accessible to the public anyway. But Dawn had studied the documents Joe Trunko had emailed her after their call, so she knew there was more to the story. Joe had even called the next day to make sure she'd received all the files. That made her feel more worried than anything else. "It's like he wanted this information to get out," she told me. "Like he was waiting for someone to call and ask."

Dawn printed out everything Joe had sent and took it to her parents' house that weekend, where she and her mother were planning to host her daughter's fifth-birthday party in a few weeks. Dawn had planned to talk to her mother about balloons and cupcake recipes but instead spread out all the documents on the kitchen table. Her brother and husband and both her parents pulled up chairs as she explained about the landfill and the waste. They shook their heads in disbelief. "Someone should have told us about this," said her father, shaking his head.

———

After her daughter's birthday party, Dawn Chapman got to work. Each day she would wake up, make breakfast for her two school-aged children, and put them on the bus. While her younger son watched *Sesame Street* and ate Cheerios out of a plastic bowl, she searched the Internet, printing out any information on the landfill she could find. During her youngest child's nap time, she spread the documents out on the kitchen table, leaving the floor unswept, the dishes unwashed, the laundry unfolded in a basket by the couch. She learned that in 1990, the EPA had listed the West Lake Land-fill Superfund site, which encompasses both the West Lake Landfill and the nearby Bridgeton Landfill, on its National Priorities List. Eighteen years later, when it finally got around to making a decision on the site, its proposed remedy was to install an engineered cap and leave the waste exactly where it is. At that time, in 2008, only a few people in the community knew there was a nuclear dump in their backyards, and the EPA did little to alert them. "If it weren't for the fire," Dawn realized, "we never would have known."

Weeks later, she found herself standing outside the chain-link fence that surrounds the landfill with half a dozen environmental activists who had gotten some air-sampling equipment. A news crew had come, and there, shivering in the biting cold of the February wind, Dawn gave her first interview about what was causing the terrible smell. She shivered partly from the cold but also because by that point, her concern had become righteous anger. She stood with the others on a patch of frozen grass watching the meters and dials on the handheld monitor jump and buzz and whir.

She looked up and locked eyes with a woman she'd never seen before.

Karen Nickel didn't know much about the landfill—she'd only just learned about it a few weeks before—but she knew about the waste. Unlike Dawn, she'd grown up in North St. Louis County, and this waste had been here, making her neighbors sick, since before she was born. Karen was nine years old when her parents moved to North County in 1973 in pursuit of good schools, a safe neighborhood, and a big yard for all the children. Her father worked in the lumberyards, and her mother stayed home to care for Karen and her siblings.

On their quiet cul-de-sac in North County, sometimes as many as fifteen or twenty children would play kick the can in the street or chase lightning bugs in the park until the streetlights clicked on. A creek ran behind the houses on one side of the road, and the kids splashed through the water in the mid-August swelter. They fished in the creek for minnows and crawdads and often followed it all the way to McDonald's to get shakes and fries. All the children attended the same elementary school, which also backed up to the creek, and heavy rains would bring the water into the field behind the school, a field where they played sports when it was dry. Karen played softball throughout middle school and high school. She was healthy and active and outside all the time.

When Karen and her husband bought a house in North County for their own growing family, they chose one not far from the neighborhood where she'd splashed through the creek as a girl. But one summer day in 1999, she ran across a parking lot in the rain and then couldn't get out of bed for days. Maybe she had come down with the flu, she thought. Her doctor didn't know what to make of her symptoms, but Karen's blood work showed signs that antibodies were attacking the proteins in the nuclei of her cells. "Lupus," the doctor finally told her years later. He prescribed steroids to manage the symptoms of the disease, and mostly they did manage them. She felt healthy more often than ill. But in July 2012 she collapsed at her daughter's softball game and didn't bounce back, didn't return to work, or to feeling healthy. Her doctor said this might be the new normal.

Karen went to a new doctor, who told her that there's increasing consensus that lupus can be brought on by environmental triggers, including exposure to contaminants and chemicals like cigarette smoke, silica, and mercury. In particular, he said, recent studies have shown a link between lupus and uranium exposure. That night over dinner, Karen's husband asked if she remembered a story on the news from a few months before about the creek that ran through her neighborhood. She remembered only vaguely. "Well, it was something about uranium contamination," he said, looking up from his plate.

"And?" she said.

"And, well, maybe you should look into that."

Karen did look into it and learned that many of her classmates and neighbors and childhood friends had died of leukemias and brain cancers and appendix cancers—rare in the general population but apparently common among those who live or have lived near the creek. It couldn't possibly be a coincidence.

On the day they met at the air sampling event at West Lake Landfill in early 2013, Dawn followed Karen back to her house and the two stood out in the driveway talking for hours—Dawn about the landfill, Karen about the waste. The next day, first thing in the morning, they were on the phone together. "I'll bring my kids and come over," Dawn said. They stayed until late in the evening. "That's what life looked like, and has looked like ever since," Dawn tells me on the phone.

When Dawn and Karen learned what the EPA had proposed years earlier in the Record of Decision, they immediately pushed back. They called the media, gave interviews, started a Facebook page. "I remember getting so excited when we hit two hundred members," Karen told me. "Now we have over seventeen thousand." They all lobbied their representatives, their senators, city council members, mayors— even Missouri's attorney general at the time, Chris Koster, who responded to Karen and Dawn by hiring his own scientific teams to reinvestigate the EPA's findings and then sued the landfill operators. At one point Karen and Dawn had become so fluent in the relevant jargon that public officials began to suspect they were working for some kind of law firm. "Who are you again?" the officials kept asking. "What group are you with?"

"We're just moms!" Karen and Dawn would answer. "We're

just citizens concerned about the health and safety of our kids and our community!"

Soon after, Karen and Dawn, along with another resident, Beth Strohmeyer, officially formed Just Moms STL, an advocacy group that hosts monthly meetings to update their neighbors and community on the progress of their collective efforts. They learned that many of their neighbors near the landfill had developed respiratory diseases and chronic nosebleeds, and some had lost all the hair on their bodies. When they asked the EPA about these illnesses, officials refused to acknowledge any link or even entertain the possibility that the "exothermic reaction" might be causing them. Their scientists had studied the site, they kept saying, and concluded that there was nothing dangerous happening at the landfill, that there is no disaster approaching, that the landfill poses no threat.

But each day, Dawn and Karen could see the containment vehicles that arrived to siphon off the thick black leachate seeping from the burning refuse into the ground. The vehicles took the leachate to be treated off-site before it was dumped into the sewer or the river, which supplies the water they drink.

Dawn and Karen decided to look into the fire for themselves. During the day, Dawn downloaded temperature reports from the well monitors at the landfill. At night, she and Karen would sit at the kitchen table with crayons and markers, mapping the temperatures of the wells, using graph paper and trying to remember how to calculate equations they had learned in high school. After a few weeks of making these graphs, they realized the fire wasn't under control; it wasn't going out. It was, in fact, moving toward the waste, inching toward the known edge, spreading through the old limestone quarry: now one thousand feet away, now seven hundred. In the best-case scenario, the fire chief told them, people need only close their windows, turn off their air-conditioning, and shelter in place. In the worst-case scenario, there is nuclear fallout. A disaster is coming, they realized. And worse than that: nothing is standing in its way.

*   *   *

As the plane circles downward toward the city, a familiar green stretches for miles in every direction, familiar enough to me that I could call this home. I'm not from St. Louis, but I grew up near enough that I came often to watch the Cardinals play in the second Busch Stadium and ride in a claustrophobic tram capsule to the top of the Gateway Arch. In high school I drove to St. Louis on the weekends to see my favorite bands play in what was then called the Riverport Amphitheatre. A few years later, as a senior in college, I flew out of St. Louis Lambert Airport with a man I loved on a two-month trip to Europe and flew back here changed and alone.

It's July when I land this time at the airport. I take the bus to the rental car office to collect the car I've reserved, an exercise in patience since the pace of all things—conversation and business and traffic—moves more slowly in St. Louis than in Houston. The calm navigation voice coming through the car speakers leads me onto and off the highway, down a business strip of big-box stores lined with swarming parking lots, onto a narrow road past a farm, and into a subdivision of ranches and split-level homes. I stop in front of a raised ranch at the end of the street.

Robbin Dailey opens the door and welcomes me into her home, less than half a mile from the burning landfill. She reminds me of so many other mothers I've known: the same hair, the same loose-fitting shirt and capri pants, the same open-hearted laugh. Robbin's husband, Mike, stands to greet me in the entryway, shakes my hand, and then gestures for me to follow him into the living room and sit on the couch. He leans into his brown corduroy recliner, eyes on the muted TV. Robbin sits in a stiff chair across from me, crosses her legs.

Robbin and Mike moved to this house in 1999, after their kids had moved out and started families of their own. It's a relief their children never lived here, she tells me. In this neighborhood, children fall ill. There are brain cancers and appendix cancers, leukemias and salivary gland cancers. Up the street from Robbin and Mike is a couple with lung and stomach cancer. They bought their home just after it was built in the late 1960s.

I ask what they think might happen if the fire ever reaches the waste. The question hangs in the air for a moment as the TV flickers from the far wall. "Look, we know it won't explode," Robbin explains. "We're not stupid. We know that's not how it works. But just because there's no explosion doesn't mean there won't be fallout."

"They let Pandora out of the box," Mike interrupts. "Splitting the atom opened the box." It's actually a jar in Hesiod's version, but I don't correct Mike here. "Pandora's box" has a better ring to it anyway, makes a better metaphor for original sin. The box, like the atom, he is saying, each contained within itself a capacity for ruin beyond imagining.

Eventually Robbin claps her hands on her knees and says, "Well, let's take a look." We leave the house and climb into her maroon SUV. She lights a long cigarette, then rolls down the windows. We drive up the street a few houses, pause as she watches a uniformed man open a gate into one of the backyards and enter—"Testing," she explains—and then she drives out of the mouth of the street, left at the corner where the street meets the old farm, and suddenly we're there.

"Jesus," I say out loud. I've looked at thousands of pictures of this landfill, aerial photos and historical photos, elevation photos and topographical maps, but nothing has prepared me for seeing it in person, this giant belching mound of tubes and pumps and pipes. There's some kind of engineered cover over the dirt itself, which is supposed to suffocate the fire and capture the fumes. It looks like little more than a green plastic tarp patched together over a hundred acres of sagging hills.

"This is the burning side," Robbin tells me. "The radwaste is on the other side." The patchwork is topographical and bureaucratic. The burning side is the southern section of the landfill and falls under the jurisdiction of the Missouri Department of Natural Resources; the radioactive waste is mostly on the northern side and under EPA jurisdiction. On the burning side, workers drive over the tarp on utility carts, wearing hard hats and work clothes. No gloves, no masks, no protection from the destruction buried underneath their feet. Robbin waves her cigarette at them, and we take off down the road, driving the full circumference of the site. It's bigger than I imagined: two hundred acres in all.

Robbin shows me the pond to the west of the landfill where the leachate is collected, the fence where Franciscan nuns hang ribbons at the prayer vigil they hold every other Wednesday. We drive up to the adjacent property onto which radioactive soil has eroded. There's a chain-link fence around the entire site. "We call it the magic fence," Robbin says, laughing in that open-hearted way.

On the way back, Robbin takes a detour through a series of empty streets that used to be a "nice" neighborhood. "Carrollton," the sign at the entrance still reads. "They demolished it all," Robbin explains. "The government bought everyone out because of noise pollution from the airport." She shakes her head, gives a little cough, tightens her grip on the steering wheel. "Noise pollution!"

It seems like we are driving past countless streets and intersections and cul-de-sacs, all the infrastructure without any of the houses—without streetlights or driveways or gardens or people. "Mike and I used to come out here and dig up bulbs and plants from the yards," she says, slowing down and looking out the window. "It was too sad to leave them. When they built this neighborhood, it was like a magazine. The American Dream. Look at it now."

We drive past a parking lot marking the former site of a community center, where children once swam in the pool, spending whole days in the water without sunscreen, riding their bikes home without helmets as the streetlights flickered on.

"Do you think your neighborhood will end up like this someday?" I ask, goose bumps forming on my arms and legs.

"I sure as hell hope so," she says, tossing her cigarette butt out the window.

*   *   *

"Seventy-one years ago, on a bright cloudless morning, death fell from the sky and the world was changed," President Obama's speech in Hiroshima begins. It's May and he's standing next to Prime Minister Shinzō Abe at a podium in front of the Peace Memorial in Hiroshima. His choice of words is interesting, as if death arrived in Japan that morning of its own volition. As if the US government didn't have everything to do with it.

"A flash of light and a wall of fire destroyed a city," he continues, "and demonstrated that mankind possessed the means to destroy itself." But at that point, in August 1945, there was only one government in the world that had succeeded in generating a self-sustaining nuclear chain reaction, only one military with an atomic weapon, only one aircraft that opened its bay doors on the morning of August 6 over Hiroshima and dropped a fission bomb containing 141 pounds of uranium, which fell for forty-three seconds before incinerating several square miles of a city and every person, animal, and structure in it.

At first, the Manhattan Project didn't have a name; it

consisted of a loose affiliation of military personnel, politicians, and scientists linked together by special government committees. Arthur Holly Compton, the Nobel-winning physicist leading the team working on fission at the Metallurgical Laboratory in Chicago, was on one of these special committees. At that time, the idea of a self-sustaining uranium fission chain reaction was still purely theoretical. To prove it was possible, his team needed forty tons of uranium, and they needed it urgently. Rumors had been circulating that the Germans were two years ahead of the Allies in the race for the bomb. This brought Compton to St. Louis, to Mallinckrodt Chemical Works, where he convinced his old friend Edward Mallinckrodt Jr. to enlist his chemists in the secret government project over a gentlemen's lunch.

The uranium ore, several thousand pounds of it, arrived at Mallinckrodt in hundreds of containers of various shapes and sizes ranging from large wooden crates to one-gallon paint cans. The twenty-four workers in the new uranium division at Mallinckrodt Chemical Works labored around the clock to process the uranium. Within a month of that gentlemen's lunch, they began sending the purified uranium back to Compton's lab in Chicago. Within three months, they were sending a ton of it a day.

Three days after Hiroshima, after the Japanese refused to surrender sovereignty to the US government, a plutonium bomb exploded over a small community in the Urakami River Valley. A ring of fire spreading outward for miles from the hypocenter became a ball of fire, and then a pillar of fire rising forty-five thousand feet into the air.

When Japan surrendered on August 14, 1945, *Life* magazine reported that people across the United States celebrated without reservation, "as if joy had been rationed and saved up for the three years, eight months and seven days" since the attack on Pearl Harbor. Two million people from all over the New York City area flocked to Times Square, where they kissed and drank and danced in conga lines through the streets. Scraps of cloth snowed down from windows in the garment district onto people parading below. In Chicago, enormous crowds flocked to the Loop and celebrated with wild abandon.

In St. Louis, the news came over the radio at 2:30 a.m. Bar owners rushed to reopen, and the parents of deployed soldiers tapped kegs in their front yards, pouring beer for their neighbors into pails and buckets. Those who bothered to go to work the next morning threw reams of paper out the windows of office buildings and then descended the stairs to dance through the piles of paper in the street. Impromptu parades sprang up all over the city.

At the Mallinckrodt plant in downtown St. Louis, workers were given the day off. For many of them, it was only the second or third day off since they'd begun purifying uranium for a project with a strange name and a secret purpose. Only as they joined the celebrations did they understand what that purpose had been.

*   *   *

It's dark when I spread a stack of government reports out on the hotel bed—each report held inside a binder clip, each hundreds of pages thick. I've spent the whole summer wading through thousands of pages of documents like these, all of them full of disturbing concessions and impenetrable jargon. Months ago, a high school friend reached out to me asking that I give my attention to this story. She told me that a company tasked decades ago with disposing of nuclear waste for the federal government had instead dumped thousands of barrels of the waste somewhere in North St. Louis County. The barrels were left exposed to the elements for decades, and the waste leaked into the ground and into the water of a nearby creek.

I did start looking into it, and I haven't been able to stop. I have learned that although there wasn't anything especially dangerous about the first ore Mallinckrodt processed in the downtown facility, after the "Pile-1" experiment in Chicago succeeded in generating a self-sustaining chain reaction, the focus of Mallinckrodt's work for the Manhattan Project shifted from purifying uranium for lab experiments to purifying uranium for use in an atomic bomb. A different kind of ore began arriving in fifty-five-gallon drums marked plainly URANIUM ORE—PRODUCT OF BELGIAN CONGO. The new ore was more concentrated than any other uranium ore on the planet—up to 65 percent pure uranium (versus the 0.3 percent they had previously considered "a good find"). The workers had to handle this new ore differently. It arrived on vented freight cars, and they needed to take care to store it separately from the other ore, the other wastes, and the processing equipment, and to put all the residue back in the barrels after the uranium was extracted and save it. For what they did not know.

By all accounts, the government knew about the dangers of working with this new material but allowed the uranium workers to continue working with it anyway. Weeks after the bombing of Hiroshima and Nagasaki, safety officials arrived at Mallinckrodt and demanded that the uranium workers begin wearing badges to monitor their radiation exposure and that they stop using their hands to scoop the uranium salts into bins and pick through the unrefined ore.

The officials also began looking for a place to store the radioactive wastes and settled on a 21.7-acre property just north of Lambert Field—at that time it was a municipal airport and an airplane manufacturing base—far outside the edge of town. The base sat on one side of the property; a small creek ran down the other. Beyond the creek was nothing but sparsely populated farmland. When the federal government filed suit to acquire the property under eminent domain, officials refused to disclose the exact nature of the waste "for security reasons." They assured the local government that the waste they'd be storing there wasn't dangerous. They shook hands and signed papers. They looked people squarely in the eye.

During the next twenty years, truckload by truckload, the green patchwork of farm fields by the airfield turned into a foreign world. Mountains of raffinate rose up alongside row after row of rusty black drums, stacked two or three high. But even as those mountains grew taller, the

American Dream transformed the fields into subdivisions, brought houses and streets right up to the airport site, right up to the black sand, right up to the borders of the creek. Every time the wind blew, it carried radioactive dust into the brand-new parks and gardens and backyards. Every time it rained, the water flowed between the barrels, into their rusting holes, and all the things that water can carry flowed into that small creek.

The reports tell only so much, only certain parts of certain versions of the story. The rest I have to piece together using articles in the local newspaper, phone calls with residents, oral histories collected by others, newsletters from various companies celebrating one anniversary or another. I have learned through months of this piecing together that in 1966, the government abruptly canceled the Mallinckrodt contract, but not why. The Atomic Energy Commission (AEC) advertised a public auction and sold the wastes to the highest bidder, Continental Mining and Milling Company, for a lump-sum payment of $126,550. Things get a little foggy at this point. There isn't a single unbroken paper trail, a single history, any one person who has nothing to lose, but it appears that after the sale, Continental moved the Mallinckrodt wastes to a private storage site about a mile away on Latty Avenue and then promptly went bankrupt. The radioactive wastes were then repossessed by a bank in Chicago (which did not have the required license to own radioactive waste) and were quickly sold again to another private company, Cotter Corporation of Colorado. Records from this second sale indicate that the inventory included 74,000 tons of the Belgian Congo pitchblende raffinate, containing about 113 tons of uranium; 32,500 tons of Colorado raffinate, containing about 48 tons of uranium; and 8,700 tons of leached barium sulfate, containing about 7 tons of uranium. Surprisingly, the sale also included a few hundred barrels filled with contaminated junk—boots and uniforms and bricks from the Mallinckrodt plant downtown that were hot with radiation. Cotter began drying the piles of raffinate in a giant kiln and shipping the dried material in open train cars to its facility in Colorado. After a few months, nothing was left except the barrels and the 8,700-ton pile of leached barium sulfate.

In my pile of reports is a series of letters from Cotter to the AEC in which Cotter tries to convince the government to take these wastes back. Commercial disposal would cost upwards of $2 million (about $12 million today). Cotter couldn't afford it, but they knew that the AEC was using a quarry at the recently decommissioned second Mallinckrodt facility at Weldon Spring, roughly twenty miles southwest of the airport, as a dump for nuclear waste. It asked the AEC if it could use it, asked for guidance, and for help.

That help never came.

In 1974, a government inspector arrived at the storage site on Latty Avenue and casually asked where the barrels and the leached barium sulfate had gone. Someone working at the site—a driver or a security guard, maybe—mentioned he thought they had been put in a landfill. A lengthy investigation discovered that from August to October 1973, a private construction firm drove truckloads of the leached barium sulfate, along with roughly forty thousand tons of soil removed from the top eighteen inches of the Latty Avenue site, to West Lake Landfill, around the clock. To the landfill operator, it looked like dirt, so he waved the trucks in and charged them nothing, using it as landfill cover for the municipal refuse.

I keep hoping I'll find something in these reports—a graph, a chart, a single sentence or letter or memo—that will make all of this make sense. But the reports express the detection of this contamination in charts, as numbers and statistics. They've found contamination at the airport, in the drainage ditches leading away from the airport, and all along the creek—along the trucking routes, in ballfields and in parks and gardens and backyards, in driveways, in people's basements and under their kitchen cabinets. Even now, as I write this, they are still trying to figure out just how far it has spread.

The reports measure the health risk of exposure to this contamination as an equation, with a threshold of acceptable risk. But what the reports don't say is that the contamination has already done so much damage that cannot be measured or undone. The Mallinckrodt uranium workers are some of the most contaminated in the history of the atomic age—so contaminated, in fact, that in 2009, all former Mallinckrodt uranium workers were added as a "special exposure cohort" to the Energy Employees Occupational Illness Compensation Program Act. The act provides compensation and lifetime medical benefits to employees who became ill with any of twenty-two named cancers as a result of working in the nuclear weapons industry. Because of this special cohort status, if a former Mallinckrodt worker develops any of these named illnesses, exposure to the uranium is assumed. But the people who live near the creek never worked for Mallinckrodt, which means that according to the government, they aren't entitled to compensation or medical benefits.

A woman named Mary Oscko, for instance, has lived her whole life in North St. Louis County, most of it near that small creek. Now she is dying of stage 4 lung cancer, though she has never smoked a day in her life. Shari Riley, a nurse who lived near the creek, died recently of appendix cancer. My friend, the one who contacted me about this story, never lived in St. Louis, but her mother grew up two houses away from that creek. My friend suspects that her mother's exposure to the contamination as a child changed her DNA in ways she passed on to her children, which would explain why my friend was diagnosed with an aggressive form of cancer a few years ago at the age of thirty-five. Could it also explain why my friend's mother once gave birth to a set of conjoined twins? Conjoined twins are an anomaly in the general population, but these were the fourth set born to women who grew up near that creek. And those are just the ones we know about.

———

The reports don't acknowledge these stories, these illnesses, those who are dying or dead. Most residents of St. Louis—including and especially the residents of predominantly African American neighborhoods—don't even know the contamination is there. It creates an impossible situation for health professionals in St. Louis, like Dr. Faisal Khan, director of the St. Louis County Health Department. "In community meetings people have narrated heartrending stories to me," he says, "stories about their own cancers or their loved ones or their children. I've had people walk up to me and hand me pictures of their children who have died of cancer. They've given me hair and teeth and nail-clipping samples and say, 'Could you please have these tested?'"

They're looking for a cause, looking for someone to blame, looking for a location toward which to direct their rage and bewilderment and grief. More than anything else, they want to know *why*.

Dr. Khan told me he often finds himself saying, "I just don't know."

*   *   *

I don't recognize the woman who answers the door at Kay Drey's house. I've never met Kay Drey but I've seen her photo countless times: her silver hair cut in a short wavy bob, her tall, slender frame standing slightly slouched. She's in her eighties, I think, but this woman answering her door is my age, my height. She flashes a broad smile and leads me to the dining room, where the table is piled with papers sorted into

the lids of cardboard boxes, then into the kitchen, where Kay
is writing something at her desk. Kay stands to greet me; we
shake hands, and I follow her to the dining room table, where
we sit. A paraplegic dog comes over to my leg and demands
to be scratched. "Moxie," Kay tells me, introducing the dog.
"You might as well go ahead and scratch her because she
won't leave you alone until you do."

Kay Drey lives in University City, another suburb of St.
Louis, but one where the homes are older and larger and set
farther back from the streets. Kay's husband, Leo Drey, was
a conservationist, a forester, and Missouri's largest private
landowner before he donated most of the land to charity. He
passed away in 2015 of complications from a stroke. Kay's
health is also failing now, a fact that becomes apparent as she
tells me multiple times that her memory is not what it used
to be. She relies on sticky notes, she says, which she sticks
to the shelves above her desk in the kitchen. On one orange
note she's copied a quote from Hugh Hammond Bennett, the
first director of the US Soil Conservation Service: "It takes
nature," she has written in the erratic scrawl of someone
who cannot hold a pen without difficulty, "under the most
favorable conditions, including a good cover of trees, grass,
or other protective vegetation, anywhere from 300 to 1,000
years or more to build a single inch of topsoil." She pokes this
note, hard, with the bent tip of her finger and tells me, "The
topsoil around that landfill is ninety feet deep. Some of the
richest soil in the world, and it is ruined forever."

Kay repeats herself only a few times during the three hours
we sit in her dining room, and it's in these repetitions that I

learn what is important to her: that she spent her life fighting for housing integration before she began the fight against nuclear proliferation, that any amount of radiation exposure is bad for one's health, and that she gave her first speech against nuclear power on November 13, 1974, the day that, as is widely believed, Karen Silkwood was run off the road in Oklahoma. In that speech, Kay argued against the building of a nuclear power plant in Callaway County in the middle of the state, about one hundred miles from her home in St. Louis. Originally the plan was to build two reactors, but activists like Kay fought the plan and only one was built. "That was a victory," she says. She's had other victories too: she tells me that she's the one who got the Department of Energy to acknowledge the radioactive waste at Lambert and won a twenty-year battle to get it removed. She also tells me she identified contaminated water near the second Mallinckrodt plant at Weldon Spring and made sure a water treatment plant was constructed so that radioactive waste wouldn't be dumped into the Missouri River. "It is important to pause to celebrate those victories, no matter how small," she says, "because that is what gives you courage to fight the really big battles, the ones you have to fight even though there's no chance of winning."

She asks if I'd like to see her basement. "Most people do," she adds. We climb down a set of steep stairs and she flips a switch, illuminating an overhead fluorescent light. "LED," she corrects me, even as I think it. Four-drawer file cabinets line two walls, all meticulously indexed and cross-indexed in an ancient oak card catalog that sits in the center of the room. Thousands of documents are housed here, and she knows exactly where to find any given report. "In St. Louis we have the oldest nuclear waste in the country," she observes, "because we purified all of the uranium that went into the world's first self-sustaining chain reaction."

The moment I mention the EPA, she puts her hand directly on the drawer where the woman upstairs—"my librarian," Kay tells me—has filed the EPA's Record of Decision for the West Lake Landfill and then on the drawer where I might find studies that contradict the EPA's assessment that the radioactive waste in the landfill doesn't pose a threat to residents: the radiological surveys of the site conducted in the 1970s and 1980s by the Nuclear Regulatory Commission and the Department of Energy, as well as more current studies by independent researchers. She explains that the radioactive waste buried in West Lake Landfill covers about twenty acres in two locations in one or many layers, estimated at two to fifteen feet thick, some of it mixed in with municipal refuse and some of it sitting right at the surface. It is in the trees surrounding the landfill and the vacuum bags in nearby homes. This waste contains not only uranium but also thorium and radium, all long-lived, highly radiotoxic elements. And because Mallinckrodt removed most of the naturally occurring uranium from this ore, the Cotter Corporation, in effect, created an enriched thorium deposit when it dumped the residues at West Lake Landfill. "In fact," Kay muses, "West Lake Landfill might now be the richest deposit of thorium in the world."

Thorium and uranium in particular are among the radio-active primordial nuclides, radioactive elements that have existed in their current form since before the Earth was formed, since before the formation of the solar system even, and will remain radioactive and toxic to life long after humans are gone. We're sitting back in Kay's dining room when she pulls out a tiny booklet titled "Nuclear Wallet Cards." What its intended purpose is, I don't know, but Kay flips to the back to show me the half-life of thorium 232: 14 billion years, a half-life so long that by the time this element is safe for human exposure, the Appalachian Mountains will have eroded away, every ocean on Earth's surface will have evaporated, Antarctica will be free of ice, and all the rings of Saturn will have decayed. Earth's rotation will have slowed so much that days will have become twenty-five hours long, photosynthesis will have ceased, and multicellular life will have become a physical impossibility.

"You know, tritium is my favorite," Kay tells me before I leave. It's produced as a side effect of operating nuclear reactors and released into the air, or leaks into the waterways; it contaminates the water supply and condenses in our food. One official who worked at the nuclear reactor Kay had tried to prevent once told her that tritium was no big deal: "It only destroys DNA molecules." A few years ago they found tritium in the groundwater in Callaway County. "There is no way to remove it," she says.

As I'm standing to gather my things, Kay goes to retrieve an extra copy of the "Nuclear Wallet Cards" booklet that she wants me to have. The woman who answered the door,

Kay's librarian, comes back to keep me company while Kay is out of the room. "I was her husband's caretaker," she tells me. "When he left, I stayed to take care of her." Kay returns with a warning of a nasty thunderstorm blowing in. I mention my disappointment that the storm might prevent my visit to the Weldon Spring site. After it was decommissioned, the plant, a second one run by Mallinckrodt, was found to be so contaminated that the Department of Energy eventually entombed the whole site in layers upon layers of clay and soil, gravel, engineered filters, and limestone rocks, creating a mountain covering forty-five acres, containing approximately 1.5 million cubic yards of hazardous waste. With its own educational center located near the base, the containment dome, the top of which is the highest point in the entire county, has become a kind of memorial for a tragedy that hasn't finished happening yet.

"Oh, you don't want to go there anyway," Kay says, waving the idea away with her slender hand. "It's leaking."

*　　*　　*

The rain comes down in sheets so thick I have to pull my car over to the side of the road. It's early afternoon, but the sky has turned dark as dusk. It's not the first time I've been stuck in a storm like this, the kind that comes up out of nowhere and falls all at once. Wipers and headlights become useless; nothing to do but stop and wait it out. It's a thin little sliver of a storm, I see on the radar on my phone, so I know it will pass as quickly as it arrived, but even still, this time I'm wasting makes that tired, burning feeling I've been carrying around in my back more acute.

It's caused, perhaps, by a contradiction I can't resolve: that the massive crime here began with a belief in a kind of care, a belief that protection comes only in the form of wars and bombs, and that its ultimate expression is a technology that can destroy in a single instant any threat to our safety with perfect precision and efficiency. But hundreds of thousands lost their lives to those bombs in Japan, and the fallout from building them has claimed at least as many lives right here at home.

There is no one to arrest for this, to send to jail, to fine or execute or drag to his humiliation in the city square. Even if Karen and Dawn win their fight and convince the government to remove every gram of radioactive waste in the landfill and the creek and the airport and the backyards and gardens here, people will still be sick. Thousands of them. Chronic exposure to radiation has changed their DNA, and they'll likely pass those changes on to their children, and to their children's children, and on and on through every generation. In this regard, no one is immune.

My mom puts dinner on the table, but my grandmother refuses to eat. "Not again," my mom groans, slamming her silverware down and rolling her eyes.

"It happens," my mom's husband explains to me behind the cover of his raised hand, "when something throws off her routine."

My grandfather died a month ago, and now that Grandma is living in the spare bedroom, my mom has learned there was a lot my grandfather did not tell her. My mom is stretched thin with the sudden responsibility of it all: taking care of my grandmother, who has apparently been suffering from dementia for the last twenty years; cleaning out the house; selling all of their possessions at auction; her own inconsolable grief.

"You don't have to eat if you don't want to," she says, her tone as calm and even as she can muster. "But I'm not making you anything else."

Grandma throws a weak tantrum at this: she pushes her chair out from the table, arranges her walker, shuffles out of the room. She is too old and feeble to storm out, but I think that is how she wants us to understand her actions. I laugh a little to myself when the television clicks on, Pat Sajak's voice on *Wheel of Fortune* bellowing through the house full blast: "Do we have a U?"

"It's not funny," my mom scolds, retrieving a bottle of wine from the fridge. "Let's change the subject. What are you doing here anyway?"

I tell her a short version of the story: there's a landfill, there's a fire, there's nuclear waste left over from the Manhattan Project. People are dying of rare cancers. But the short version of the story always leads into the long version, and soon the bottle of wine is empty. My mom's husband is doing the dishes, half listening. His health has been deteriorating in the years since he retired—he gets lightheaded and can't always feel his feet or his hands. "Peripheral neuropathy" is the term for it, I think. It's becoming harder and harder for him to help around the house. The dishes are one thing he can do to feel helpful, balancing his weight against the sink.

"So then all this waste is just sitting in giant piles at the airport," I say.

"Right there by the ballfields," he interrupts, putting a plate into the dishwasher, but I don't fully hear him. He is a man who likes to know things and to explain them even if they do not need explaining. I've learned to tune it out.

"Then the government holds an auction and sells the waste to a private company. Who knew there was a market for nuclear waste?" I say while my mom opens another bottle and refills my glass. "And then the company that bought it went broke and another company took it over. They shipped most of it to themselves out in Utah—"

"Colorado," my mom's husband interrupts again. I look up this time. "We were shipping it to Colorado." He comes over, places his hand on the back of a chair to steady himself. "It was months out there shoveling that dirt into the train cars. Yellow and red and white: odd colors for dirt, if you ask me. We'd fill up the gondolas and then ride them over into the dryer, then jump off and ride the dry ones out the other side."

Suddenly I am completely sober. "You have to tell your doctor this," I say. "Mike! You were right there in it! You have to tell your doctor. You have to file a claim with the government."

He shrugs his shoulders, sitting down in the chair. "What good would that do? I'm seventy-five years old."

_____

Later, I watch him as he shuffles from the kitchen to the living room. He moves so slowly, each step so tentative. He sits down on the couch to catch his breath.

Peripheral neuropathy can be one side effect of radiation exposure, but it might also be caused by having smoked for sixty years or by having worked on trains for fifty years; years after he shoveled those radioactive wastes, he was exposed to Agent Orange during a train wreck. It would be an impossible case to make with the government, to pinpoint radiation as the one thing. Besides, he's the kind of man who thinks it is unpatriotic to accuse the federal government of making mistakes.

His eyes droop, losing focus, and then his head sags to his chest. Grandma falls asleep too, both of them folding over on themselves. My mom shouts for them to go to bed. She isn't angry, just loud because they are both nearly deaf. I hear the sounds of running water, of doors opening and shutting, of ancient bodies surrendering to gravity and age. My mom sighs, pats my hand, tells me she'd better get off to bed also. When the bedroom door closes behind her, I turn off all the lamps and sit in the blue light of the flickering TV.

*   *   *

It is afternoon when I park my car in the EPA Region 7 parking lot and rush toward the door. The Region 7 offices are located in a sprawling modern government building in a suburb of Kansas City. The small conference room just to the side of the main entrance is filled with a surprising number of people. Curtis Carey introduces himself as the director of public affairs. He's the one who arranged this meeting after our phone call last week. He was vetting me then and told me he'd try to set something up with a few of the technicians. I wasn't expecting much. He introduces me to Mark Hague, the federally appointed administrator for Region 7, and also to Mary Peterson, director of the Superfund Division. Also present: Brad Vann, the new project director at the West Lake Landfill, and Ben Washburn, who does public affairs work too. To break the ice, I tell a quick story about getting lost in the backwoods while my phone was dying on the way here. "I thought I was going to have to get married to a farmer and start my life over again!" I say. No one laughs.

"Here are the ground rules," Curtis Carey begins. "Everything is on the record. You have one hour."

An hour isn't much time to get anywhere with anyone, much less the five humorless strangers in this room. During our too-short conversation I learn that the EPA has more than thirteen hundred sites in the Superfund program, and Region 7 alone has ninety-eight sites on the National Priorities List. Each of these communities is demanding that their toxic sites be scrubbed clean. "And the process is lengthy," Brad Vann tells me. "The investigations are lengthy, and then there's all the time to collect [and] evaluate the data—to get to this point where you can make a decision on a remedy takes time. And unfortunately, sometimes it takes a lot of time, depending on the complexity of the site."

"Why not remove the waste?" I blurt out. "Just to be sure. Just to be safe."

"It's not as clear-cut as it might seem," Brad says. "There's more to excavating a landfill than sticking a backhoe in it. There is a process we must follow by law." The law he's referring to is the Comprehensive Environmental Response, Compensation, and Liability Act (CERCLA), known more commonly as Superfund, which mandates that the risk to human health must cross a certain threshold before the EPA can take any action at all. He sighs heavily.

"Our decisions have to be based on science," Mary Peterson interrupts. "They can't be based on emotion. They can't be based on fear. They have to be based on sound science and the law."

According to the EPA, the science shows that there is low-level nuclear waste buried in a landfill in suburban St. Louis. Mostly it's covered; mostly it's inaccessible. But these findings do not alleviate the community's concern. The landfill sits in the floodplain of the Mississippi River. What if there is a flood? What if the fire spreads and comes in contact with the radiological material? Either of these would create a disaster, and neither requires a great feat of imagination to bring into the realm of the possible. But the law doesn't offer a framework within which to consider anything that hasn't already actually happened yet.

"So the community is asking us to use our imagination," Mary explains, "and generate hypothetical scenarios in order to evaluate the risk. We don't have any real data to rely on because that's not the reality. Those things have not happened. If it had become reality, then we could collect real data and say, okay, this is the impact."

I know this isn't how risk evaluation works, but I've heard Mary say this before, in footage of a community meeting several years ago when she gave a PowerPoint presentation about the health risk assessment for the site. That presentation is convoluted and technical, and the whole thing comes down to an equation. One woman in the audience can't handle this. She stands and takes the mic. She wants to know about the process, why the EPA is withholding certain information. "Did a cost-benefit analysis determine whether we are worth saving?" she asks, dropping the mic, fighting back tears. Behind her, her husband holds up photographs of their two children, both dead of rare cancers.

Dan Gravatt—the project manager for the West Lake site at that time, their point of contact, the man who should be their advocate and ally—stands up and strides to the front of the room, laughing to his colleague as he takes the mic. He explains the process in simple language, speaking slowly, raising his voice oddly on certain syllables in a kind of singsong, clearly straining to keep his tone neutral and calm and flat. The effect is deeply patronizing, infuriating even. He goes on for some time about the bureaucratic machinery behind the scenes of the EPA, the process through which its decisions are reviewed and re-reviewed. "The National Remedy Review Board asked for more tests," he says. "That work is still being done. When that work is done, and the supplemental feasibility study is amended to include that new information, we'll go back to the National Remedy Review Board, and they'll have another crack at it." He's interrupted here by someone in the audience shouting something I can't make out.

This is an important moment because it's when a lot of things go wrong. The interruption unnerves Gravatt, and the strain to remain calm and neutral becomes too much. He shouts, "I'm not done!" and lowers the mic for a moment to collect himself. Many people begin shouting—the parents holding up the pictures of their dead children, Dawn and Karen, Robbin and Mike. The camera pans across the room. Mostly it's impossible to make out what the crowd is saying, but I hear the words, "They're not your dead children!" and then a shuffling of chairs. Gravatt tries to continue, raises the mic to his mouth, is interrupted again. He laughs—a nervous response maybe, but the optics are not good. At this instant, the meeting breaks down, and Karen and Dawn and most of the other community members storm out.

After that meeting, Gravatt stopped working on West Lake—moved to another project, another division. The head of Region 7 was also suddenly working in a new position, and Mary Peterson, formerly the deputy director of public affairs, became director of the Region 7 Superfund program. That's when Brad Vann came on board and immediately tried to get the project back on track, improve transparency, expedite certain studies, move forward on a final remedy for the site. But none of this has repaired the relationship with the community, which might have been irrevocably broken from the start.

———

At the end of the hour, the room empties except for the public affairs director, Curtis, who watches me turn off the recorder and pack up. There are documents and links he wants to send to me, he says, things that came up in the meeting. He wants, very much, to be helpful. He admits they are trying hard to mend their relationship with the community, but their efforts just aren't really going anywhere. I suspect they see the community—the moms in particular—as problematic, difficult.

"Look," I say, still telling myself that I am neutral in all of this. "They have no power whatsoever to change their situation. They can't get out there with shovels and dig this stuff out of the landfill. They can't put out the fire or stop the leachate from seeping into the groundwater. They feel like they can't protect their children, or go outside, or breathe the air. They're powerless." He looks down toward his hands, nodding as I speak. I do not envy him. I say, "From their perspective, you have all the power. And you're choosing to do nothing at all."

*   *   *

Uranium, thorium, Agent Orange, dioxin, DDT. I am thinking of all the ways our government has poisoned its citizens as I board the plane that will take me back home. The sky grows darker; blue gives way to purple, to red and orange near the horizon. I read recently about a housing project in

St. Louis, the infamous Pruitt-Igoe, where the government sprayed nerve gases off the roof to see what effect it would have on the people living there—testing it for its potential use as a weapon in war.

"On every continent, the history of civilization is filled with war, whether driven by scarcity of grain or hunger for gold, compelled by nationalist fervor or religious zeal," President Obama says during his speech at the Peace Memorial in Hiroshima. "Empires have risen and fallen. Peoples have been subjugated and liberated. And at each juncture, innocents have suffered, a countless toll, their names forgotten by time." At no point during this speech does he apologize for what some have called a war crime. The closest he comes is this: "Technological progress without an equivalent progress in human institutions can doom us. The scientific revolution that led to the splitting of an atom requires a moral revolution as well."

A 2005 Gallup poll showed that a majority of Americans still approve of having bombed Japan. Admittedly this is down from near-total approval in August 1945, but it's hardly a "moral revolution." One factor in the decision to use the bomb was that its destructive power would end the war and save American lives—some estimated that as many as a million American soldiers would have perished in a ground invasion of Japan. Does saving one life require taking another? Must they both be soldiers, loyal to their countries and their neighbors? After Nagasaki was bombed, a woman walked through the burning streets asking for water for her headless baby. A four-year-old boy, burned alive under the rubble of his crushed house, was crying out, "Mommy, it's hot. It's so hot." President Truman called this bombing an "achievement" in his solemn radio broadcast from the USS *Augusta*: "The Japanese began the war from the air at Pearl Harbor. They have been repaid many fold."

In the last few months of his term, President Obama was reportedly considering the idea of adopting a no-first-use policy on nuclear weapons—an official promise that we would use them only in response to an attack by our enemies—but ultimately his advisers talked him out of it, arguing that it is our responsibility to our allies to maintain the illusion of ultimate power. Now that we have a new president with access to the nuclear codes, we must face the consequences of projecting, and protecting, that illusion.

There are about sixteen thousand nuclear warheads in the world right now, enough to destroy the planet many times over. The United States and Russia own 90 percent of these, and though various treaties prevent them from making additional weapons, both are working to modernize the bomb-delivery systems they do have. The US government recently approved a plan to spend $1 trillion over the next thirty years to make our arsenal more modern, accurate, and efficient.

One trillion dollars. This number is staggering, not least of all because one factor—a minor one but still a factor—deterring the EPA from fully excavating the radioactive waste created by the program that developed these nuclear weapons in the first place is how much it will cost—maybe as much as $400 million. That's a lot of money for an EPA project. Budgets are not so simple that one government program, like the Department of Defense, could direct money to another, but the fact that they are not does makes our priorities apparent.

Even if every gram of radioactive waste was removed from the landfill, where would it go? Facilities in Idaho and Utah are willing to accept it, but those facilities are located in communities, or near them, and the nearby residents don't want this waste in their backyards or their gardens or their rivers or their drinking water either. Even if we box it up and send it in train cars to remote places, it will be there, ready and waiting to kill any of us long after we've forgotten where we put it, or what "it" even is.

"Why should we tolerate a diet of weak poisons, a home in insipid surroundings, a circle of acquaintances who are not quite our enemies, the noise of motors with just enough relief to prevent insanity?" Rachel Carson asks in *Silent Spring*. Nothing is sacred, or safe, or protected. As a species we have evolved to recognize threats to survival: plants we cannot eat, animals we should not approach, places we cannot safely go. Fear of the other is perhaps an enduring trace of this ancient instinct: that barbaric impulse to attack and destroy anyone different from ourselves, anything we do not understand. But increasingly it seems our ability to invent technologies that destroy one another has evolved faster than our ability to survive them. Carson asks, "Who would want to live in a world which is just not quite fatal?"

Not all radiation is fatal. Radiation is around us always, and each of us is exposed to radiation daily: from the sun, from the dirt, from sources we would never think to suspect. We ourselves are a source of radiation, since each of us carries radioactive elements inside our bodies from birth. Throughout our lives, we are constantly irradiating one another, not only with charged microscopic particles but also with suspicion and fear and blame. We find infinite directions in which to project our rage and bewilderment and grief.

"Do you ever think about just walking away?" I asked Dawn Chapman recently. She's just learned that her own daughter has developed a tumor on her salivary gland. It's not cancer, the doctors say. Not yet.

"I don't know. I dream," she answers. "This weekend my husband and I dropped the kids off with my family and drove around and dreamed for a while about what it would be like to walk away. But I don't know how to walk away from it even if I wanted to, knowing what I know about what's going on, how it's hurt people. In the end, I'm not even fighting to win. And even if we could win, a win isn't what you think it is. A buyout isn't a win because we could move but this poison would still be inside us."

For Karen, winning means the government finally caring for its citizens like it has always promised it would. "I am shattered. I am broken," she says. "And now my children and my grandchildren have those chances of being sick as well. Our human rights are being violated and it has to stop. It has to stop here."

As the plane lifts off the ground, I open the tiny window shade to see, one last time, that familiar green that never fails to make some bell in me ring. This place has always been a confluence of things, like the two rivers that converge just north of the city, where the glaciated plains meet the Ozark Highlands, where an eroded mountain range called the Lincoln Hills rises now only a few hundred meters above the alluvial floodplain, all of it pushed into place by the Laurentide Ice Sheet half a million years ago. All of it divided into neat rectangles and squares by city streets, subdivided, fenced into single lots—as if a few planks of wood and slabs of concrete could isolate any one place from the world.

We are all connected. The rivers and streams and tiny creeks wind through the city and go on winding. They twist and bend and run backward on themselves, changing course and direction a thousand times over the ages. The water swells and leaves its banks with the seasons, swells into the streets we build, and our backyards and gardens, into the places we never think of because we do not want to see them: our landfills, our factories, our toxic dumps, all of the remote places we send our worst creations. There is no fence to keep it all out. The disaster that approaches is ourselves.

ART IN THE AGE
OF APOCALYPSES

The first semester in my new job, I taught one class only, a nonfiction writing class, which met on Tuesday afternoons. We spent September and October talking about facts, about narrative, about evidence and ethics, but then November arrived and because voting is more important than nonfiction, I insisted that if anyone needed to miss class in order to vote, they would be excused. On Election Day, only a few were missing from the circle we had made with our desks. I checked in with those who were present: Did you vote yet? Did you? Most said yes, they definitely voted earlier in the day, or during early voting, or they had mailed absentee ballots back to the states where they are registered. A handful did not vote at all. One, registered in Florida, said she just wasn't very excited about either of the candidates. (I regret the ways my face registered the horror with which I reacted to this.) Another, registered two hundred miles away in San Antonio, said her vote wouldn't make any difference anyway. I looked at my watch: 3:15. The polls closed at 7:00. "You can make it," I said. "Go there. Drive now." My students didn't understand why I was so worried.

They believed in the data, in the arc of history. One said, "The outcome is certain."

I raced home after class to prepare for guests. I warmed appetizers, opened bottles of wine. Our neighbors arrived with food in their hands. The children raced from room to room — from inside to outside through wide-open doors — in a shrieking, tumbling pack. The adults laughed and clinked our glasses together and turned on the television. Nervous laughter rose as one said, "It's early." "There's still New York," said another. We stuffed ourselves with cheese. It was nearly midnight when the children were gathered and returned to their homes. My daughter asked, as I tucked her into bed, whether a woman was president and I said, "No, darling. Not yet."

A week later, I found myself back in the same classroom with my students, now living in a different world. Or it was the same world, but revealed to us, and we were all different for having seen it as it is. They looked a little gray and unwashed, wrung out or strung out; their eyes were swollen or sunken or bloodshot. They wouldn't look me in the eye, didn't meet my gaze. They stared at the floor, slouched low in their seats.

Neat piles of pages were stacked on every desk in our circle: three brave writers had shared their essays about trauma and desire and loss, written before any of us knew what we know now, but my students did not want to workshop. "Workshopping," one said, "is the last thing in the world I want to be doing right now." As if it was completely clear to everyone that art cannot rise to an occasion like this.

"What do you want to be doing right now?" I asked. One shrugged her shoulders. "Go back in time," one said. "Die," said another. I had not prepared a speech—I had felt too distraught, too much a hunted animal to do anything but rage and grieve—so instead I listened and pretended to be wise and calm. It is hard to find the words, they insisted. One gestured broadly over her head with her hands. "There is nothing we can do," she said.

"What are the words you do not yet have?" Audre Lorde asked attendees of the Modern Language Association Convention in 1977. "What do you need to say? What are the tyrannies you swallow day by day and attempt to make your own, until you will sicken and die of them, still in silence?"

In my life, as in my art, the uncertainties of the world often strike me silent, but I find my voice again by describing things I know. I know, for example, that William Carlos Williams famously said that a poem is a "small (or large) machine made of words." I love this quote, and I have repeated it often to my students because it offers an inroad to thinking about what our words can do when it seems there is nothing to be done.

Every semester my students struggle with this idea that art is not an object but a *machine*. Some arrive believing—insisting, even—that art exists to communicate "hidden meanings." I don't want to disparage my students for thinking this way, because in fact they do learn to let go of it. But the misconceptions illustrate one of the many drawbacks to coming of age in a culture at war with itself. When daily life is saturated with the devastating spectacle of the so-called real—visualize, for a moment, what reality television has obscured about actual reality—we are asked to pledge allegiance to the appearance of fact, even as we observe its fabrication.

Machines don't have meanings; they have functions, I tell them. It is difficult for them to accept that a painting or poem has no meaning just as a toaster has no meaning, though they do perform their work for us. Just as high-speed Internet, email, the twenty-four-hour news cycle, the three-strikes law, the private prison industrial complex, the war on terror, and, perhaps more alarming, the broadly shared experience of terror also perform their work for us. The result is that my students have no memory of a time when the world was not, as one so aptly put it, "deeply and profoundly fucked." If the function of saturating our experience with horror is to make us accept this as inevitable, perhaps art, that doorway to the symbolic, can make us see something more.

When I was a much younger woman, long before I began teaching or writing even, I found myself unemployed after having been kidnapped and raped and very nearly murdered by a man I had once loved, so I frequently visited the Nelson-Atkins Museum of Art in Kansas City, which houses one of Monet's *Water Lilies* in its permanent collection. For hours I sat in front of the painting, only looking. "We only see what we look at," John Berger writes in *Ways of Seeing*. "To look is an act of choice." Looking is a form of recognition, a method for contemplation that can approximate a form of prayer. "If we accept that we can see that hill over there," Berger continues, "we propose that from that hill we can be seen." This is not to say, exactly, that as I sat looking at Monet's *Water Lilies*, I felt the painting look back at me, but rather that perhaps my looking was not only a meditation on a sublime visual cue, but part of a desire to comprehend the world, and my place in it, differently.

In this way, the act of making art also begins with looking. When I sat for many hours looking at the Monet, I had not yet found essays. Or perhaps essays had not yet found me. Years later, I would discover in essays a way of reseeing the world in which the world could be changed—in which no ocean was ever just a rising body of water, and no mistake had ever been inevitable, and no bruise was ever just an accident. Not even, I would conclude, the ones I had sometimes worn on my face.

What later unfolded in me for essays began unfolding in me as I sat for hours, looking only at the Monet. All those hours I meditated on the water, the flowers in the water, the clouds reflected in the water, I also looked closer at myself. I saw myself, and all the ways in which I might be a better, stronger person. I had no words yet to describe the person I might be, but it was a version of myself I could not unsee.

In my classroom one week after the election, my students did not want to think or talk about art because the apocalypse had arrived on our doorstep. "There is nothing we can do," one said again. "Then what is art for?" I asked. This question met their blank faces. "What is art for if not precisely this moment?" I asked again. Their eyebrows furrowed. This was not the speech they came to hear.

There's a story I've heard Project Row Houses founder and MacArthur Fellow Rick Lowe tell about his evolution as an artist. He began as a painter whose work documented social problems, but one day a high school student came by his studio and asked him why he made work about problems. "We don't need people showing us what's happening. We already know what's happening. If you're an artist and you're so creative, why can't you create a solution?" the student asked. It was an important question. Afterward, Lowe gave up trying to document problems and instead began wrestling with the problems themselves. Along with several other artists, he purchased and renovated twenty-two shotgun-style houses in Houston's Third Ward, one of the city's oldest African American neighborhoods. The work became known as Project Row Houses, which is simultaneously a residential program for young mothers, an education program for their children, a residency program for artists, a historic preservation program for the neighborhood, and a work of art.

It's this last statement that's a point of some contention. Is it activism, or is it art? Is it protest or performance? Am I making art or making a point? "Real" art, we are told, must be commodifiable to have value. "Political art" is a small, stigmatized domain, a ghetto for the radical few.

But the art that has shaped and continues to shape my

trajectory as an artist proves this untrue: William Kentridge's *9 Drawings for Projection*, a series of charcoal animations protesting South African apartheid, which I watched in a poetic forms class in graduate school even as I was learning that *racism* was a term that also implicated me. Or *El año en que nací*, a recent work of documentary theater in which eleven artists born during Augusto Pinochet's dictatorship in Chile take the stage to reckon with the crimes of the generation before, alternately implicating and exonerating their very own parents, and revealing the ways that history and memory can be remade, old divisions can be redrawn or, sometimes—and only with great patience and generosity— erased. There is also *The Way Black Machine*, an installation of flickering monitors that acts as an archive of footage of both traditional media and social media coverage of the events at that time still freshly unfolding in Ferguson, Missouri. There are the series of public die-ins that were staged across the country by medical students, clergy members, lawyers, and even university presidents, all in solidarity with the protests against police brutality across the country.

Critics call these works "disturbing" and disparage their status as art, but I think that means they're working exactly as art should. If these works disturb us, it's because in looking at the work, we see ourselves looking at the work, and doing little else. We watch the events on television unfold in total horror, and then do nothing. We turn off the television and go back to our own problems: How will I buy groceries this week? How can I pay the bills? Maybe we'll go out of our way to post something on Facebook and pat ourselves on the back for it. It's not enough and we all know it. These works incriminate, indict. They demand that we do more.

Chekov says that art exists to prepare the soul for tenderness, and if this is true, I wonder how it could possibly succeed. I look up from my desk at the news even now as I write this—there is a war, and we have lost it; we are moving toward a future from which there is no escape—and see all the ways in which the world is, without a doubt, "utterly fucked."

But what I finally told my students one week after the election—or maybe I'm now telling myself—is that our art has the power to change this, but we must dedicate ourselves to the task of making apparent what our despair has obscured. Where the irrefutable evidence of science has failed, and where the slippery logic and grand rhetoric of public debate fail, and where the cruel and biased vengeance of the judicial system fails and goes on failing, our writing can succeed in unfolding a subtle shift in intellect, a change in perspective, a new way of seeing that is then impossible to unsee.

I know how hopeless things now seem, but that isn't a reason to give up. A few years ago, when the writer Rebecca Solnit came to the campus where I worked at the time, she talked about the difference between optimism and hope. "Optimism," she said, "is when you believe something good will happen, no matter what." Optimism is blind that way, and maybe even a little bit silly. "But hope," she said, "is when the odds are stacked against you, when you choose, in spite of these odds, to believe something good can happen." Hope is powerful that way, radical even. She was paraphrasing Václav Havel, I think, who spent years in prison as a dissident before he was freed and elected president of the country that had condemned him. "Hope is an orientation of the spirit," he writes. "It's not the conviction that something will turn out well, but the certainty that something makes sense, regardless of how it turns out. It is this hope, above all, that gives us strength to live and to continually try new things, even in conditions that seem as hopeless as ours do, here and now."

None of this is to say we don't need beauty. On the contrary: we need beauty now more than ever before. But I have grown impatient with the beautiful art of galleries and museums, with auctions and collections and commissions, with curators and prizes and award galas. They operate in a world where beautiful things are made and sold and that transaction is final and enough. But what I have learned about being an artist is that for each of us who makes giant mirrored-steel balloon-animal sculptures that sell for a zillion dollars, there are a thousand more in suburban garages and church basements, in pediatric cancer wards and recovery shelters where nearly every hand shudders with the palsy of addiction, under bridges and on street corners with spray cans, in after-school programs and on playgrounds where sometimes a collective hunger unites as a single gut-wrenching wail, and all of them are putting their hands and voices to work each day trying to remake the world.

I have exactly zero hard evidence to prove that any of

us will succeed in this. But I know for certain that what art first unfolded for me unfolds in me still, and it's what leads me to choose, in spite of the odds, to believe that, yes, we can put something into the world that is greater than what is being taken from it every damn day of our lives. We can make good things happen. Writing can change us, make us better, stronger people whose actions, though they may seem small and inconsequential at the time, can matter, for ourselves and for the world.

My students left class that week, still wrung out and slouching, and came back slouching the next week, and the next. They watched the news unfolding in total horror and went on feeling there was nothing they could do. And when they did begin writing again, their essays did not rise to the occasion of this particular apocalypse. It was disappointing, I admit. Sometimes young writers come to the page as if there is nothing at stake in the matter, as if they have no skin in the game. Maybe they write to impress those they admire, or to belong, or to be seen. Many will never make the kind of art I'm talking about; they would not wish to risk their reputation or privilege and could not tolerate accusations against their character or craft—not after working so long and so hard to hone it. They would not wish to displease anyone who might possibly be pleased.

How many tyrannies will they swallow in exactly this way?

"[Art] means nothing if it simply decorates the dinner table of the power which holds it hostage," Adrienne Rich once wrote in a letter explaining her decision to reject the National Medal of Arts. "In the end," she continues, "I don't think we can separate art from overall human dignity and hope."

Nor can we separate art from the power of those who make it, I think. We are not powerless, and the situation, though bleak, is hopeless only if we reject the tools we already have. If there is to be a revolution against this madness, we can write it, build it, lead it into the streets. We may look at the world in despairing horror—as everyone looks—but as artists, we owe it to the world to look again, and to keep looking until we see in ourselves the way the world can be changed. The art we make can remind ourselves and others of all the beauty and justice there still can be.

THE FLOOD

For three days and three nights, the rain falls in sheets, in swirls. It falls in gentle showers and falls sideways and is dumped like a bucket all at once. Tornados spin overhead as thunder and lightning rattle the walls and the roof, and families gather in their closets, squeeze together in the bathtub, pull mattresses over their heads.

The bayous fill, and the water runs into the streets; the streets fill, and the water fills the highways and the underpasses. The water swallows cars and trucks and entire families of people. It swallows fathers and mothers and tiny brand-new babies. The water turns the highway into an ocean; the white peaks of waves crest and crash against the sides of buildings. People wade out of their houses, through the water, toward one another and dry land. They climb to the second floor, and then the third; they scramble to their roofs and wave white T-shirts or towels toward the rescue they believe will come. Cages like open coffins descend from helicopters, and people climb into them, one at a time or as an inseparable group. A mother clings to her children as they ascend from the water toward safety. She never lets them go.

My husband and I watch the rescues on the news. There aren't enough helicopters for everyone who needs saving, aren't enough high-water vehicles, or boats, or flashlights, or meals, or warm beds. We watch the water rising in our own neighborhood, filling the streets up to our ankles, our knees, up to our waists. We are trapped here, on the little island of our address. We occupy ourselves and the children in the ways we can: we eat, we drink, we play board games and curl together in the bed. My husband and I take turns going outside to check the water, watch it rising. When we wake on the fourth day of rain, it is still rising.

We hear that a shelter has opened up the road from us and that supplies there are low. We gather a large backpack full of clothing and towels and blankets, and my husband leaves, trudging through the floodwater, to deliver it. On the way home, he sees an emergency crew attempting a deep-water rescue at one house on a street where all the houses are underwater. He calls two of our neighbors, who pull a canoe from the garage, and the three of them begin knocking on doors. They find people in houses with water up to their waists, people sheltering on the second floor of their houses, people who refuse to come downstairs because they are afraid of being electrocuted by their own submerged appliances. My husband and our neighbors kick down fences and garage doors to find breaker boxes and cut power to the houses. They rescue elderly couples, a woman with more dogs than teeth, people who are in denial about the state of their homes. The hardest thing for so many, he tells me when he returns wet and exhausted, is leaving, letting all the things they have held so tightly go.

While he is out rescuing these neighbors, I am at home with the children. They are bored of playing games, of being indoors and watching the rain. They want to move and squeal and run. I want them to stay very still, to enter a kind of quiet stasis until the storm passes. I search for news, read the weather forecast, imagine worst-case scenarios while they stand on the back of the couches and dive headfirst into deep pools of pillows.

I have just put on yet another animated movie when there is a break in the rain. The river in the street subsides a little, and the children come outside to splash at the water's edge. The woman who lives three doors down from us has a son, I learn, about the same age as my son. We make plans for them to play another time, when we aren't all so focused on staying dry. Another neighbor approaches to tells us that the dam just west of our neighborhood is full to capacity already and that the Army Corps of Engineers has announced it will be releasing water from the reservoir in order to avoid "catastrophic failure." There is a long silence in which we all try to process the meaning of those words: *water, dam, failure*. I am still processing when the rain begins falling again, and I shoo my children back inside.

There are two dams, I learn. One, Addicks Reservoir, which is north of the interstate, began overflowing in the early hours this morning. Officials are calling this an "uncontrolled release." This has never happened before, not since construction on that reservoir was completed in 1948. The dam nearer to us, Barker Reservoir, still has a few feet to go before it spills over. With more rain ahead of us, that might happen, but it's not the thing that will keep me up all night, which is a paralyzing terror that the dams will fail, and all of west Houston will drown in a quiet tsunami in our sleep.

When my husband returns late in the evening, he showers and we scramble around trying to put together emergency bags in case we have to climb onto the roof and wait for our own rescue. We eat dinner and the children lie down for sleep on an air mattress we've put on the floor of our bedroom: the mattress will float, I tell myself, so that I too can close my eyes for even a moment to sleep.

On the morning of the fifth day, the water is higher still— it's over the sidewalks now—and it isn't clear like rainwater anymore. The water is brown—dirt brown, shit brown, the color of sand or silt or maybe beef stew. And it smells like one might expect fetid floodwater to smell—like sewage, like contagion.

Officials are saying that we should leave our homes if there is water in the house because the water is a danger—leave if we cannot come and go with ease, that our homes will be monitored, that if we return in a few weeks, we will find everything in one piece. And if we stay? I don't even want to imagine the wretched surprises this water will have in store for our bodies when the evidence of it recedes.

In a press conference, a spokesperson from the Army Corps of Engineers admits it has never before released water from the dam while it is still raining, and also that it has very little information about how exactly this will have an impact on communities downstream. It calls for voluntary evacuations to the west of the dam, in the county neighboring ours, and for mandatory evacuations along the Brazos River to our south. It warns us to stay out of the water, which is infested with all manner of disease—*E. coli* and Staphylococcus at the very least—but also snakes, alligators, and live downed electrical wires, which have claimed the lives of three volunteer rescuers I know of so far. And yet there is no way to stay out of the water, to come or go without entering and submerging up to one's knees, or waist, or neck.

For the second day in a row, my husband and our neighbors paddle away from our home through the floodwaters in the canoe, heading to another neighborhood where people are calling out their windows for rescue. Our children are still sleeping—later and more deeply than at any time of nondisaster—and there is little I can think to do. I turn to reading, to research, to learning all I can.

I discover that decades ago, the two reservoirs were built far outside what were then considered the city limits in order to protect the city itself—the business district downtown, the ship channel, and the refineries and network of pipelines that form the heart of the nation's oil industry—from the comparatively minor floods that happen in Houston nearly every single time we have a good rain. The reservoirs are normally bone dry, but in the event of rain, they store the water and then release it slowly over a period of many days. Unfortunately, this storm is not like a regular storm, not even like a very unusual storm. It is not like anything Texas has ever seen. Over the past several days, some places in Houston have seen up to 51 inches of rain. If we were in Colorado and this had been a snowstorm, we would be sitting under 750 inches of snow; if you are, like me, slow to calculate, that's roughly 62.5 feet. There isn't a city in the world designed to handle that.

The reservoirs are now completely full—overflowing, in fact—and the engineers are releasing the water as fast as they can in order to save the city: the dam, the infrastructure, the businesses downtown, the ship channel, all of the millions of people who live here. And in order to save these other very important parts of the city, they will be flooding a less important part of the city—my neighborhood and others—"for the near foreseeable future." My neighbors and I have joked that we should rename ourselves the Venice of the West.

All of this is to say that I don't resent the water. Flooding is almost a way of life in this city: the water comes, it floods us, it recedes. Not every disaster is an injustice. I don't even entirely resent that they're flooding my neighborhood on purpose. I understand the concept of sacrifice, why some people might be asked to give up something that benefits the group. We do this every day without thinking: we give up a seat on the bus, a place in the checkout line, our time and talents, and sometimes our lives or money.

A friend posts a photo of the line of cars waiting to drop off donations at the Convention Center in the dry part of town, hundreds of cars long. Heroes appear everywhere: teenagers in canoes rescuing homeless veterans, beer brewers out in their giant trucks plucking people off their roofs, volunteers arriving at their neighbors' doors with supplies, clothes, helping hands. People are very good at showing up for one another in their times of desperate need. What we are less good at is maintaining that kind of deep, abiding empathy on the scale that will give us any hope of surviving the next storm like this: like how to care for one another equally.

Elsewhere in the world, people argue about whether *Game of Thrones* has lost its mojo, their favorite kind of shoes. I don't begrudge anyone this normalcy. I don't begrudge anyone who is safe, and well fed, and warm. Life goes on, here and elsewhere, despite tragedy, despite disaster, despite devastating loss. Most people I know who are trying to salvage their belongings, or their homes, or their families do not have time or energy to pay attention to what is happening in the rest of the city—or in the country, or the rest of the world—where people go about their days, posting photos of their good hair, and their Labor Day weekend getaways, and, as ever, their favorite cat memes. No doubt these people have already started feeling the effects of what is known as compassion fatigue, which feels like a form of suffering, I suppose—a deficit of emotional energy to expend on other people, their problems, their needs.

Here, there seems to be almost no end to the need. The city of Beaumont, to our east along the coast, is an island in the floodwaters—no way in or out—and they have no clean water to drink. Did you catch that? Water everywhere and none of it is drinkable. In fact, it's poison. Before the hurricane, this whole region, devastated as it is, was home to some of this country's most dangerously contaminated EPA Superfund sites, and those sites are still here, except now they're underwater. It's all mixed together: the water in the dump sites, and the factories, and in our homes. There's no separating good water from bad. No separating water that might be drinkable from water that drowned a father, a police officer, the bat colony, a family of six, a factory, a Superfund site, the power station, the pretty woman who lived on the first floor of the apartment building. Over the past few days, a chemical plant near the ship channel has been exploding. That's in the water too. Officials have told us to stay inside, to stand well back, to avoid breathing the air if possible—and for those who are closest to the ship channel, to close the windows and turn off the air-conditioning. We're all trapped in a state of suspended, horrified grief.

On social media, I have seen some spirited debate about whether Texas might have deserved this, as if this catastrophe is some kind of cosmic climate karma for having hosted the oil industry all these years, or that the hurricane was delivered to us as cosmic retribution for our state having once elected two compassionless senators who voted against aid for Hurricane Sandy, or that maybe this is God's way of punishing us for having elected the country's first lesbian mayor. I don't believe in some kind of cosmic register that keeps a tally of all our worst misdeeds, but if I did, I would not count that last one among them.

Who is to say what each of us deserves? My children deserve to be fed, I think, and cared for; our neighbors deserve food, supplies, power, and relief. There are literally thousands of people around Houston who deserve rescue, and the monumental task of coordinating the efforts of getting to all of them nearly boggles the mind. Perhaps you have seen the photo of elderly folks in a nursing home, waist deep in water, waiting for rescue. It's making the rounds. Boats are on their way from everywhere in the country—some as far away as Minnesota, I've seen. They're using an app to coordinate, and they've been criticized for this, because, well, according to the criticism, to assume that people are able to download an app or that seniors have smartphones is completely inexcusable. The perfect has always been the enemy of the good.

I have seen so many crazy things the last few days. People from far afield are so gleeful to criticize how we are feeling and processing and talking about what is going on here. People I've never met have mocked me on social media, mocked friends and strangers who show their support. I do not understand this impulse. What makes a person rejoice in the misfortune of another? To find pleasure in another person's pain?

What must we do to ourselves to make us hate one another beyond reason? I may never find an answer to this question, but I know that whatever structures to hate we have built within ourselves, they can fall away in the moment when someone reaches out a hand—whether asking for help or offering it—and you grab hold.

My husband returns from a day of rescuing neighbors just as I learn that our own neighbors have lost power. They arrive, soaking wet, and we join together our meager provisions, have dinner, watch movies, play a trivia game. (I win.) Another neighbor crosses the flooded street to join us, and we swap rescue stories over wine and beers. I laugh, really hard, for the first time in days.

My friend—the one who crosses the river to sit at my table—tells us stories about the people he rescued today. The youngest of these, who is twenty-five and relies on a wheelchair for mobility, didn't want to leave his house. My friend told him about a camp where he volunteers, where young people are often at the end of their lives. "You haven't been there yet," my friend told this young man, and somehow, the idea that there might be something else, some as yet unimagined possible future, convinced the young man to let my friend carry him to the boat, to safety, to warm towels, and diligent care. These two men, strangers to one another, held each other in their arms, and both found their own comfort in that. This friend has told me he actually knows no strangers, and this was no exception. Today he met two volunteers from out of town, and the three of them went out on an airboat and pulled around 120 new friends out of the flood and hauled them to dry land, to safety, to tender, loving care.

It's been decades since I claimed any manner of religious practice, but as I remember it, a blessing is what we say before a meal, or when a child is born, or has become a particularly zealous way to sign an email in what translates to "have a nice day." The idea is somewhat synonymous with grace. In Judaism, a blessing is a slightly different idea, often called a *mitzvah*—a word that also carries the weight of a command-ment—and the focus is less on words than it is on deeds. The point being, in both cases, that you're not supposed to get paid, or to expect to be repaid, even in karma points, for everything you do. You can let some of it be a blessing. And if there is one thing I have learned in my thirty-nine short years on this Earth, it is that anyone who can afford to give a blessing is wealthy beyond measure. My friend isn't rich, but right now he's the wealthiest man I know.

He's wealthier even than the man who came to Texas today, the one who stood on the bumper of a firetruck for a photograph and said, "What a great crowd!" Our neighbors to the south, in Mexico, have offered to send us aid, even as this man demands they pay to put up a wall between them and ourselves, that we close our border to them and all of their needs. Today he placed supplies into the trunks of cars. He met with elected officials in a dry, air-conditioned building, took a few selfies with evacuees, and kissed their babies before he got back on his plane without even getting his shoes wet. Has he ever risked anything to help a stranger in need? I suspect he has not, because there's an idea he has been circulating for some time now—and every decision he makes is part of it—that America is a small boat and there just aren't enough seats. He built his campaign on that idea—that we should make the boat smaller, not bigger. But even as he chooses to peddle that cruel vision of the world, everyone at my table in Houston is choosing another. Here, we'll make room in the boat for everyone, and we'll row together to shore.

I don't believe in the god of any organized religion, but I do believe in grace. What kind of blessings can each of us afford to give? No doubt more than we actually do. I fully admit that I am no saint in this regard: I don't have a deep reservoir of patience for my children couch-diving in my living room, or for fools who peddle lies and division and hate. But probably there are people on my street, or in this neighborhood, or elsewhere in this city, friends I haven't met yet, who desperately need a little grace. My family may yet lose our house to the water that is still rising all around us, but for now, we have power, and warm water, and clean sheets. That's far more than we need.

Elsewhere in Houston, where the water has already receded, a friend helped to gut a house in a subdivision where every house had a water line to the second floor—the soggy, molding guts puked onto the curbs as far as the eye could see. Across the street from where my friend was working, a neighbor said that he had to float his baby out in the cooler. It wasn't even the first time he'd done this. This is only one neighborhood in a metro area of nearly 7 million, where it is still unclear what percentage of people have lost their homes. I've heard a third of the people. I've heard more than a hundred thousand homes. Or three hundred thousand homes. It will take time to get a reliable accounting. They're not entirely sure how many homes are still underwater, and by the time we know, there likely won't be anything left of them.

There is no way to help them all. So instead, we help who we can. A friend does laundry. Another coordinates teams of volunteers. One of my daughter's friends from school left her home as the floodwaters rose, left even without shoes. I've been calling, sending emails and text messages for days to find a furnished apartment where they can stay. One Realtor I spoke to has been working all week trying to place families that have been displaced. She's been working day and night, sleeping on an air mattress in her office because she too lost everything. She is still wearing the clothes she wore to evacuate. Some neighbors' homes are underwater, and a group of us are planning a flotilla recovery mission: all the neighbors will meet, and among the group of us, we'll bring all our lives back to shore.

At least once a day, I have a good cry. An ugly cry; a shoulder-shaking, whole-body cry. Sometimes it comes while I am standing in the kitchen, as the weight of the water begins to sink in. Sometimes, like tonight, I have a good cry when I finish putting the children to bed on the air mattress, realizing that the ways I need them are so different, though no less acute, from how they need me.

We say our good-byes to the friend who crosses the river back to his own home, and we all settle down to sleep, to the extent that sleep is even possible. We all have our minds on the water. It is underneath us, around us, running past our every thought, every gesture, saturating every word we say. We are all so very weary, but I stay awake all night anyway, checking the gauge levels at various points along the bayou, looking out the window at the water slowly approaching our house, searching for news. Is the water rising or falling? Is the dam leaking or holding strong? Will we live, or will we drown?

This is the new normal. Today is the sixth day, I think. When the sun came up this morning, I found a wide rushing river outside my home: three feet deep and thirty feet across. My neighbor was standing there, crying too. She and I shouted softly to each other over the flooded street: "At least it isn't hot," I offered. "At least the water is moving," she returned. Now, hours later, there is blue sky, barely a cloud, neighbors picking their way over dry land to walk their dogs. It could be the first spring weekend, or the first autumn one, with so many people bustling about. Meanwhile, the Coast Guard helicopters pass and pass overhead; airboats can be heard shuttling people to and fro. A giant military convoy plane keeps circling and circling.

While I am drinking my coffee and watching airboats fly up and down the street, a group of rescue officers approach on foot. One tells me about a house that had waist-high water at the door. He knocked, rang the doorbell. Someone answered, also standing in waist-high water. As they were talking, a mother duck and her ducklings jumped from the stairs into the water and floated through the living room out the door. Our favorite neighbors have left a pork shoulder to smoke in the driveway all day while they are out pulling heirlooms from a flooded house. At the end of the day, they'll have an enormous party. A pontoon boat will cruise around on one of the most flooded streets in our neighborhood: at least six people on board, drinking, smoking maybe more than cigarettes. Who will stop them? Each of us, in our desperation, is following our natural human inclination: toward the future, toward joy.

My husband comes outside to share bad news: the Army Corps of Engineers, in its meticulously calculated wisdom, has decided overnight that it will open the floodgates at the overspilling reservoirs even more. There will be an additional one to three feet of water, it says, but people who have not already flooded likely will still not flood, not unless the water is already close to the house. How close is "close"? we wonder. Inches? Feet? Inside, I watch government officials say murkily reassuring things in press conferences: everything is fine, we have everything under control, all y'all will be okay.

We hear from neighbors that water is rising quickly at the back of the neighborhood, where people have woken to find themselves stranded, water chest-deep rising in their houses; their voices heard outside calling for help. My husband and our neighbors once again drag the canoe from the garage and row toward them.

The National Guard passes with a flatbed full of evacuees; SWAT teams trudge upriver in their giant canoes. One neighbor looks overhead and says, "I think we're on the news." I ask one Guardsman passing through to tell me what he knows: "You're gonna get more water tonight," he says, "but we don't know how much. We're taking people out who want to go; we won't be here after dark when the water really starts rising." Another neighbor hears from a state trooper "maybe two more feet." When my husband returns, we talk it over. He says, "What I've been telling people who need to leave their houses is that it's never a mistake to leave, but it might be a mistake to stay."

It is one of the hardest things I've ever had to do: to choose what belongings in my house I cannot live without, to figure out which of those things I value enough to carry through waist-high water on my back. And then: how to explain to my children how to place value on their most precious things. To explain that we are leaving, that we don't know when we will return, that they can bring along only what their tiny bodies can carry.

We pack our things. We trudge through water filthy with sewage up to our knees and very slowly make it to the end of the street, where we leave our flooded neighborhood and enter a military zone: army trucks lined with uniformed soldiers in the back, airboats surrounded by emergency responders lifting people onto stretchers, EMTs, volunteers lining the entire street. The sight of them brings the reality of the situation down in all its force. I admit: it breaks me, even the part of me I've worked so long to make solid and hard. A man approaches us as we emerge from the water and offers to walk with us, to carry our bags as far as we need to go.

We walk past fire trucks, ambulances, past volunteers offering us water and something to eat. I feel so visible passing them with tears streaming down my cheeks. One man—I don't know him—approaches me and holds me in his arms. "We will rebuild it," he says, "and it will be even better next time. Next time, we can make it even more beautiful."

We make our way eventually to the parking lot where we are supposed to meet the person my husband has arranged to pick us up, but that person can't reach us, we learn, because of the water on every street between us and him. Just as my husband dials the phone to call someone else for help, a woman approaches and asks whether we have a ride, where we are going. "Halfway across the city," I tell her, "as far from the bayou as we can go." She offers to drive us. It takes nearly an hour to reach our destination, in the care of this stranger. I never even get her last name.

I have often told my students that I find the theory of the Stranger more useful than the idea of the Other, because the Stranger is a person who is in the group but not of the group, who arrives from elsewhere but never departs, and who embodies that elsewhereness no matter how long she stays. The Stranger is usually treated with contempt and suspicion because she exists in the presence of those who believe they are known to one another and performs the function of consolidating difference in a single body, allowing all other differences among the group to seem to fall away. The Stranger gives the group cohesion, and a language rises up to describe it: good/evil, citizen/immigrant, homesteader/refugee. And yet it is strangers who sometimes arrive with the help they are able to offer, and this simple act confirms our common humanity.

Cornel West has said that "justice is what love looks like in public." But love is not the conclusion of a risk assessment. The lesser factor in a calculation. We cannot love our fellow humans in the abstract. Already there is another hurricane forming somewhere in the Gulf or in the ocean; it is heading our way, maybe. Or it is headed elsewhere: to Florida, the Virgin Islands, Puerto Rico. That storm, like this one, will ravage neighborhoods without regard for inequalities of status. But love will ask us to reckon with those inequalities when the storm reveals them.

Houston is the most diverse city in the country. We're proud of that fact. If Houston were a country, it would be fourth in terms of the number of refugees it accepts. We are also a sanctuary city, though we mostly keep that to ourselves while our local law enforcement refuses to enforce racist federal laws. I have lived here for nine years total, longer than I've lived any other place in my life. This city is beautiful and amazing because of the people who live here, not in spite of it. And if we didn't know it before, we have learned since the hurricane made landfall six days ago that each of us makes a choice to help another, or not to, every single day. We can bear witness to another person's need and do nothing, or we can choose to help. Everyone I know has chosen to open their homes to strangers, to feed them, clothe them, raise money for the restoration of their homes. Even people whose own houses were destroyed are helping others in the ways they can. The choice to help is never the wrong one. It is never a mistake to show compassion to our fellow human beings.

Water destroys what it touches: carves canyons out of deserts, swallows people, ice, whole cities and continents. It also destroys the trivial things we spend our lives worshipping: our houses, our streets, our pride, our temples to bigotry and greed. I have heard now a story of a man who escaped his flooding neighborhood, only to row back in his kayak to save one more person or one more thing and capsized in the current. He was missing all night, and in the morning they found him holding on to a tree. A teenager was swept away in the current of the bayou and caught the grate of a bridge and held on there until rescuers found her in the morning. An infant was taken from her mother by the current and the current offered that brand-new life back to the churning sea.

But water also washes, gives life, makes new. The water has destroyed this city—there are no two ways about it—but the outpouring of love I have witnessed here among neighbors and strangers, arriving from all over the world, is the most beautiful thing I have ever seen.

The donations and prayers and well wishes flowing toward us are so welcome, but there's something else we will need, something that can help us better in the long run: whatever ideas you hold about people from Houston, or Texas, or Sri Lanka or Trinidad or the Bronx or Palestine, or whatever kinds of ideas you have about people who come from wherever you are not from, stop holding on to them. They serve no one. Please surrender them to the current that is lapping at the doorstep of this moment. Leave them behind and just let them go.

MAKE WAY FOR JOY

The alarm rings somewhere in the darkness, and I rise from the bed. I dress in the bathroom in my usual uniform: sneakers, bandanna, a blue belt that holds my water bottles and phone. I wake the dog from the crescent he's made with his snoring body on the rug. He stretches and yawns while I clasp the pinch collar around his neck. I lock my sleeping family inside the dark house; outside, a yard of sprinklers sputters awake as I walk through the streets. I begin running at the corner. There is no one in the world but me.

It is nearly six o'clock when I reach the entrance to the park and continue running along the trail. The moon illuminates a pale field to my left where, until recently, tall native grasses grew alongside wildflowers: bluebonnets, castillejas, phlox. They'll grow here again soon. To my right, trees tangle with twisting vines to form a curtain against the bayou: the water ripples, leaves rustle, a squirrel startles awake in its nest.

I have run this section of the path so many times that I nearly have it memorized. The path meanders alongside the bayou, through a wide basin cut over all the years of its existence. I cross a bridge over a small creek that feeds the larger one, through a tunnel carved between trees, past the ferns and mosses that grow on the forest floor, the sweet damp smell of their rot seeping back into the earth. There are three bridges like this one between here and the water fountain. I convince the dog to keep running on the promise I'll let him stop there to smell the wildflowers while I stretch my hip.

I run despite the aches and pains, old injuries from the thousands of miles of running since I began as a teenager. Then, as now, I would wake up before the rest of my family and tiptoe out the door. I drove my father's blue '68 Ford F-150 out to the lake at the edge of town and ran along the dam. There was almost never any traffic, almost never any other people. Only me—just a girl—and the lake stretching out under the fog. I didn't have a care in the world.

Probably the world cared more to harm me then than it does now, but I didn't know that yet. I knew to wear reflective colors, keep my body covered, run against the direction of traffic instead of with it. Now I know that wearing a ponytail on the wrong path at the wrong time could have meant the end for a girl like me. Back then, all I knew was that I felt an agitation with the world that running helped me air out. I could stretch my legs, sing loudly, throw my arms into a cloud of gnats above my head. I could stop or skip or keep moving. I could talk to myself or simply listen. Running became a kind of church I attended, a religion between the world and me.

I tried running on my school's track team for a year or two, but I wasn't particularly good at any of the events. I can't make my body move fast enough to be a sprinter, and at that time I didn't yet have the stamina to go long distances either. My coach—a man, it should be said—couldn't figure out what to do with me on the team. He put me in hurdle events, on relays, sent me to the weight room. I wasn't good at anything, he told me. At practice one day I stepped in a hole on the track by mistake and twisted my knee; there was a surgery, rehabilitation. I didn't compete on the team after that. In truth, the injury saved me. Running had never been a way for me to win something, but rather a way to simply *be*.

In college I ran laps around the outdoor track after class; on the weekends, I ran through the neighborhood where I lived. When I moved in with the man who would later try to kill me, I ran in long circles—away from the apartment we shared toward the shops downtown, where people sat at little tables together drinking coffee or reading books—and back again, and all the while I imagined the life I could have if only I were brave enough to leave him. I ran no matter the weather—through the snow, and the falling leaves, and the driving rain—because he didn't watch me, didn't follow me, had no idea where I was. He believed I belonged to him—my body, my words, my every action and gesture and thought. Running, I knew I belonged only to myself.

After I left him, after he tried but failed to kill me, I didn't run for years. I was too afraid. I adopted the dog maybe for this reason, because eventually I felt that old agitation. I wanted to be brave enough to run again and felt I needed company, or protection. I needed a very large dog with very sharp teeth. I needed to cover myself in tattoos. And maybe to carry a hammer.

All these years later, I run because sometimes I am still afraid and I am trying not to be. The dog is as alert as I am, pointing his hearing in the direction of every sound: that pounding is only the echo of my shoes; that rustling is only a rabbit diving under the leaves—as afraid of the very large dog appearing out of nowhere as I feel of whatever danger might wait in the darkness for me.

I have learned during all these years of being afraid that fear has a force and momentum all its own. First, I see a shadow in some dark corner—nothing more than a memory, maybe—and then the shadow becomes electric and every neuron fires with it, a charge that shocks the blood pumping in my chest, the air I pull into my lungs; it buzzes in the street lamps, the rippling water, every blade of grass. Even the tips of my fingers prickle with its current. I take deep breaths. I time my steps to the dog's. We are a team, the two of us. He knows the drill. He keeps me running while my heart slows, while the shadow inside me retreats.

It's been decades of this now. This is the single longest and most enduring effect of having been kidnapped and raped all those years ago by a man I once loved: I am unable to live in the present. I'm always in some other time, either trying to see the danger that might evolve in the future, or trying to understand some heartbreak or accident in the past. I am too afraid, too angry. I'm too vigilant. Too worried. Too ready to catastrophize. Too quick to lose my temper and implode. And all of that work that I do to be in some other place, some other time, worrying about something terrible that just might happen, keeps me from experiencing all the joy that is all around me in the right here and now.

Lately, I have found myself running longer and longer distances, have found it harder to air the agitation out. It started when the Republican candidate for president admitted to being a serial sexual assailant on the *Access Hollywood* tape. I had mostly tried to avoid listening to him until that point, since he reminds me in so many ways of that man I used to love, the one who believed even my happiness belonged to only him. Suddenly I was a hunted animal all over again, crouching, slinking, trying to remain alive and unseen. That none of this disqualified the candidate only gave speed and endurance to all the things I had been trying for so long to outrun.

The day after the election, after it was clear he'd won, I woke even earlier than usual from a nightmare in which my house was falling apart, my family was missing, everything I loved was either ruined or gone. It wasn't safe to go outside and look for them. This dream came after months of nightmares: dreams where every building I entered had no floor, nothing to stand on; dreams where everyone walked around with guns in both hands, aiming. I went for a run that morning, hoping to run myself empty of that feeling, or to erase it, like a stain I could wash out if I just scrubbed hard enough, like a bad meal I could purge in a single furious fit and then be done.

But that's not how grief works. Later that morning, over breakfast, I told my kids who had won the election. They were shocked and dismayed and deeply sad, as I was. As all our friends were. They wanted to know how this could happen, what we do now. I told them that now, as before, we have to be kind—so, so kind to one another—we have to stick together, to take care of our community, and to protect our friends. "Yesterday, and all the days before that, it was our job to stand up to bullies," I said. "That is still true today, especially true today, even if that job seems so much harder now." It means we will have to be very strong, and very brave. "But more than anything else," I said, "we have to love one another fiercely—so, so fiercely." They asked why I was crying, and I said it is because I am so, so angry.

I called it anger because they don't know about rage and would be frightened if they did. After they left for school and I was home alone, I wanted to let that rage consume me. I wanted to rage at anyone who voted for that racist, sexist, xenophobic demagogue, who voted third party because they didn't like what they perceived to be two equally bad choices, who didn't vote at all. The candidate wasn't the only person who won, it seemed—also all of the men who are like him in their own toxic ways, even the man I used to love. I had an appointment for a mammogram that day and glared at all the white women in the waiting room in their fresh white robes. *Which one of you did this to us?* I thought. I was contemplating the various ways I could make them suffer when I realized I was beginning to feel something I hadn't before. *Oh*, I thought, *so this is what hate feels like.*

Hate is "a hideous ecstasy," Orwell once wrote, and it can turn anyone, myself included, into "a grimacing, screaming lunatic." I don't hate anyone—not even that man who became president, not even the man I used to love. I refuse to, because I meant what I said to my children about loving fiercely. I took them with me to cast my vote in that election out of a fierce love: for this country, for all of its people, for our planet. We all pushed the button together and called it history. On the day after the inauguration, I marched in Washington out of a fierce love for the millions of women who planned to gather there: my sisters, my friends, women I knew and those I hadn't met until then. My family came along, marched out of a fierce love for me. It was a moment to take our rage outside, give it oxygen, and let it burn off clean. It seemed, at the time, like a consolation—or if not consolation, a transformation. A woman's rage can transform many things, including herself.

I've held on to my rage for precisely that reason. I've gathered it, decades of it. I carry so much rage with me that I grind my teeth at night, and grind them all throughout the day. I am careful not to become a woman who is "hysterical," "militant," "shrill," "unhinged"; I try to "control" myself because my rage is too much, and the too-muchness would make my friends and enemies uncomfortable in nearly equal measure. But sometimes the rage is so large that nothing else can live alongside it, and because everything I've been taught to do with rage means harming myself or another person, I run. Now fifteen miles. Now twenty.

Rage has transformed me from a woman who runs away, to one who runs toward, who runs against and despite, who runs through. Running harms no one—takes only time and energy. I run because running requires that I be present wherever I actually am: in my legs, which carry me; in my hip, which I injured during a recent fall; in my arms, where the sweat is dripping from my elbows; in my chest, where my heart pumps dark red blood out to my fingers and back again; in my feet, which pound the dark streets and the path through the park, up hills and over bridges through trees. Running turns me into a body that can breathe, that can arrive here, in precisely this moment, despite sometimes paralyzing fear, despite everything.

And then there's this: each morning I run through the darkness for miles. I cannot escape all the terrible news I've heard or seen the day before, but the thoughts arrive and pass over me like waves. I cannot hold on to them, do not even try. I run over the first bridge, the second, the third, through a gap in the trees, and then enter the field and look up to see the sunrise greet me. Every morning! Beauty finds me despite everything, and in a thousand different ways every morning.

And suddenly I can see it: how things seem to be coming together instead of falling apart. My body is stronger than it used to be, I can run farther than I used to, I take chances that I wouldn't have before. I am here, alone, in the darkness, for instance, and I do not feel small and scared, but free and capable and strong. I feel something begin to open—that shut place I carry—and what stampedes inside me is a feeling of being unrestrained, unencumbered, unlimited. It is a joy that has no bottom and no top; it shines inside my body, faster, stronger, more brilliant than ever before. Running makes a tiny space for joy to enter my life, and I find my own justice in that.

Joy comes in the morning, or so the familiar saying goes. In the morning I run with the dog. I run with my neighbor. I run with two friends. I finished a half-marathon with blood on my knees and a smile on my face, another with tears streaming down my cheeks. In a few weeks I'll run a full marathon. Twenty-six miles. I can see it already: how I cross over the finish line with my hands in the air. Everyone watches, but no one I know. They cheer, these strangers; they can't possibly know how this story began, but they rejoice with me to see how it ends.

"The happiest person in the world is one who learns lessons of worship from nature," Emerson wrote. Running allows me to recognize the way that beauty sometimes arrives in my life almost entirely unbidden, like the clouds that tower in the air, tumbling upward, higher than mountains; like how the sky grows lighter as black gives way to indigo, to blue and purple, to red and orange near the horizon; like how a layer of mist hangs only feet above the field even as it condenses and gathers on the leaves as tiny gemstones glinting in the rising sun; like the sunrise. Sometimes I stop running to watch the sunrise. I watch in a kind of rapt wonder that never gets old—the play of light on our atmosphere that turns the sky all red and gold except for the darkness receding behind me.

Someone once told me that his grandmother told him that an injustice is anything that gets between a person and their joy. I don't know if that covers all of what an injustice is, but I like the idea that justice is anything that makes way for joy, that makes the condition of joy a possibility again.

Can this be what justice is? I think it can be, at least for me. I think justice means that I work together with others for our mutual joy. It means rejoicing in the joy of another, fostering the lives and good fortune of everyone, not only the people we consider "our own." Justice means we value the lives of everyone equally, and protect and support them equally. It means we recognize and protect what is radical and unique about every single person—even those who cannot return this recognition. Justice means that children are allowed to be children, and then to enter adulthood with safe passage, at their own pace, in their own way. Justice means we pass responsibility for keeping peace from one generation to another. That we return our children from war and teach them to put down their guns; it means we never pick them up again, not ever. It means we teach everyone, from birth, that they are capable of nurturing, of healing, of compassion, of love. Justice means we repair instead of repeat. Justice is the permission I give myself to go out running, to trust my own strength and fortitude to fight off danger; or better yet, to trust that no danger will befall me at all. Justice is what makes it possible for me to be sitting on the kitchen floor with my children, who are laughing and telling each other silly jokes, and to stay right here in this moment, laughing also. This is a new moment in my life, a new place to simply be; it didn't exist before and I couldn't have made it alone. Justice means everyone has a place like this — places we make together, for one another, for us all.

NOTES

THE RECKONINGS

2   *a local man has been convicted*: During the trial, a jury of seven women and five men heard testimony that the local man (in addition to raping the boy and burning him alive) had molested a six-year-old girl and had stomped a kitten to death. His defense argued that the local man had been a troubled boy, whose mother had died when he was eight and whose father had been absent; his guardians almost never interacted with him. It took the jury only three and a half hours of deliberation to return a guilty verdict on the four charges of capital murder. Months later, during his sentencing hearing, the jury deliberated only an hour and fifteen minutes before giving the local man the maximum sentence of forty years in prison for a crime committed when he was thirteen. The mother of the murdered boy told reporters, "I'm happy. I'm just going to enjoy this day and not worry about anything else."

5   *a retrieval of all I had lost*: I have come to dislike the term *recovery* for precisely this reason. There is no going back for me, and there's no re-becoming the person I once was. I will

never again be a woman who has not been kidnapped and raped by a man I once loved. That woman is gone. Writing that book, my previous one, helped me to grieve that loss maybe, if only because it forced me to fully acknowledge the ways that recovery was not possible. *Discovery*, on the other hand . . . well, that is always possible.

5 *Now* that *would be justice, they think*: Alec Walen writes in the *Stanford Encyclopedia of Philosophy* that retributive justice can be best understood as a form of justice committed to the following three principles: "(1) that those who commit certain kinds of wrongful acts . . . morally deserve to suffer a proportionate punishment; (2) that it is intrinsically morally good—good without reference to any other goods that might arise—if some legitimate punisher gives them the punishment they deserve; and (3) that it is morally impermissible intentionally to punish the innocent or to inflict disproportionately large punishments on wrongdoers."

7 *"one mina of silver"*: Despite this seeming endorsement of barbarism, the most common form of criminal punishment was actually a fine, which varied according to a person's gender, status, and rank. Only equals had rights to retaliation; serfs did not have the right to break the bones of a magistrate or snatch out one of his eyes. That would be preposterous, since inequalities of status and power are so assumed throughout ancient Babylonian society that they are written into the law. Not surprisingly, there's nothing in the code that suggests this unequal social order was considered unjust or that anyone

thought to question it. In fact, the fine of one mina of silver for a crime against a serf was imposed in order to protect the serf's rights, even if those rights were not equal to those of a "free man." When a serf made a claim to justice, he did so as an assertion of his rights, not as a plea for charity.

In ancient Greece, the laws reflect a similar hierarchy of justice. The crime of rape, for example, incurred a fine of a hundred drachmas, payable to the woman's father or head of household. The crimes of adultery and battery also carried standardized fines, though a fine might be raised or lowered depending on a variety of factors: the time of day, the place the crime was committed, whether a weapon had been used, the social class of the victim, the severity of injury, and whether the victim could be expected to recover. The standard fine was tripled if the victim was a magistrate.

In ancient Germanic societies, every person had an agreed-on monetary value, known as a *wergild*—*wer* meaning "man" and *gild* here meaning "price," but like the much later word *shuld*, also meaning both "guilt" and "debt." The value of a wergild was different for different people depending on the specific culture and on norms associated with gender and age and social rank. In some cultures, a noble was worth twice what a free man was worth, in some cases as much as six times the value. A woman's wergild was worth twice a man's, or in some places, only half. Codes of law in these societies, such as the Frankish Salic Code, compiled in the first decade of the sixth century, established fixed monetary penalties for a wide variety of alarmingly specific violent or otherwise damaging acts, such as "striking a man on the head so the brain shows" or "skinning a dead horse without consent of the owner." Regardless of the amount and form of the wergild or, for that matter, the nature of the crime, any time a crime was committed, the criminal would be required to pay wergild to the victim or to the family of the victim as restitution. The only exception was for slaves, who could not pay a monetary wergild and could therefore instead expect to pay the wergild through lashings and even sometimes castration. In any case, only after the wergild had been paid would the criminal be redeemed.

We see in these ancient laws something that is still true today: that any person who commits a crime against someone higher in the social order is punished more severely than a person who commits a crime against his social equal, and that anyone who commits a crime against someone who is lower in the social order is punished less severely. Low-status criminals tend to suffer physical punishments: lashings, imprisonment, castration, beheadings. High-status criminals suffer a punishment against their status or wealth: they offer land, or titles, or some token of their wealth.

David Graeber points out in *Debt: The First 5,000 Years* that money evolved in order to transform the abstract concept of a debt into a concrete form through the use of a common currency. But others, such as David Johnston, have argued that this evolution is inseparable from how money has always been used as an expression of injustice among unequals.

See in particular Johnston's *A Brief History of Justice* for a thorough discussion of how social hierarchy was written into ancient law. See also *Women, Crime and Punishment in*

Ancient Law and Society, Vol. 2: *Ancient Greece* by Elisabeth Meier Tetlow; and Mitchel P. Roth's *An Eye for an Eye: A Global History of Crime and Punishment*.

8   *what humans understood to be our baser instincts*: In Book II of Plato's *Republic*, Glaucon suggests to Socrates that humans generally want to outdo others by getting and having as much as possible. "Uncurbed, this attribute would undermine cooperation and lead to perpetual conflict," David Johnston writes in *A Brief History of Justice.* "Justice, then, is a human invention designed to curb the natural inclinations of human beings, which would have radically unsociable consequences if left unchecked."

8   *every injury has some equivalent of pain or sacrifice*: It is worth quoting from *The Genealogy of Morals* (Second Essay) at length here:

> Have these genealogists of morality up to now allowed themselves to dream, even remotely, that, for instance, the major moral principle "guilt" [*Schuld*] derived its origin from the very materialistic idea "debt" [*Schulden*]? Or that punishment developed as a repayment, completely without reference to any assumption about freedom or lack of freedom of the will?—and did so, by contrast, to the point where it always first required a high degree of human development so that the animal "man" began to make those much more primitive distinctions between "intentional," "negligent," "accidental," "responsible," and their opposites and bring them to bear

when meting out punishment? That idea, nowadays so trite, apparently so natural, so unavoidable, which has even had to serve as the explanation how the feeling of justice in general came into existence on earth, "The criminal deserves punishment because he could have acted otherwise," this idea is, in fact, an extremely late achievement, indeed, a sophisticated form of human judgment and decision making. Anyone who moves this idea back to the beginnings is sticking his coarse fingers inappropriately into the psychology of older humanity. For the most extensive period of human history, punishment was certainly not meted out because people held the instigator of evil responsible for his actions, and thus it was not assumed that only the guilty party should be punished:—it was much more as it still is now when parents punish their children out of anger over some harm they have suffered, anger vented on the perpetrator—but anger restrained and modified through the idea that every injury has some equivalent and that compensation for it could, in fact, be paid out, even if that is through the pain of the perpetrator.

10   *"We must do what we can to add weight to the lighter scale"*: See Simone Weil, *Gravity and Grace*.

10   *he threw Christians to the beasts in the Colosseum*: Tacitus writes in his *Annals*, Book XV, Chapter 44:

Mockery of every sort was added to their deaths. Covered with the skins of beasts, they were torn by dogs and perished, or were nailed to crosses, or were doomed to the flames and burnt, to serve as a nightly illumination, when daylight had expired.

Nero offered his gardens for the spectacle, and was exhibiting a show in the circus, while he mingled with the people in the dress of a charioteer or stood aloft on a car. Hence, even for criminals who deserved extreme and exemplary punishment, there arose a feeling of compassion; for it was not, as it seemed, for the public good, but to glut one man's cruelty, that they were being destroyed.

10   *justice, like language, is a "special characteristic" of humans*: Aristotle writes (translated by Welldon):

Nature, as we are fond of asserting, creates nothing without a purpose and man is the only animal endowed with speech. . . . The object of speech . . . is to indicate advantage and disadvantage and therefore also justice and injustice. For it is a special characteristic which distinguishes man from all other animals that he alone enjoys perception of good and evil, justice and injustice and the like.

10   *Plato suggested that justice is "an inward grace"*: Sir Ernest Barker writes in *Greek Political Theory* of how the concept of justice evolved from previous conceptions into the version we see in Plato's *Republic*: "Whereas it had been regarded . . . as something outward—a body of material precepts confronting the soul, and claiming to control it in virtue of a power external to it—it is now regarded as an

inward grace, and its understanding is shown to involve a study of the inner man."

GIRLHOOD IN A SEMIBARBAROUS AGE

14   *the black triangle of the Venus*: A few years ago, a team of German archaeologists found a Venus figurine in the bottom of a vaulted cave in a low mountain range bounded by the Danube and Neckar rivers in the German Alps. This figurine, like the Chauvet Cave Venus and the well-known Venus of Willendorf, is undoubtedly meant to signify a female body: a pair of giant breasts balloon above a round belly; the elaborately carved labia gape open; there is a small ring in the place of a head, a void in the place of feet. The discovery of the figurine created quite a splash, with magazines announcing proof of Upper Paleolithic pornography. "You couldn't get more female than this," Nicholas Conard (the archaeologist whose team found the figurine) tells *Smithsonian Magazine*. "Head and legs don't matter," he said. "This is about sex, reproduction." At the time, they thought the figurine was maybe as much as forty thousand years old, and named it the Venus of Hohle Fels, after the cave where it was discovered, and in the tradition of calling all such "fertility" totems "Venus."

There are something like 149 so-called Venus figurines from the Upper Paleolithic that have been discovered, dating from thirty-five thousand years ago to nine thousand years ago, ranging from Europe to Siberia and elsewhere. The first of these was found in the mid-1860s in the Abri of

Laugerie-Basse by Paul Hurault, an amateur archaeologist and the eighth marquis of Vibraye, who called his discovery of the nude figurine Venus Impudique (or "Immodest Venus"), in contrast to Venus Pudica ("Modest Venus"), a fourth-century BC sculpture of Aphrodite of Knidos by the Greek sculptor Praxiteles of Athens. The "Modest Venus" was also a nude sculpture but is depicted covering herself with her hand in the proper Hellenistic tradition. The uncovered Upper Paleolithic nude, in contrast, was considered obscene, pornographic even.

And yet unlike the Venus of Hohle Fels, or the Venus of Willendorf, or the Chauvet Cave Venus, this "Immodest Venus" did not have ballooning breasts or a round abdomen—what Conard now calls "the essence of being female"—but rather is slender, elongated, perhaps even juvenile. What about a juvenile female body is less "essentially" female than a pregnant woman's?

In fact, many of the lesser-known Venuses do not fit the "Venus" type at all: the Venus of Galgenberg is a slender Venus, one leg extended, one arm raised: dancing; the Venus of Buret' wears heavy fur from head to foot and is also slender, like most of the other Venus figurines found at Malta. The Venus of Willendorf—often considered the quintessential Venus—was only one of two figurines discovered at that archaeological site in Austria. The other figurine was also female, but tall and slender, more roughly made, and many archaeologists have dismissed it from consideration as being "unfinished" in some way.

By singling out the Venuses with exaggerated sexual features as if they were the only type, the only message, the only idea of what has been and will always be "sacred" throughout the ages, we are saying more about what women's bodies mean to us in the present than anything about what they might have meant in the past.

For a more thorough discussion, see Andrew Curry's "The Cave Art Debate" in *Smithsonian,* as well as April Nowell and Melanie L. Chang's "Science, the Media, and Interpretations of Upper Paleolithic Figurines," in *American Anthropologist.*

14   *"the myth that has endured until our days"*: There are so many myths to choose from! But here I'll focus on the Greek one in which the young goddess Persephone was picking wild-flowers in a field when Hades, Lord of the Underworld, burst through a cleft in the earth and carried her off. After searching desperately for months, her mother, Demeter, goddess of fer-tility and harvest, learned what had happened and convinced Zeus to persuade Hades to release the girl. Before doing so, Hades tricked Persephone into eating pomegranate seeds, which doomed her to return to the underworld for a portion of each year. This, the myth tells us, is why we have seasons.

But it's not why the myth fascinates us. For millennia, artists and writers working in nearly every form, genre, and media have appropriated and claimed this myth as their own, reenacting the mythological violence over and over again.

In a fourth-century BC fresco, Hades abducts Perse-phone. His expression, despite the degradation of the image over time, shows clear purpose and intent. He carries the screaming woman off in his chariot; her pink robes shred and trail behind her while the Fates and Demeter cower nearby. The fresco, or *The Rape of Persephone* as it is now called, was discovered on the front of a tomb in 1977 when a Greek archaeologist became convinced that a hill called the Great Tumulus concealed the burial site of the great Macedonian kings. He uncovered the tombs, including the so-called Tomb of Persephone, which may have belonged to Philip II, father of Alexander the Great, at the end of a six-week dig.

In a fresco titled *The Rape of Proserpine*, commissioned in the early 1680s, Luca Giordano, a late baroque painter, depicts the Roman version of the abduction myth in a series of interlocking visual narratives. On one side of the fresco, Ceres sows seeds in a field while other gods plow the soil, water it, prune branches in a nearby tree, ride across the sky in a chariot, or look up in fear at the other side of the painting, where Pluto carries off Proserpine, daughter of Ceres. His three-headed dog, Cerberus, guards the entrance to the underworld, while Charon's boat waits to ferry them across the River Styx. Giordano completed the series in 1683, in plenty of time to celebrate the arranged marriage of Ferdinand de Medici (who preferred men) to the dull daughter of a politician.

Earlier that same century, Gian Lorenzo Bernini completed a nearly ten-foot-tall marble sculpture depicting the abduction scene. Proserpina's hand creases Pluto's skin, where it pushes back against his face, while his fingers sink into the flesh of her thigh and hip. Proserpina's lips open in a near-scream, and delicately crafted marble tears drip down her face. This sculpture, which is also called *The Rape of Persephone*, has, more than the other works discussed above, been especially lauded for its realism.

Recently Jeff Koons unveiled a sculpture at the Whitney Museum in New York City. *Pluto and Proserpina* it is called, standing nearly ten feet tall, cast in his signature mirror-polished stainless steel, a poor imitation of the much earlier Bernini from which it has unabashedly copied. In Koons's imitation, the god of the underworld is not nearly as imposing as Bernini's: he doesn't seem to abduct the girl so much as carry her. That is, she isn't struggling but appears to go along willingly: her hand is behind her head in a classic pin-up pose, her breasts perky and pointed upward, her eyes closed and mouth slightly open. Her expression conveys not terror but ecstasy.

What does it mean to retell a story of rape as one about seduction?

What does it tell us that this retelling happens all the time in real life?

16   *an ongoing, even obsessive infatuation with prepubescent girls*: See, for instance, his *Thérèse Dreaming*, and *The Guitar Lesson*. More recently, a controversy at the Metropolitan Museum of Art ensued over *Thérèse Dreaming* in particular. A petition called for its removal or for a plaque of some sort that gives the painting clearer context within the exhibition. The author writes, "Given the current climate around sexual assault and allegations that become more public each day, in showcasing this work for the masses, The Met is romanticizing voyeurism and the objectification of children."

The Met refused to remove the painting, saying through a spokesperson, "Moments such as this provide an opportunity for conversation, and visual art is one of the most significant means we have for reflecting on both the past and the present and encouraging the continuing evolution of existing culture through informed discussion and respect for creative expression." When the retrospective opened in 2013, the art critic Jed Perl, writing for *The New Republic*, suggested that these paintings should not stand in the way of a full appreciation of Balthus's artistic achievement. Paintings such as *Thérèse Dreaming*, and *The Guitar Lesson* "can be properly appreciated only when we accept them as unabashedly mystical, the flesh a symbol of the spirit, the girl's dawning self-awareness an emblem of the artist's engagement with the world."

19   *"How is this not pornography?"*: My student doesn't realize that he is several decades late to this debate. In 1990, after the *Washington Times* revealed that the University of the District of Columbia had acquired Judy Chicago's *Dinner Party* as a gift, members of the House of Representatives debated the work's merits and whether to cut off funding for the institution. "It's not art! It's pornography!" shouts Representative Robert K. Dornan during the heated eighty-seven-minute exchange. Dornan waves a copy of the *Times* article at his colleagues in the chamber: "full color photographs!" of "women's genitalia area!" He's flustered, red in the face. Eventually he folds the paper back on itself and huffs away from the podium, shouting: "It's obscene!"

It is worth quoting Representative Ronald Dellums's response in full:

> [Representative Dornan] used the term pornography and raised the question of the difficulty of dealing with moral issues. With respect to the issue of pornography: I think that it is pornography to see nuclear weapons standing erect with only one function and that is to destroy human life on this planet beyond comprehension. Pornographic are military weapons that look like phallic symbols capable of doing nothing but destroying human life on this planet. You want to talk about pornography? You want to talk about deadly art? We deal with pornography every single day but we don't talk about it in that context. Mr. Chairman, obscenities and immoral issues: I find war immoral, I find poverty immoral, I find the fact that we can all drive from our jobs to our various homes throughout this country and see thousands of human beings eating from garbage cans and living in homelessness. That's immoral. We can address the real immorality of this nation, but we sit here pompously and arrogantly talking about immoralities and obscenities and profanity and pornography, when the real pornography, the real scandal, the real pain, the real obscenities and immorality are not really fully addressed and adequately dealt with. Yes, Mr. Chairman, members of the committee, sound and fury: signifying NOTHING.

21   *Or the* Venus of Urbino, *which depicts a naked woman reclining coyly*: Mark Twain, in his 1880 travelogue *Tramp*

Abroad, describes this painting as "the obscenest picture the world possesses" because of a certain "attitude" of one of her hands. He writes:

> If I ventured to describe that attitude, there would be a fine howl—but there the Venus lies, for anybody to gloat over that wants to—and there she has a right to lie, for she is a work of art, and Art has its privileges. I saw young girls stealing furtive glances at her; I saw young men gaze long and absorbedly at her; I saw aged, infirm men hang upon her charms with a pathetic interest. How I should like to describe her—just to see what a holy indignation I could stir up in the world—just to hear the unreflecting average man deliver himself about my grossness and coarseness, and all that. The world says that no worded description of a moving spectacle is a hundredth part as moving as the same spectacle seen with one's own eyes—yet the world is willing to let its son and its daughter and itself look at Titian's beast, but won't stand a description of it in words. Which shows that the world is not as consistent as it might be.

22   *there likely won't be justice for the girls*: All at once, it seemed, a hashtag campaign was launched to save the Nigerian schoolgirls. Friends changed their profile pictures to an image that read "BRING BACK OUR GIRLS." One friend posted an Instagram photo of all the names of the missing girls tagged #bringbackourgirls. There was an absurd photograph circulating of Sylvester Stallone parading down the

red carpet in a shimmering purple suit, with his entourage of minor celebrities all in red carpet finery, each carrying a white paper sign that read "BRING BACK OUR GIRLS." An image of Michelle Obama appeared on the cover of the *New York Post* in which she holds a sign that reads #BringBackOur-Girls. In the ensuing hours, this image was turned back on the First Lady as a meme, with people Photoshopping their own messages onto her sign. Of these, #TakeBackYourDrones was the most popular and pointed, a clear indictment of her husband's reliance on drone strikes, which some estimate killed thousands of young girls throughout the world—more than Boko Haram ever could—while they were at school, or in the kitchen washing dishes, or playing with friends in the yard.

THE PRECARIOUS

28   *a single proto-Indo-European syllable*: In English we have so many words that mean "to see." Among the oldest of these is the proto-Indo-European root word *okw*, from which we derive terms like *autopsy*, *binocular*, and *optics*, as well as words like *amblyopia*, which means "a weakening of the eyesight without any apparent defect in the eyes," and words like *ferocious* and *window*. *Okw* gives us the word *atrocity*, a term we think of as meaning a terrible horror, but is in fact a word that emphasizes that someone survives the horror to *see* it. "Atrocity" similarly requires a witness, a person to see for oneself, with one's own eyes.

30   *rumored to show real footage of people dying*: There were actually two movies: the first was *Faces of Death*, originally released in the late 1970s. People were said to pass out from the sheer gore of it, though the creators of the film have since admitted that they used B–horror movie techniques to make fake footage appear real. In response, another film, *Traces of Death*, followed in 1993 and did show actual archival footage of people dying or being killed, including the televised suicide of R. Budd Dwyer, a Pennsylvania state treasurer who shot himself during a press conference in January 1987.

The day of Dwyer's suicide had been a snow day in much of Pennsylvania, and children were home from school watching television when the press conference interrupted regularly scheduled programming. The press conference aired in the morning, without redaction, while children looked on. After that, the news outlets began spinning different versions of the press conference into existence: one in which the footage pauses after Dwyer puts the gun in his mouth but before he pulls the trigger, one that pauses before he puts the gun in his mouth, another in which he does not pull the trigger, does not take out the gun, never even opens the envelope.

31   *But the violence changes the person who looks*: The particular phenomenon of observing another's suffering through photography is the subject of Sarah Sentilles's *Draw Your Weapons*. She writes:

This is what happens when you see a violent photograph. . . . First, shock. The other's suffering engulfs you. Then, either despair or indignation. If despair, you take on some of the other's suffering to no purpose; if indignation, you decide to act.

To be able to act, you must emerge from the moment of the photograph and reenter your own life. But as you leave the world of the photograph and return to your life, the contrast between the two—the photograph's world and your world—is so vast you know whatever you might be able to do, whatever action you might be able to take, will be a hopelessly inadequate response to what you have just seen.

The object of your shock has shifted. No longer is it the violence in the image that shocks you. It is your sense of inadequacy. You are too small. Violence is too big. You have failed before you have even begun.

31   *The photographs were taken by Harold Edgerton*: Edgerton was a mechanical engineer and taught engineering at MIT. He had invented something he called a stroboscope—a bulb full of inert gas connected to a battery that, when ignited by a current, created a flash of bright light, controllable down to fractions of microseconds, which allowed him to capture on film the fastest bullet or rapidly beating hummingbird wing. Among his most famous works are the photographs of atomic bomb explosions, including the Trinity test in July 1945. He had been commissioned by the government to take these particular photographs.

The Trinity test was just that: a test. But the test, along with Edgerton's photographs, proved that the government would be successful if it unleashed the real thing. For years after the bombing of Hiroshima and Nagasaki, photographs of the destruction were suppressed. Under the Allied Powers' Press Code rule that "nothing shall be printed which might, directly or by inference, disturb public tranquility," prints were routinely confiscated in order to squelch any evidence of atrocity. But in 1952, when US forces ended their occupation of Japan, photos began appearing in waves. In one, a woman nurses her baby in the back of a pickup truck. The woman has a smear of blood on her cheek; she looks at nothing in particular. The baby fiddles with the open neck of her shirt; its face and head are burned, charred, caked, and splattered with blood.

"Don't make me out to be an artist," Edgerton once said. "I am an engineer. I am after the facts. Only the facts."

31   *photographs of birds in flight*: Edgerton's motion studies are in many ways reminiscent of the much earlier motion studies conducted by the French physiologist Étienne-Jules Marey, who in 1882 invented something called the chrono-photographic gun. The chronophotographic gun looked very much like a regular gun and worked similarly as well, except that when a person squeezed the trigger, the gun turned a pair of discs that captured twelve successive images in a single second instead of delivering a quick and painful death. Using these photographs, Marey studied the motion of horses, birds, dogs, chickens, sheep, donkeys,

elephants, fish, microscopic creatures, mollusks, insects, reptiles—even the famous photographic study about cats always landing on their feet. Marey came to think of motion as a force, alongside weight and gravity, light, heat, and attraction, and decided that all forces lie in wait for an opportunity to become manifest. "Thus, a *stretched* spring will at the end of an indefinite time give back the force which has been used to stretch it," he wrote in *Animal Mechanism*, "and a weight, lifted to a certain height, will restore, the instant it falls, the work that has been employed upon raising it."

This principle of stored force, or *tension*, inspired Hiram Maxim with an idea for an automatic weapon that could use the recoil force of firing a bullet to at once eject the spent cartridge and reload a new one. Even his earliest "machine gun" was capable of continuous fire of four hundred to six hundred rounds per minute, equivalent to the firepower of one hundred ordinary rifles. Maxim's invention forever changed the way people fight and think about war by giving a handful of soldiers the capability of creating casualties on a scale like never before. Armed with only four Maxim guns, four soldiers mowed down five thousand indigenous rebel warriors in Rhodesia in 1893. Machine guns became more widely used in World War I, which saw carnage previously unequaled in human history. In just the first battle of the war, the German army killed twenty-one thousand British soldiers along the Somme River in France.

Some of the very earliest films show footage of the carnage of this war: footage of dead soldiers in ditches, wounded soldiers climbing over their bodies to escape to safety, soldiers checking dead bodies for a pulse, bloody bodies, piles of bodies, dozens of bodies by the side of the road, soldiers loading giant bullets into cannons over and over and over, giant casings piling on the ground, bodies hanging from nooses or decapitated, bodies burned to a crisp. I have to remind myself these are not just bodies but humans: old men, young men, old women, girls, children, babies.

This footage might not exist were it not for Marey's chronophotographic gun, an essential step in the evolution of film photography, although it is usually Eadweard Muybridge who gets the credit for this innovation. As it happens, Muybridge visited Marey in France in 1881, just as Marey was turning his attention to his motion studies. By that time, Muybridge had succeeded in capturing the motion of a galloping horse. Marey delighted in these photos and suggested he also try birds, noting the method of the chronophotographic gun. Muybridge declined, though historians don't say much about why. Some suggest he was too proud or perhaps too committed to his own methods. I suspect it had something to do with the gun itself, with the fact that it looked almost identical to the kind of gun one uses as a weapon: point, aim, shoot. Years earlier, Muybridge had been charged with murder for shooting his wife's lover with a revolver point-blank in the chest. During the trial, his defense argued that any reasonable man would have done the same thing. The all-male jury agreed and ruled the murder a justifiable homicide. Hearing this, Muybridge collapsed on the floor, wailing, shaking. He had to be carried out of the room, had to leave the country, had to go to Central America on a photographic expedition for a year, perhaps proving what the prosecutor had suggested to the jury during his closing arguments: that "no man suffers this kind of insanity without some permanent mark."

34   *by making us more capable of violence ourselves*: While I was working as an Americorps VISTA peace educator in 2001, just after the attacks on the World Trade Center, I learned that by the time most children have reached the age of ten, they have witnessed at least a hundred thousand acts of violence in the media and that bearing witness to so much violence damages our empathy in profound and devastating ways. Our natural orientation as humans is toward one another. To see another harmed harms us also. We are a little destroyed every time we watch another destroyed. As we age, we learn to turn inward, increasingly orient our care and attention away from others and toward only ourselves, not out of apathy but rather as a response to ongoing trauma, until we finally abandon empathy entirely out of self-preservation.

36   *"What allows a life to be visible in its precariousness"*: See Judith Butler, *Precarious Life*.

37   *"When we are afraid, we shoot"*: See Susan Sontag, *On Photography*.

38   See Søren Kierkegaard, *Purity of Heart is to Will One Thing*.

ON MERCY

44 *"To have great pain is to have certainty"*: See Elaine Scarry's *The Body in Pain.*

44 *What makes pain subject to doubt*: So many scientific revolutions are quiet ones. In 1971 the McGill Pain Questionnaire was developed by two researchers, Ronald Melzack, a psychologist, and Warren Torgerson, a statistician, as a means to give patients and medical practitioners a shared language of pain. Melzack began collecting pain words as a postdoc while researching phantom limb pain. He worked with Torgerson to organize the words and divide them into classes and categories and an intensity scale to determine the pain experience.

48 *people like Brewer, who can kill with no remorse*: "Life unworthy of life" is perhaps a way to paraphrase every death sentence in the modern era. It is troubling, then, that this exact phrase was used to justify the early eugenics movement in Germany and was a designation for certain segments of the population that, according to the Nazi regime, had no right to live and consequently were euthanized. The same three drugs used to execute those condemned to die by the state are also used to end the suffering of the terminally ill.

49 *"I hope you find comfort in my execution"*: I first encountered many of the last words collected here at *Goodbye, Warden* (www.goodbyewarden.com), and confirmed them with the Texas Department of Criminal Justice, which maintains a database of all inmates executed in the state of Texas (549, as of this writing). Each inmate's record supplies demographic information for the inmate (name, date of birth, highest education level completed, race, height, age, etc.), as well as a brief summary of the incident for which they were sentenced to death; each record also offers the inmate's last statement: some go on for paragraphs, others only a few words.

51   *"The flakes are skyflowers"*: From "The Snowfall Is So Silent" by Miguel de Unamuno, from *Roots and Wings: Poetry from Spain 1900–1975*, translated by Robert Bly.

53   *They leave the chamber with smiles on their faces*: "The instinct for retribution is part of the nature of man," wrote Justice Potter Stewart in *Furman v. Georgia*, the 1972 Supreme Court case that placed a four-year moratorium on the death penalty in the United States, "and channeling that instinct in the administration of criminal justice serves an important purpose in promoting the stability of a society governed by law. When people begin to believe that organized society is unwilling or unable to impose upon criminal offenders the punishment they 'deserve,' then there are sown the seeds of anarchy—of self-help, vigilante justice, and lynch law." When this verdict was overturned in 1976 in *Gregg v. Georgia*, it was in the spirit of honoring this "instinct for retribution." Retribution is as valid a justification for execution as any other,

or so the prevailing opinion goes, because some crimes are so heinous that to deny retribution would be an affront to human dignity.

53 *"Twenty-two years we've been going through this"*: See "Even After Execution, No Finality for Mother" by Moni Basu at CNN.com, including embedded video interviews; and "Troy Davis, Victim of Judicial Lynching" by Amy Goodman, writing for *The Guardian*.

54 *"the contention that violence is inevitable"*: See Stephen P. Wink and Walter Wink's "Domination, Justice and the Cult of Violence" in *St. Louis University Law Journal*.

56 *"a kindly and pleasant sleep"*: See Book II, "To the King," in Francis Bacon's *The Advancement of Learning*.

56 *"but when it may serve to make a fair and easy passage"*: On April 26, 1990, Dr. Jack Kevorkian appeared on *The Phil Donahue Show* to debut an invention: the Thanatron, or "death machine," the purpose of which was to facilitate suicide for patients in the final stages of crippling disease. The Thanatron was engineered so that the patient could pull a trigger that initiated a sequence, beginning with a drip of saline solution; another push of the button began releasing thiopental, which would put the patient into a deep coma; sixty seconds later, the machine would release a dose of potassium chloride sufficient enough to stop the patient's heart.

After the State of Michigan revoked his medical license in 1991, Kevorkian no longer had access to the drugs required for the Thanatron, and thus the Mercitron was born: a simple suicide machine that employed a gas mask fed by a canister of carbon monoxide. Kevorkian would often counsel his patients to take muscle relaxers or sedatives before the procedure began so that they would not panic or feel pain while gasping for air.

59   *we don't treat what ails their bodies*: There is some debate about this. According to the Gate Control Theory of Pain, authored by Ronald Melzack (the same Ronald Melzack as the one who developed the McGill Pain Questionnaire with Warren Torgerson) and Patrick David Wall in 1965, pain messages originate in the body and flow along the nerves to the spinal cord and on up to the brain, where they encounter "nerve gates" in the spinal cord that may be open or closed depending on a number of factors, including whether any messages are at that time "coming down" from the brain. These pain messages are influenced by emotion and cognition, and because creative expression work on and by these same forces, one theory proposes that art therapy may assist in pain management, though this theory remains largely untested.

60   *I think there are different kinds of mercy*: I owe credit for this idea to Arthur Chu's discussion of "big faith" and "little faith" in "How 'Orange Is the New Black' Found God" in the *Daily Beast.*

62   *"It didn't bring me any sense of peace or relief"*: In "A Hanging," George Orwell writes:

> It is curious, but till that moment I had never realized what it means to destroy a healthy, conscious man. When I saw the prisoner step aside to avoid the puddle, I saw the mystery, the unspeakable wrongness, of cutting a life short when it is in full tide. This man was not dying, he was alive just as we were alive. All the organs of his body were working—bowels digesting food, skin renewing itself, nails growing, tissues forming—all toiling away in solemn foolery. His nails would still be growing when he stood on the drop, when he was falling through the air with a tenth of a second to live. His eyes saw the yellow gravel and the grey walls, and his brain still remembered, foresaw, reasoned—reasoned even about puddles. He and we were a party of men walking together, seeing, hearing, feeling, understanding the same world; and in two minutes, with a sudden snap, one of us would be gone—one mind less, one world less.

62   *He wishes the state would have shown his father's killer mercy*: "It's not that I believe people don't deserve to die for the crimes that they commit," Bryan Stevenson often says in his public lectures. "It's just that I think that we don't deserve to kill." The entire argument over capital punishment hinges on what each of us deserves: a victim deserves peace, and if necessary, retribution, or so the argument goes; murderers deserve nothing less than death, and certainly nothing more.

63   "*Poetry has its uses for despair*": From Christian Wiman, "Mortify Our Wolves," in *The American Scholar*.

SPEAK TRUTH TO POWER

67   *Speak Truth to Power*: An earlier version of this essay was delivered as the John F. Eberhardt Memorial Lecture at the University of Kansas on April 23, 2015. I had been invited to speak on this subject after it was revealed that the university was being investigated for Title IX violations.

68   *she curses Tereus and vows to tell everyone what he has done*: See, in particular, *Metamorphosis* (the Slavitt translation), Book Six, lines 817–824, in which Philomela is speaking:

> My self, abandon'd, and devoid of shame,
> Thro' the wide world your actions will proclaim;
> Or tho' I'm prison'd in this lonely den,
> Obscur'd, and bury'd from the sight of men,
> My mournful voice the pitying rocks shall move,
> And my complainings eccho thro' the grove.
> Hear me, o Heav'n! and, if a God be there,
> Let him regard me, and accept my pray'r.

68   *I learn first from social media*: The Steubenville case probably would have become like every other case were it not for the early efforts of Alexandria Goddard, a crime blogger who once lived in Steubenville and began following the case only after seeing tweets making death threats toward the

girl after the arrest of the football players on August 22. She followed those tweets back to the night of the party, when those same football players were posting explicit photos and jokes about a "dead girl." "Within about two hours, I had a pretty decent outline of what was going on that night," Ms. Goddard told the *New York Times*. "I was sickened. . . . It was amazing the stuff that was out there and that so many people who saw what was going on recorded it in real time and yet not one person stopped it."

71   "*The finest trick of the devil*": See Charles Baudelaire, *Paris Spleen*: "La plus belle des ruses du diable est de vous persuader qu'il n'existe pas."

71   *a sixteen-year-old girl known simply as "Jada"*: See *Jezebel*, CNN.com, *The Guardian*, the *Houston Chronicle*, and *Houstonia* for original coverage of this story.

74   *some kind of James Frey reference*: When, in 2005, Oprah chose James Frey's 2003 memoir, *A Million Little Pieces*, for her book club, it shot to the top of bestsellers lists. Several months later, reports exposed parts of the book as false, fictionalized, fabricated, and the media responded with uproar. Oprah confronted Frey on her daytime talk show: "I don't know what is true, and I don't know what isn't," she told him before asking him to apologize to her, and to the world. Despite this scandal, the book (now marketed as a semi-fictional novel) remains a strong seller, fifteen years after its original release.

75   *"No advanced step taken by women"*: See "Fifty Years of Work for Woman," *Independent*.

81   *The insults boys learn*: Consider, for example, the following abbreviated list: *pussy, bitch, twat, sissy, cunt, faggot, girl*.

81   *Cosby's language is playful*: Denial itself could entail a pleasurable act if, as Freud maintains, the logic of the pleasure principle acknowledges only what has the narcissistically pleasing characteristics of being good and everything else must remain unacknowledged. See Wilfried Ver Eecke's *Denial, Negation, and the Forces of the Negative*, especially "The Complex Phenomenon of Denial."

82   *an allegation, a suggestion, a rumor*: After every atrocity, one can expect to hear the same predictable apologies, writes Judith Lewis Herman in *Trauma and Recovery*: "It never happened; the victim lies; the victim exaggerates; the victim brought it on herself; and in any case it is time to forget the past and move on. The more powerful the perpetrator, the greater is his prerogative to name and define reality, and the more completely his arguments prevail."

82   *The lawyers for Owen Labrie*: See the *New York Times*, the *New Yorker, Vanity Fair*, *Vice, Jezebel,* and the *Concord Monitor* for original coverage of this story.

83   *"may have been a little carried away"*: He is thinking, perhaps, of the play between the word *rape* and its Latin root,

raptus, for "seized," from *rapere*, "to seize." Not like forcible sex, the word for that being *stuprum*: "disgrace." But like the word *raptio* refers to the seizures of women by Zeus. Like the way property is seized and carried off. Like rapture, or the transport of one's soul.

85   *I was fourteen the first time a man raped me*: This section of this essay has appeared in a different form as "Trigger" in *Guernica* and in Brian Turner, ed., *The Kiss: Intimacies from Writers*.

87   *"Power"*: This quote from Michel Foucault comes from an interview conducted by Michael Bess on November 3, 1980, "Power, Moral Values, and the Intellectual," and transcribed for the journal *History of the Present*; both the Voltaire and the Arendt quotes on power appear in Hannah Arendt's *On Violence*.

89   *"speak truth to power"*: See *I Must Resist: Bayard Rustin's Life in Letters*.

WHAT WE PAY

94   *when news that the* Deepwater Horizon *had exploded*: On the morning of April 20, 2010, news reports said there had been an explosion on an oil rig out at sea and the fire had been burning all night. Eleven people were missing, and the Coast Guard was searching the Gulf in boats and from helicopters. All day long, the crews battled the fire that threatened to consume the rig: wide streams of water

shooting into the blaze from every direction, while a pillar of black smoke billowed upward and upward until the wind caught it and carried it darkly to the east. The fire burned the next night too, and in the morning the rig began creaking—cranes falling over, whole decks collapsing, explosions sending debris into the air. Within minutes there was only a ring of fire, the wreckage sinking toward the ocean floor.

Reports emerged of a five-mile-long oil slick extending away from the sunken rig. Three Norwegian crews sent remotely operated underwater vehicles to the seabed to locate the source of the spill. They found giant plumes of oil—much larger than the oil company or the Coast Guard admitted publicly—but no evidence of oil leaking from the rig itself, which they discovered upside down on the ocean floor. The next day, Coast Guard Rear Admiral Mary Landry told CBS News's Harry Smith, "At this time, there is no crude emanating from that well-head at the ocean floor." That afternoon the search for the eleven missing crew members was called off. The oil company executive expressed his condolences in a press release: "On behalf of all of us at BP, my deepest sympathies go out to the families and friends who have suffered such a terrible loss."

Rear Admiral Landry claimed the situation was "contained," that disaster had been "narrowly averted," that there would be "zero environmental impact." People watching television breathed a collective sigh of relief. A BP spokesperson claimed perhaps up to five thousand barrels of oil had been spilled. The Coast Guard offered a higher estimate, maybe eight thousand barrels. Meanwhile, the oil company set up a command post on the Louisiana coast to "prepare for potential release."

The slick continued to grow. In the morning, the broken wellhead was discovered by a pair of remotely operated underwater exploring vehicles. At that time Rear Admiral Landry said, "This is a very serious spill."

Ships set up containment booms to try to capture what they could of the oil: a sheen covering 580 square miles, now 100 miles long, now approaching the coast of Louisiana. Booms were placed along the coast to protect delicate ecosystems, though oil washed ashore anyway in giant, slopping waves.

After weeks of pressure, the oil company released a live feed of the leaking well. Mud-colored crude gushed from the broken pipe in plumes so vast they boggle the mind. Spokespeople for the oil company insisted it looked worse than it actually was, sticking with the initial estimate of a thousand barrels a day. The company's top executive asked the public to remember that the spill is "relatively tiny" in comparison to the size of the "very big" Gulf. Scientists analyzing the video said, no, the leak must be at least sixty thousand barrels a day, perhaps as many as a hundred thousand barrels a day. The president's adviser on climate and energy said, "This is probably the biggest environmental disaster we have ever faced in this country."

The oil company tried to close the well, to cap the well, to contain the leak, it pumped oil from the leaking wellhead to a ship at sea; to several ships at sea; it placed a smaller pipe inside the larger broken pipe; it drilled a second well, and a third; it jammed drilling mud into the well to stop its flow; someone suggested blowing the whole thing up with a nuclear bomb.

But the oil kept gushing and gushing and gushing. The National Oceanic and Atmospheric Administration created a no-fishing zone in the Gulf, and then a larger one. Dead sea turtles washed ashore. Dead dolphins washed ashore. Oil washed ashore and covered the wetlands: birds and frogs and grasses. Experts said up to 1 million gallons of oil were flowing into the Gulf every day, which meant that the equivalent of the *Exxon Valdez* disaster repeated itself once every eleven days. After eighty-seven days, when crews finally succeeded in capping and sealing the broken wellhead, the oil spill covered an area the size of Oklahoma, drifting on the surface of the Gulf toward the coast, where it had already devastated entire ecosystems and economies. Miles-long oil plumes drifted under the surface of the Gulf toward underwater rain forests, toward reefs and canyons, toward currents that have since carried them who knows where. "Never in my career have I used the word *hopeless*," environmentalist John Wathen told *Tuscaloosa News*, "but I think this is absolutely hopeless."

See also the *New York Times, The Guardian,* CNN, CBS News, *Mother Jones*, the *Houston Chronicle*, the *Times-Picayune*, *Propublica*, *Rolling Stone*, and *Smithsonian* for original coverage of the BP oil spill in the Gulf of Mexico.

98   *never really their dream in the first place*: The Dream, writes Ta-Nehisi Coates in *Between the World and Me*, "is perfect houses with nice lawns. It is Memorial Day cookouts, block associations, and driveways. The Dream is treehouse and

Cub Scouts. The Dream smells like peppermint but tastes like strawberry shortcake. And for so long I have wanted to escape into the Dream, to fold my country over my head like a blanket. But this has never been an option because the Dream rests on our backs, the bedding made from our bodies."

99   *"they were putting poison in the ocean"*: The data are spotty, but it appears that BP employed roughly 140,000 people in cleanup work related to the spill; of those, nearly 90,000 workers were exposed to the controversial dispersant Corexit. Despite BP's assurances that Corexit is "safe enough to drink," the dispersant contains five chemicals associated with cancer and ten chemicals that are or may be toxic to kidneys; the label states it can cause red blood cells to burst and kidney and liver problems. Studies have found that Corexit causes damage to respiratory and nervous systems; skin irritation, burning and lesions, and in some cases temporary paralysis. BP sprayed 1.8 million gallons of that into the Gulf of Mexico.

See "Cleanup in the Gulf: Oil Spill Dispersants and Health Symptoms in *Deepwater Horizon* Responders" in *Environmental Health Perspectives* and "The Gulf Study: A Prospective Study of Persons Involved in the *Deepwater Horizon* Oil Spill Response and Clean-Up" in *Environmental Health Perspectives*. See also Dahr Jamail's feature article, "BP's 'Widespread Human Health Crisis,'" in *Al Jazeera*.

101   *a number of dangerous chemicals into the air*: Among these chemicals are ammonia, benzene, acetaldehyde, allyl alcohol, carbon disulfide, chlorine, hydrochloric acid, lead, mercury

compounds, methanol, methadone sodium salt, sulfuric acid, tert-Butyl alcohol, vanadium compounds, vinyl acetate, and butadiene. Butadiene in particular has been linked over and over again to rare forms of leukemia and other aggressive cancers.

The ship channel is, for instance, home to Rhodia Eco Services, a chemical company that produces sulfuric acid, the most widely used chemical in industry—used, at least, in unleaded gasoline, automobile batteries, paper bleaching, sugar bleaching, water treatment, fertilizers, steel manufacturing, and dye. Rhodia Eco Services is the leading producer of sulfuric acid in North America.

Less than a mile away from Rhodia Eco Services stands J. R. Harris Elementary School, named after John Richardson Harris, the founder of Harrisburg, the namesake of Harris County, Texas. The J. R. Harris Elementary School was originally known as the Harrisburg School and operated out of a different facility that was built in 1895, nearly sixty years after General Santa Anna burned the city of Harrisburg and twenty years before Texas Chemical Company built the plant that has now become the single greatest source of pollution on the Houston Ship Channel. The Harrisburg School was rebuilt as J. R. Harris Elementary in 1958, at which time the Texas Chemical Company had been operating from its location on the Houston Ship Channel for more than forty years. Today, there are laws that can deny air permits to any chemical facility built within three thousand feet of a school, but there are no regulations preventing a school from operating within three thousand feet of a toxic chemical facility.

This means there are no regulations protecting the 693 students between the ages of five and eleven currently enrolled at the J. R. Harris Elementary School: 97 percent are Hispanic, 3 percent are black; 94 percent are considered economically disadvantaged; and all live within two miles of the Houston Ship Channel, which means they too have a 56 percent greater chance of developing leukemia than kids who live anywhere else. And though this is a staggering fact in itself, the health risks from the plants and refineries that are located along the Houston Ship Channel are not limited exclusively to leukemia.

101 *than for people who live anywhere else*: See "A Preliminary Investigation of the Association between Hazardous Air Pollutants and Lymphohematopoietic Cancer Risk among Residents of Harris County Texas," a report to the Houston Department of Health and Human Services, by Kristina M. Walker, Ann L. Coker, Elaine Symanski, and Philip J. Lupo.

102 *why are we okay with it for anyone else?*: "Why are some citizens exposed to intense pollution while the vast majority of Americans can afford to avoid this contamination?" environmental activist Steve Lerner asks in his book *Zones*. He continues, "There are no comfortable answers to these questions because sacrifice zones do not exist by accident." Reverend Benjamin Chavis, who coined the term *environmental racism*, describes what activists often mean by the term *environmental justice*: "The environmental justice movement is a movement that confronts the 'immorality of upper- and

middle-class people consuming the most energy and producing the most waste, while it is the health of the poor that is most affected by the resulting pollution.'" This definition is echoed by Robert D. Bullard, in some circles considered the father of environmental justice, who adds: "Low income and minority communities continue to bear greater health and environmental burdens, while more affluent whites receive the bulk of the benefits."

111   *the oil spill changed nothing*: In the early days of the oil spill, BP blamed the explosion and ensuing ecological disaster on BP's business partners in the *Deepwater Horizon* venture, Halliburton and Transocean. Transocean and Halliburton executives blamed each other and BP. All of them together blamed a variety of technicalities, including the fact that the *Deepwater Horizon* was owned by Transocean but was simply leased and operated by BP. Halliburton owned the cement in the well and maybe some of the equipment, but definitely none of the faulty equipment. The details are difficult to glean. Everyone agrees, though, that the oil itself was owned by BP, since the company paid tens of millions of dollars to the US government—which claims exclusive economic rights to anything above or below the surface of the water across a large swath of the Gulf of Mexico—in order to lease the mineral rights to the Macondo Prospect, where the *Deepwater Horizon* was drilling when it blew up. President Obama called their finger pointing a "ridiculous spectacle," which was, perhaps, all part of the spectacle.

Finally, the chief executives of the five major oil and gas

companies appeared before the US House of Representatives Subcommittee on Energy and Environment in June of 2010. The session was one long self-righteous admonishment, beginning and ending with committee members criticizing how the companies spent and didn't spend their money. One particular gripe was that though BP, Shell, Chevron, ExxonMobile, and ConocoPhillips had together amassed nearly $289 billion in profits over the previous three years, their average investment for safety was less than one-tenth of 1 percent of those profits.

Mostly the executives maintained their composure, remaining calm and expressionless. Then, under combined pressure from Representatives Bart Stupak of Michigan and Henry Waxman of California asking specifically about the companies' disaster response plans, ExxonMobile CEO Rex Tillerson became uncharacteristically flustered. His face reddened and his voice cracked as he admitted that, yes, when it comes to oil spills, his oil company—every oil company, in fact—is "not well-equipped to handle them. There will be impacts, as we are seeing."

To be perfectly honest, each of these companies' disaster response plans is a bit of a joke, some only five pages long. Several of the plans list, for instance, "walruses" under "Sensitive Biological and Human Resources" in the Gulf Coast. Luckily, no walruses were harmed in the Gulf Coast oil spill, but maybe that's because walruses haven't occupied the Gulf of Mexico for 300 million years.

Soon after the hearing, BP set up the BP Disaster Victim Compensation Fund for people living on the coast whose lives and livelihoods had been "adversely affected" by the spill. It seemed like a gesture of good faith until the fund began litigating all claims at every step, arguing it was too easy for businesses and individuals to claim economic damage without evidence. This same line of argument was at least part of the reason BP CEO Tony Hayward was fired three months after the spill. Officially, spokespeople for BP claimed he had resigned, but it seems clear that what led him to be transferred to a BP outpost in Siberia was, in fact, the public's ire. People weren't pissed so much about the spill, but rather that Hayward had suggested that Americans were likely to file bogus claims with the compensation fund. His comments drew criticism from President Obama and former chief of staff Rahm Emanuel, among others, but that didn't stop Hayward from taking a vacation to England's Isle of Wight to watch his yacht compete in a race, or from saying, fresh off his private transatlantic flight, "There's no one who wants this [spill] over more than I do. I want my life back." In the end, it's likely he was fired because he did not prove himself to be capable of behaving "in ways that earn the trust of others" (one of the self-stated values of BP) and not, in fact, because his company broke an oil well at the bottom of the Gulf of Mexico. That, it seems, might have been forgivable on its own, since it wasn't even the first time oil was spilled in the Gulf of Mexico.

In 1979 Pemex, a state-owned Mexican petroleum company, was drilling an oil well when a blowout occurred. The oil ignited and the drilling rig collapsed, just like the *Deepwater Horizon* did a little over thirty years later. Oil from the rig, the *Ixtoc I*, began gushing out into the Gulf at a rate of ten thousand to thirty thousand barrels a day for almost an entire year before workers were finally able to cap the well. Ten years later, in 1989, the *Exxon Valdez* hit a reef off Prince William Sound in southern Alaska, piercing the hull and dumping thirty-nine thousand tons of oil into the sound. Compared to the Gulf spill, the *Exxon Valdez* was small, but it created a complete ecological disaster for a coastal community. Despite attempts to use dispersing agents and oil-skimming ships, oil washed onto thirteen hundred miles of Alaskan coastline. It's unclear exactly how much marine life was affected, but an estimated 250,000 seabirds, 2,800 sea otters, 300 harbor seals, 250 bald eagles, and up to 22 killer whales died, along with billions of salmon and herring eggs. Even today, oil remains a few inches below the surface on many of Alaska's beaches.

Eventually, the US government appointed Kenneth Feinberg as the administrator of the BP Disaster Victim Compensation Fund. Feinberg had spent his career in this sort of role as a court-appointed special settlement master in cases involving Vietnam veterans and the Agent Orange product liability litigation, as well as the September 11th Victim Compensation Fund. As had become usual, he was appointed by the government to manage the fund; however, in this case, his salary was paid by BP, including a flat fee to his firm of $1.25 million a month for labor and overhead costs. The terms of his lucrative compensation arrangement with BP are somewhat murky. It is unclear, for example, whether even one unspoken condition was that Feinberg find any number of reasons to refuse payment to 116,000 of the 331,560 claims, as when the claimants provided no documentation or insufficient documentation or were just plain ineligible.

111   *what we Americans consume in our automobiles in a single day*: In 2010 alone, Americans consumed roughly 377 million gallons of gasoline per day, which would have been refined from no less than 833 million gallons of crude.

112   *"Gifts from the earth or from each other"*: See Robin Wall Kimmerer's "The Gift of Strawberries" in *Braiding Sweetgrass*.

AGAINST WHITENESS

114   *"If white American feminist theory"*: Audre Lorde continues:

> What is the theory behind racist feminism?
> In a world of possibility for us all, our personal visions help lay the groundwork for political action. The failure . . . to recognize difference as a crucial strength is a failure to reach beyond the first patriarchal lesson. In our world, divide and conquer must become define and empower.

116   *"No one was white before he/she came to America"*: James Baldwin writes in "On Being White . . . And Other Lies":

> There is, for example—at least, in principle—an Irish community: here, there, anywhere, or, more precisely, Belfast,

Dublin and Boston. There is a German community: both sides of Berlin, Bavaria and Yorkville. There is an Italian community: Rome, Naples, the Bank of the Holy Ghost and Mulberry Street. And there is a Jewish community, stretching from Jerusalem to California to New York. There are English communities. There are French communities. There are Swiss consortiums. There are Poles: in Warsaw (where they would like us to be friends) and in Chicago (where because they are white we are enemies). There are, for that matter, Indian restaurants and Turkish baths. There is the underworld—the poor (to say nothing of those who intend to become rich) are always with us—but this does not describe a community. It bears terrifying witness to what happened to everyone who got here, and paid the price of the ticket. The price was to become "white."

116   *in order to become intelligible to others*: For some, the process of becoming white was a process of simply "passing" for white. For others, who had formerly been labeled "ethnic whites," the process of officially being defined as white by law often came about in court disputes over the Immigration Act of 1790, which offered naturalization only to "any alien, being a free white person." Courts denied the status of "whiteness" to individuals in at least fifty-two cases. By 1923, courts began using a "common-knowledge" standard, concluding that "scientific evidence" for whiteness was inconsistent and incoherent.

In *How the Irish Became White,* Noel Ignatiev argues that becoming white wasn't simply a matter of erasing difference or of legal status. During the 1840s and 1850s, Irish immigrants were able to lay claim to a lesser and inferior whiteness in America by distancing themselves from former slaves, whose economic circumstances were not unlike their own and with whom they often found themselves competing for jobs. Whiteness meant they didn't have to compete as much for these jobs, but it required that they ally themselves with their oppressors against their economic equals.

117   *a system of racial hierarchy*: Theodore Allen, author of *The Invention of the White Race*, writes:

> The introduction of this counterfeit of social mobility was an act of "social engineering," the essence of which was to reissue long-established common law rights, "incident to every free man," but in the form of "white" privileges: the presumption of liberty, the right to get married, the right to carry a gun, the right to read and write, the right to testify in legal proceedings, the right of self-directed physical mobility, and the enjoyment of male prerogatives over women. The successful societal function of this status required that not only African-American bond-laborers, but most emphatically, free African-Americans be excluded from it. It is that status and realigning of the laboring-class European-Americans that transformed class oppression into racial oppression.

118   *the jury ultimately acquitted them of these charges*: After the acquittal of the four officers—Stacey Koon, Laurence Powell,

Timothy Wind, and Theodore Briseno—the Department of Justice sought indictments at the federal level, and the grand jury returned indictments against Powell, Wind, and Briseno for "willfully and intentionally using unreasonable force" and against Sergeant Koon for "failing to take action to stop the unlawful assault." The subsequent federal trial returned a guilty verdict for Powell and Koon, who subsequently served thirty months in prison despite Judge John Davies's acceptance of much of the white officers' version of the beating, finding that King had likely provoked the actions by "failing to comply."

118   *"Can we all get along?"*: Although I remember this as a plea to the entire world, King was very much making a direct plea to people of color to end what must have seemed to him a campaign of retributive violence on his behalf. He continues:

> Can we? Can we get along? Can we stop making it horrible for the older people and the kids? And . . . I mean we've got enough smog in Los Angeles let alone to deal with setting these fires and things . . . it's just not right. It's not right. And it's not going to change anything. We'll get our justice; they've won the battle, but they haven't won the war. We'll get our day in court and that's all we want. And, just, uh, I love—I'm neutral, I love every—I love people of color. I'm not like they're making me out to be. We've got to quit. We've got to quit; I mean after-all, I could understand the first upset for the first two hours after

the verdict, but to go on, to keep going on like this and to see the security guard shot on the ground—it's just not right; it's just not right, because those people will never go home to their families again. And uh, I mean please, we can, we can get along here. We all can get along. We just gotta, we gotta. I mean, we're all stuck here for a while, let's, you know let's try to work it out, let's try to beat it, you know. Let's try to work it out.

120 *Rachel Dolezal notoriously decided to reject whiteness*: For nearly ten years, a white woman named Rachel Dolezal passed herself off as a black woman, working as a lecturer in the African American studies department at Eastern Washington University (where she taught such classes as "African and African-American Art History," "African-American Culture," and "The Black Woman's Struggle"), as a freelance black hair stylist, and also as the head of the Spokane chapter of the NAACP. She was "outed" in early June 2015 during a TV interview on KXLY by reporter Jeff Humphrey. The pretext for the interview was to ask questions about the hate mail Dolezal had received at her home. At one point Humphrey asked, "Are you African American?" Dolezal looked stunned; several moments passed before she answered, "I don't understand the question." He asked, "Your parents: are they white?" Dolezal lowered her head, walked off camera; she was saying "I refuse . . ." when the recording stopped.

In June 2015, many people spent a lot of time talking and thinking and writing about the Rachel Dolezal scandal. Mostly people were baffled, I think: about her decades-long hoax, about her claim of being "transracial," about her hair. On June 17, 2015, Dolezal sat down for an interview with NBC's Savannah Guthrie, who said to Dolezal, "It's one thing to embrace the questions [of race] as an academic matter; it's another thing to just actually be honest and transparent about who you really are." "Right," Dolezal responded. "I definitely am not white. Nothing about being white describes who I am. So, what's the word for it? You know I mean, the closest thing I can come to is if you're black or white, I'm black. I'm more black than I am white."

Writing in *The Stranger*, Ijeoma Oluo offers what is, in my opinion, the best take on Rachel Dolezal:

> Dolezal is simply a white woman who cannot help but center herself in all that she does—including her fight for racial justice. And if racial justice doesn't center her, she will redefine race itself in order to make that happen. It is a bit extreme, but it is in no way new for white people to take what they want from other cultures in the name of love and respect, while distorting or discarding the remainder of that culture for their comfort.

121 *Whiteness is, in fact, a fairly modern fiction*: The eighteenth century in particular was a period for a lot of theorizing about race, with Carl Linnaeus in 1758 proposing two separate species for humans: *Homo sapiens; europaeus*, the preferred category for light-skinned Europeans, and *Homo sapiens*, the category for everyone else. In 1775 Immanuel Kant used the term *weiß*, meaning white, to refer to the race "of northern

Europe." With differentiation came biases about superiority and inferiority. The writings of Thomas Jefferson in particular helped rationalize slavery in a nation otherwise dedicated to liberty and equality: "I advance it therefore, as a suspicion only, that blacks . . . are inferior to the whites in the endowments of body and mind," he wrote in 1781. Many historians have noted that the idea of an inherent inferiority was used to make it possible to deny kidnapped Africans the liberties that would be granted to European immigrants as rights.

122 *"My ancestors never owned slaves"*: In "Who Invented White People?" whiteness scholar Gregory Jay writes:

> I may not intend anything racial when I apply for a loan, or walk into a store, or hail a cab, or ask for a job—but in every circumstance my whiteness will play a role in the outcome, however "liberal" or "anti-racist" I imagine myself to be. White men have enormous economic advantages because of the disadvantages faced by women and minorities, no matter what any individual white men may intend. If discrimination means that fewer qualified applicants compete with you for the job, you benefit. You do not have to be a racist to benefit from being white. You just have to look the part.

122 *"We do not know the history / Of ourselves in this nation"*: See "Riddle" in *The Georgia Review*.

122 *public acts of racial terror*: In 1923, James Scott, a black man, was accused of sexual assault against a college professor's daughter and was lynched by a white mob in Columbia, Missouri.

In Excelsior, Missouri, Walter Mitchell, a black man, was lynched for the alleged attempted rape of a white woman in 1925.

In 1931, a mob lynched Raymond Gunn, a black man, but only after forcing him to confess to killing and attempting to rape a white schoolteacher in Maryville, Missouri.

Cleo Wright, a black man, was arrested for the alleged attempted rape of a white woman and burned alive in Sikeston, Missouri, in 1942.

In my hometown, Henry Williams, a black man, was lynched in 1898 for allegedly assaulting two white girls.

122 *We think of it as a dark exception*: Lauret Savoy writes, "How a society remembers can't be separated from how it wants to be remembered or from what it wishes it was—that is, if we believe stories of ancestors reflect who we are and how we came to be. The past is remembered and told by desire." See *Trace: Memory, History, Race, and the American Landscape*.

123 *sense of "racial superiority"*: See Leon F. Litwack's "Hellhounds," in James Allen, Hilton Als, John Lewis, and Leon Litwack, eds., *Without Sanctuary: Lynching Photography in America*.

123   *shot and killed Michael Brown in his own neighborhood*:
Comply was such an interesting word for Darren Wilson to
use in his ABC interview with George Stephanopoulos the
day after the grand jury failed to bring charges, given that
"failure to comply" is the citation of choice for the Ferguson
Police Department's fifty-three officers, who wield it often
and with impunity almost exclusively against the city's black
residents for any number of offenses that are not in fact
crimes, such as when they refuse to identify themselves,
or to take their hands out of their pockets, reach into their
pockets, take photographs or video of white police officers
using excessive force, move too slowly, move too quickly, talk
back, refuse to answer questions, ask questions, squirm while
being electrocuted with a Taser gun, leave their homes after
being told to stay there—when they refuse, in other words,
to obey. *Comply* shares the same root word as *compliment* and
compliant—to not only obey, but to do so politely, flatteringly,
with deference and courtesy.

According to the Department of Justice's *Investigation of
the Ferguson Police Department*, between 2011 and 2014, out
of all the "failure to comply" charges issued by the Ferguson
Police Department, 94 percent were lodged against the
city's black residents. Sarah Bufkin, writing in *Bustle*, asks
readers to add to that a list of the seemingly "black-specific
offenses of 'Manner of Walking' (95 percent), 'Resisting
Arrest' (92 percent), 'Peace Disturbance' (92 percent), and
'Failure to Obey' (89 percent)," and it becomes clear that
the "officers misunderstood their role and the obligations
that these communities owed to them. . . . Rather than

aiming to bolster community trust and work for the best interest of the African American residents, the Ferguson police officers seemed more bent on disciplining them and bringing them to heel."

124　*The rage is not pathological*: "If rage is not an appropriate response to injustice, I don't know what is" writer Claudia Rankine has said. This echoes a line from bell hooks's *Killing Rage*: "rage is an appropriate response to injustice."

124　*"See whose face it wears"*: I thought of this line again recently at the Women's March in Washington, DC, in 2017: the sea of pink pussy hats, of white women taking selfies and holding tone-deaf signs with slogans like "Let's Get in Formation" without any indication of concern for the actual experience of the women of color who were also at the march and to whom that song more likely refers. No one was arrested that day; police wore pink hats instead of riot gear, high-fived protesters even as they marched outside the established route. Where are these white women when black and brown men and women are being slaughtered, kidnapped, deported? Why aren't these white women using whatever power and privilege they do have to fight the oppression of people of color every single day?

125　*something I was afraid to lose*: See bell hooks, *Killing Rage*. She writes, "All our silences in the face of racist assault are acts of complicity. What does our rage at injustice mean if it can be silenced, erased by individual material comfort?"

131   *President Bush addresses a joint session*: Earlier that same day, one thousand Muslim clerics had issued a fatwa recommending a full investigation of the attacks, that the United States not invade Afghanistan, and if it did invade Afghanistan, the clerics order that "jihad become an order for the Muslims of that country."

132   *he is told that he won't recognize evil*: A few choice quotes from Anderson Cooper's March 9, 2016, interview with Donald J. Trump on CNN:

> "I think Islam hates us. There's something there. There's a tremendous hatred there. We have to get to the bottom of it. There is an unbelievable hatred of us."

> "We have to be very vigilant. We have to be very careful. And we can't allow people coming into this country who have this hatred of the United States and of people who are not Muslim."

> "And it's hard to define. It's hard to separate because you don't know who's who."

133   *I heard my first stories about evil*: I have learned from my son that the idea of evil creates fear, but I have learned from religion that the reverse is also true. The first incentive to worship is often fear, and evil looms in the remotest past

of almost every faith. In the third millennia BCE, ancient Accadians worshipped what we might now call evil gods in their pantheons—destructive deities who exacted terror as much as tribute. Ancient Egyptians paid tribute to the god Set, the embodiment of the scorching sun, the enemy of life, the drought of the desert and feverish thirst, who destroys with merciless heat. In ancient Mesopotamian mythology, Tiamat is a creator goddess before her husband is slain in war, and in her sorrow she becomes a sea dragon bent on murderous revenge. The storm god hero Marduk kills her, and the blood he spills becomes the visible heavens and creates the Earth.

This myth too—of the hero who saves the world by defeating evil single-handedly—is one that has been constantly reinventing, reviving, evolving, and resurrecting itself. In ancient Babylon, Gilgamesh, the king of Uruk, saves his kingdom by slaying not only the evil demon Humbaba, a monstrous guardian of the Cedar Forest, but also Gugalanna, Ishtar's Bull of Heaven, who devastates Uruk by drinking the Euphrates River, drying up the marshes, and opening enormous pits that swallow hundreds of men. Millennia later, the early teachings of Christianity, especially the Gospel of Nicodemus, recount a story of Christ descending after his death on the cross to battle with and conquer the devil in hell. This story isn't considered canon, but it follows the model of the story of David and Goliath, which is.

In the New Testament, evil goes by many names: Satan (which means *adversary* in Hebrew), Beelzebub, the Devil, the prince of this world, the great dragon, the old serpent, the prince of the devils, the prince of the power of the air, the spirit that works in the children of disbelief, the Antichrist. Satan is represented as the founder of an empire that struggles with and counteracts the kingdom of God on Earth.

133 *the ritual sacrifice of their children*: Maybe the deacon's wife thought I had forgotten that one time God asked Abraham to sacrifice his own son Isaac.

133 *if they are different in all of these ways*: This is a perfect example of the Manichaean allegory, which Abdul R. JanMohammed has postulated as an *economy* "based on a transformation of racial difference into moral and even metaphysical difference." He continues: "Though the phenomenological origins of this metonymic transformation may lie in the 'neutral' perception of physical difference (skin color, physical features, and such), its allegorical extensions come to dominate every facet of imperialist mentality." See "The Economy of Manichean Allegory: The Function of Racial Difference in Colonialist Literature" in Henry Louis Gates Jr. *Race, Writing, and Difference.*

134 *any story that cannot accommodate nuances*: That picture book, for example, left out the part where David overthrows his king and usurps the throne and then struggles throughout his reign to earn the allegiance of his kingdom and unify the myriad tribes and families of Israelites together in an idea of common identity and shared moral goodness. Like so many of us, he turned to the power of stories, which are at least partially immortalized in the Davidic Psalms — stories that

were meant to be set to music, to be chanted by the group, to stir the heart, to rouse the crowd, to affirm the community and establish its boundaries.

Although seventy-three of the Psalms are attributed to David, biblical scholars argue there is no hard evidence that David himself authored any of them. In particular, Adele Berlin and Marc Zvi Brettler note in *The Jewish Study Bible* that "Davidic authorship . . . is not accepted as historical fact by modern scholars, but is viewed as a way the ancients linked biblical writings with the appropriate inspired well-known biblical figure, thereby confirming the divine inspiration and the authority of those writings." Despite this consensus among biblical scholars, there is also no hard evidence that he didn't write them.

"Evil" in particular is a recurring theme in the seventy-three Psalms attributed to David. Psalm 23, for example, is perhaps the most often-quoted scripture about evil, invoked regularly at funerals, but also by President Bush in his address to the nation on the evening of the attacks on September 11: "Even though I walk through the valley of the shadow of death, I fear no evil, for you are with me." Elsewhere in the Davidic Psalms the idea of evil appears, as in Psalm 15, in order to establish an idea of shared virtue:

> Lord, who may dwell in your sacred tent?
> Who may live on your holy mountain?
> The one whose walk is blameless,
> who does what is righteous,
> who speaks the truth from their heart;

whose tongue utters no slander,
who does no wrong to a neighbor.

That word *neighbor* is important, I think. It's also important that the translation of this Psalm from Latin into Old
English in the middle of the eighth century in a monastery in
what is now England marks the introduction of the word *evil*
into the English language. Twelve centuries before my son was
born, before President Bush appeared on television to address
a grieving nation, *yfel* entered our language at another historical moment when everyone had their minds on terror—in
particular, the brutal surprise sacking of the monastery of
Lindisfarne by Vikings invading from the eastern shore. The
Vikings were England's terrorists, its savage invaders, and
the monks translating the Psalms experienced this invasion
and the slaughter of their neighbors as an unqualified evil
that escaped explanation beyond the fulfillment of biblical
prophesies of the end times, and the story of Vikings as evil,
horned-helmeted barbarians is the one that still survives
today. Alcuin, a scholar in Charlemagne's court at the time,
wrote when he heard news of the sacking: "Never before
has such terror appeared in Britain as we have now suffered
from a pagan race."

And yet even as Alcuin wrote these words, Charlemagne
was engaged in a decades-long war against evil on the main-
land. The story we have of Charlemagne imagines him as a
kind of archetypal hero who slaughtered evil single-handedly:
a romantic king; the father of modern Europe, a virtuous

savior of the Holy Roman Empire. But the truth is more complicated than that. His holy war became a brutal life-long campaign to torture and terrorize pagans into convert-ing to Christianity. At Verden, for instance, Charlemagne ordered the beheading of nearly five thousand Saxons who had been caught practicing pagan rituals. In praise of these executions, his court poet, author of the *Paderborn Epic*, writes, "What the contrary mind and perverse soul refuse to do with persuasion, / Let them leap to accomplish when compelled by fear."

134 *We hear the word* evil *applied to anyone who opposes us*: There was a time when even left-handedness was considered a sign of evil nature. The word *sinister* comes from *sinestra*, meaning "left," an association that perhaps comes from the story in Greek mythology of Cronus castrating Uranus and grasping his genitals with his left hand: "Which has ever since been the hand of ill-omen," writes Robert Graves in *The Greek Myths*.

134 *Hitler was evil*: Hannah Arendt has written at length about how Hitler would have basically been powerless were it not for low-level functionaries like Eichmann who followed along. In an interview with Joachim Fest on *Das Thema* SWR TV, Germany, on November 9, 1964, Fest asked Arendt to what extent we should tell the truth about all of this, even when legitimate interests and people's feelings come into conflict. Arendt responded:

Well, I think that such is the historian's task, as well as the task of people who live at that time and are independent—there are such people, and they need to be guardians of factual truths. What happens when these guardians are driven out by society, or driven into a corner or put up against a wall by the state—we've seen this happen in the writing of history, for example in Russia, where a new history of Russia comes out every five years. Does the state or society, with their legitimate interests that may come into conflict with the truth, still have an interest—in principle—with these guardians of factual truth? In this case I'd say yes. What then happens is of course that a whole series of apologias are brought out and put onto the market just to cover up the two or three truths that are actually quite marginal to this book. It won't succeed, as something of this kind never does.

134 *hear it from the lips of the president of the United States*: Six days into his presidency, Donald J. Trump sat down for an interview with Sean Hannity on Fox:

> HANNITY: One of the problems we have is evil in our time.
> TRUMP: True.
> HANNITY: Winston Churchill dealt with evil in his time. Roosevelt dealt with evil in his time. My father fought in World War II.
> TRUMP: But they had evil with uniforms on.
> HANNITY: That's true. This is different.
> TRUMP: We have evil that lurks around the corner without the uniforms. Ours is harder because the

people that we're going against, they don't wear uniforms. They're sneaky, dirty rats. And they blow people up in a shopping center. And they blow people up in a church. These are bad people. When you're fighting Germany, they had their uniforms, and Japan, and they had their uniforms and they had their flags on the plane and the whole thing. We are fighting sneaky rats right now that are sick and demented. And we're going to win.

The following day, Trump signed the executive order commonly referred to as "the Muslim ban," but officially titled "Protecting the Nation from Foreign Terrorist Entry into the United States," which states in part: "The United States must ensure that those admitted to this country do not bear hostile attitudes toward it and its founding principles. The United States cannot, and should not, admit those who do not support the Constitution, or those who would place violent ideologies over American law."

135 *we are fighting a global existential war*: Michael Flynn, who was briefly the national security adviser to Donald J. Trump, wrote in his book with Michael Ledeen, *The Field of Fight*, "We're in a world war against a messianic mass movement of evil people, most of them inspired by a totalitarian ideology: Radical Islam." White House aide Stephen Miller, while an undergraduate at Duke University, started the Terrorism Awareness Project as an effort to make "students aware of

the Islamic jihad and the terrorist threat, and to mobilize support for the defense of America and the civilization of the West," he wrote in a blog post. Steve Bannon, former chief strategist to Donald J. Trump, has frequently claimed that Islam is not a religion but a "political ideology." While a guest on Bannon's radio show, Trump surrogate Roger Stone warned of a future America "where hordes of Islamic madmen are raping, killing, pillaging, defecating in public fountains, harassing private citizens, elderly people — that's what's coming."

135   *And, we are told, we are losing*: See *demagogue*: "a political leader who seeks support by appealing to popular desires and prejudices rather than by using rational argument."

135   *Never react to an evil in such a way as to augment it*: See *First and Last Notebooks*. In a list from 1933 Weil writes:

LIST OF TEMPTATIONS (to be read every morning)
Temptation of idleness (by far the strongest)
Never surrender to the flow of time. Never put off what you have decided to do.
Temptation of the inner life
Deal only with those difficulties which actually confront you. Allow yourself only those feelings which are actually called upon for effective use or else are required by thought for the sake of inspiration. Cut away ruthlessly everything that is imaginary in your feelings.

Temptation of self-immolation

Subordinate to external affairs and people everything that is subjective, but never the subject itself—i.e. your judgement. Never promise and never give to another more than you would demand from yourself if you were he.

Temptation to dominate

Temptation of perversity

Never react to an evil in such a way as to augment it.

136   *"the first idea a child must acquire"*: See "Chapter V" in *The Montessori Method.*

137   *hate crimes are on the rise again*: In February 2016, Trump told supporters at a rally in Charleston, South Carolina, a widely debunked story of how General Pershing allegedly dipped fifty bullets in pig's blood and then shot forty-nine of fifty Muslims he had lined up. The fiftieth person was spared, Trump said, but Pershing gave him the blood-soaked bullet and told him to go back to his people and tell them what happened. "He went back and said what just happened, and for twenty-eight years there was no terrorism," Trump claimed. "So I'm not saying that's a good thing, I'm not saying that's a bad thing. This is history, folks. We're either going to win or lose."

137   *a mosque under construction near Austin, Texas*: After the 2016 election, the following letter was sent to mosques around the country:

To the children of satan,

You muslims are a vile and filthy people. Your mothers are whores and your fathers are dogs. You are evil. You worship the devil. But, your day of reckoning has arrived.

There's a new Sherriff in town—President Donald Trump. He is going to cleanse America and make it shine again. And he is going to start with you muslims. He's going to do to you muslims what Hitler did to the jews. You muslims would be wise to pack your bags and get out of Dodge.

This is a great time for patriotic Americans. Long live President Trump and God bless the USA!!

Americans for a Better Way

138 *What wouldn't we all give to be carried to safety by someone we love?*: Leo Tolstoy writes in "A Letter to Hindu":

The recognition that love represents the highest morality was nowhere denied or contradicted, but this truth was so interwoven everywhere with all kinds of falsehoods which distorted it, that finally nothing of it remained but words. It was taught that this highest morality was only applicable to private life—for home use, as it were—but that in public life all forms of violence—such as imprisonment, executions, and wars—might be used for the protection of the majority against a minority of evildoers, though such means were diametrically opposed to any vestige of love. And though common sense indicated that if some men claim to decide who is to be subjected to violence of all kinds for the benefit of others, these men to whom violence is applied may, in turn, arrive at a similar conclusion with regard to those who have employed violence to them, and though the great religious teachers ... foreseeing such a perversion of the law of love, have constantly drawn attention to the one invariable condition of love (namely, the enduring of injuries, insults, and violence of all kinds without resisting evil by evil) people continued— regardless of all that leads man forward—to try to unite the incompatibles: the virtue of love, and what is opposed to love, namely, the restraining of evil by violence. And such a teaching, despite its inner contradiction, was so firmly established that the very people who recognize love as a virtue accept as lawful at the same time an order of life based on violence and allowing men not merely to torture but even to kill one another.

138 *We human beings are not born with prejudices. Always they are made for us*: These two lines are drawn from *Don't Be a Sucker*, an educational film created by the War Department in 1947 to warn against the rise of fascism, which argued that whenever we sacrifice the freedom and liberty of others, we jeopardize our own. In one particularly prescient monologue, the narrator tells his nearly duped foil:

You have a right to be what you are and say what you think because here we have personal freedom. We have liberty. And these are not just fancy words. This is a practical and priceless way of living. But we must work at it. We must guard everyone's liberty or we can lose our own. If we allow any minority to lose its freedom by persecution or by prejudice, we are threatening our own freedom. And this is not simply an idea. It is good, hard common sense.

You see, in America, it is not a question of whether we tolerate minorities—America *is* minorities. And that means you and me. So let's not be suckers. We must not allow the freedom or dignity of any man to be threatened by any act or word.

139   *I have an opinion on evil*: Director Victor Salva tells Nev Pierce in an interview for the BBC, "I have a controversial opinion about evil, because I don't believe evil exists. I believe that actions are dark and destructive but I don't believe evil is a thing. I believe it's a by-product of man's fear and desperation."

139   *we do not wish to acknowledge a painful truth*: Julius Charles Hare and Augustus William Hare write in *Guesses at Truth by Two Brothers*, "A man prone to suspect evil is mostly looking in his neighbor for what he sees in himself."

THE FALLOUT

148   *Karen did look into it and learned*: In 2011 a group of North County alumni reconnected on Facebook to plan a class reunion. Members noticed that many classmates, friends, parents, siblings, and children were being diagnosed

with unusual cancers, autoimmune diseases, birth defects, and other disorders. At that time, no one had any idea what might be causing them. Two of the alums, one of whom is a statistician, began conducting a health survey and creating disease maps in an effort to learn what was behind the bizarre illnesses. They discovered a disturbing cluster of illnesses concentrated near the creek and, even more disturbing, the cause.

152 "*They let Pandora out of the box*": According to Hesiod, Pandora was molded out of clay as the first human woman, and all the gods collected their "seductive gifts" in a jar (*pithos*) to present to her on the occasion of her birth. Opening the jar released these gifts, leaving only Hope (*elpis*) inside once Pandora realized her mistake and closed the jar again. Interpretation of this myth is difficult. The jar contained all the evils of humanity but also its good. Hope is left inside the jar, which either keeps hope for humanity or keeps it from them. It's not unlike the moment Eve eats an apple from the Tree of Knowledge in Genesis, which created an understanding of both evil and good. But how do we judge the eating itself? Was it evil? Was it good? There's a similar difficulty in interpreting the consequences of opening the nucleus of the atom. Some see this scientific revolution as the promise of completely clean power; others see only the promise of complete destruction.

155 *only one aircraft that opened its bay doors*: Robert Lewis, the copilot of the *Enola Gay*, reportedly wrote in his log as he watched the city incinerate, "My God. What have we done."

155 *At first, the Manhattan Project didn't have a name*: The story of Mallinckrodt's involvement in the Manhattan Project began on April 17, 1942, over a gentlemen's lunch. Arthur Holly Compton, a renowned physicist working at the University of Chicago's Metallurgical Laboratory, was visiting St. Louis, and with all the authority of the federal government, he planned to ask a favor of his old friend Edward J. Mallinckrodt Jr. They had known each other from the time Compton was head of the Department of Physics at Washington University, where Mallinckrodt served on the board of trustees and had endowed two separate departments and the Institute of Radiology. Mallinckrodt had taken over the family's "fine chemical" business when his father died in 1928. A year before Compton had won the Nobel Prize in Physics at the age of thirty-five and had since gone on to the University of Chicago to work on something called "fission." As nice as it might have been to catch up about career developments and life changes, these days the thing most occupying both their minds was the war, and this was exactly what Compton had come to speak to his old friend about.

For the past few years, Compton had been racing the Germans, he explained. Ever since Otto Hahn and Fritz Strassmann had discovered uranium fission in 1939, physicists around the world had been racing to see who could produce the first self-sustaining chain reaction. Leo Szilard, an Austrian physicist living in the United States, was on Compton's team in Chicago. Szilard had been the first to realize that neutron-driven fission of heavy atoms like uranium could be used to create a nuclear chain reaction that could yield vast amounts of energy—vast enough to power cities or destroy them. Szilard had tried to warn his colleagues that anyone who could harness a chain reaction like this could build the ultimate weapon. He had been the one to persuade his friend Einstein to write a letter to President Roosevelt urging him to support and speed up research in pursuit of the bomb and to secure more and better uranium ore for experiments before our enemies could. "A single bomb of this type, carried by boat and exploded in a port," Einstein wrote, "might very well destroy the whole port together with some of the surrounding territory."

By the time Compton was sitting down to lunch with Mallinckrodt, it appeared that the Germans were two years closer to the ultimate weapon than the Allies were, which meant they were on the verge of losing the war. The thing holding the Allies back, Compton explained, was that fission required purified uranium. He and his team had perfected a method in the laboratory for extracting purified uranium from ore using ether, but they could achieve it in only small quantities. At that time, all the purified uranium in the world could fit into a teacup. This brought Compton to his question: Could the chemists at Mallinckrodt use the methods developed in the lab to purify uranium for the war effort?

Mallinckrodt thought it over as he finished his usual lunch of cold cereal. He knew that three other companies had already declined Compton because they were either unable or unwilling to enter into this dangerous work. But it seemed a simple enough task to him. Mallinckrodt agreed and shook Compton's hand.

Mallinckrodt didn't know whether what Compton was

asking could actually be done, but at that point in the war, an average of 220 US service personnel were dying every day, nearly 6,600 every month. Whatever he and his workers could do to help, they would do willingly. They needed equipment not readily available in wartime, so workers at the New Jersey Mallinckrodt plant salvaged pipes, kettles, motors, steel drums, and pans and sent them by train to the plant in St. Louis. Engineers drew plans on scraps of paper, or chalked them on the floor or the wall, and carpenters and pipefitters brought the drawings to life the next day. They labored around the clock to install the equipment, and then around the clock again to test it. They were working in completely uncharted territory. The chemists tried out small experiments in the alleyways between buildings and in the empty corners of warehouses so that if an explosion occurred—and they did occur—it wouldn't damage the equipment.

Meanwhile, chemists from Mallinckrodt visited the Metallurgical Laboratory in Chicago, where Compton's team had discovered that uranium ore could be dissolved in hot nitric acid—making uranyl nitrate—and that if the hot nitrate was dissolved in ether, the uranium could be extracted and all the impurities washed away. The challenge for Mallinckrodt chemists when they returned home to St. Louis was to replicate these precise laboratory methods in a hastily constructed factory on a massive scale. The work was dangerous, and the scale of the operation made the measurements imprecise. No one knew the correct proportions of ether and ore to mix or the temperatures at which any of these materials could safely be combined. Ether is extremely flammable and explosive, and adding it to the hot slurry of uranyl nitrate seemed like a recipe for a massive explosion.

The first ore that arrived had been pressed into small cylinders, which the physicists in Chicago had tried to use in early attempts to initiate a self-sustaining chain reaction. They had been unsuccessful. The ore was a high-grade Canadian concentrate, but it wasn't pure enough. The physicists needed uranium without impurities. Boron, cadmium, and rare earth impurities in particular were problematic, since those elements absorbed any neutrons that might be liberated in a chain reaction.

The Mallinckrodt workers dumped this raw uranium ore into a giant tank of nitric acid, heating it until it formed a kind of thick slurry, to which they added cooled ether and then proceeded to rinse the impurities away. In these residues were dissolved all the elements that naturally occur in uranium ore besides the uranium itself: radium, thorium, lead, and all of the other radioactive progeny in uranium's natural decay chain. Some of these early residues were collected and set aside for later processing, and some were rinsed down drains or dumped into the Mississippi River, which flowed directly behind the Mallinckrodt campus. The residues were not what mattered: workers were focused on recovering the uranium from the ether, millions of dollars' worth, concentrated and reduced to pure uranium dioxide. This is what they sent back to Compton and his team in Chicago.

That November, a team of high school dropouts stacked cast blocks of this purified uranium under the squash courts stands on the campus of the University of Chicago. By the first Wednesday of December, "Pile-1," as it was called, stood twenty feet high, six feet wide, and twenty-five feet deep, and contained fifty-six tons of uranium oxide and uranium metal, all of which had been purified by Mallinckrodt. One of the physicists on Compton's team had calculated that with the fifty-seventh layer of blocks, there would be sufficient uranium in the pile to send it into a chain reaction. At 3:25 in the afternoon, Chicago Pile-1 achieved criticality. The scientists allowed the self-sustaining chain reaction to proceed for twenty-eight minutes before radiation surpassed preset safety levels. They halted the reaction and drank Chianti from paper cups to celebrate.

See "Legacy of the Bomb: St. Louis Nuclear Waste," a six-part series in the *St. Louis Post-Dispatch*, February 12 to 19, 1989, as well as Richard Rhodes's *The Making of the Atomic Bomb*.

156   *the new uranium division at Mallinckrodt Chemical Works*: At the peak of the Manhattan Project, roughly 160,000 workers labored in more than three hundred separate locations around the country. Among the many sites that eventually came to refine uranium for the Manhattan Project, the very first was Mallinckrodt Chemical Works in St. Louis, Missouri. All of these sites were classified at first. Ironically, the once so-called secret sites—Los Alamos National Laboratory, Oak Ridge National Laboratory, and Hanford—are now among the best known. We hear less about the Fernald Feed Materials Production Center in Ohio, the Maxey Flats disposal site in Kentucky, or Mallinckrodt Chemical Works in St. Louis.

At each of these locations, the purpose of the project was kept secret from all but a very few of the most senior staff. Men came to work and did their jobs. They were paid well and asked no questions.

156 *A ring of fire spreading outward for miles*: "Awe-struck, we watched it shoot upward like a meteor coming from the Earth instead of from outer space, becoming ever more alive as it climbed skyward through the white clouds," William Laurence wrote in a press release for the War Department. He had been the only journalist allowed on board the *Bockscar* when it dropped the plutonium bomb over Nagasaki; his account was the only one the government didn't censor. "It was no longer smoke, or dust, or even a cloud of fire. It was a living thing, a new species of being, born right before our incredulous eyes."

157 *workers were given the day off*: After the bombs were dropped on Japan in 1945 and the secret project became known, Secretary of War Henry Stimson sent gold pins stamped with the letter *A* (for *A-bomb*) to anyone who had worked on the bomb as an honor for their service. In St. Louis, Mallinckrodt executives put a bronze plaque over the entrance of Building 51 that read, "In this building was refined all the uranium used in the world's first self-sustaining nuclear reaction December 2, 1942."

158 *URANIUM ORE—PRODUCT OF BELGIAN CONGO*: According to Tom Zoellner's *Uranium*, Leslie

Groves, the commander of the Manhattan Project, sent Kenneth Nichols, one of his deputies, to meet with Edgar Sengier, then director of Union Minière du Haut Katanga, the Belgian mining company in possession of the ore, who had fled to New York from the Congo when World War II broke out, bringing along with him a stockpile of twelve hundred tons of Shinkolobwe's best uranium. According to Nichols, "Our best source, the Shinkolobwe mine, represented a freak occurrence in nature. It contained a tremendously rich lode of uranium pitchblende. Nothing like it has ever again been found."

The US contract with Union Minière specified that the United States had purchased only the uranium content and that all the nonuranium residues were to be held for eventual return to Belgium. This ore contained a higher concentration of the U-235 isotope of uranium, which is what the government needed for the bomb, rather than the more abundant U-238. This purity, which was good for making bombs, made the ore highly radioactive and therefore extremely dangerous.

Over the decades, the mine has often been closed and sealed to protect local villagers and the rest of the world from what it contains, but someone always arrives to reopen it—Union Minière, the Army Corps of Engineers, men who want to wreak their havoc on the world. Legend has it that Shinkolobwe is haunted by the spirit of a woman named Madame Kipese, who had been powerful when she was alive but had grown vengeful after her death. It's Madame Kipese who guards the mine, emerging at night to even the score, to deliver justice by claiming these men's souls.

159 *a 21.7-acre property just north of Lambert Field*: In the late 1970s, as the health effects of radiological contamination were beginning to become apparent, Oak Ridge National Laboratory conducted radiological testing of the airport site to make sure it was clean and evaluate it for future land use. They found the site, as well as the nearby ditches leading to Coldwater Creek, to be contaminated "above acceptable levels," and in the early 1980s, the entire 21.7-acre site, including these ditches, was put in line for remediation under FUSRAP—the Formerly Utilized Sites Remedial Action Program. Responsibility for cleanup bounced around regulatory agencies until 1997, when FUSRAP was transferred from the Department of Energy to the US Army Corps of Engineers. Officially, the Army Corps of Engineers finished remediation activities at the airport site in 2009, but even as I write this, it is still trying to figure out how far the wastes migrated off site. It has discovered contamination in drainage ditches leading away from the airport and all along Coldwater Creek, in the ballfields and in parks and gardens and backyards, in driveways and in people's basements.

161 *a series of letters from Cotter to the AEC*: "We believe deposit in the quarry to be the most satisfactory resolution of all substantial problems involved in disposition of the contaminated material," an attorney for Cotter writes in a letter dated April 23, 1971. "No conflict exists in this situation with the Commission policy against engaging in operations with private industry, since existing privately operated waste

disposal facilities are not designed in capacity or otherwise for disposition of material in the quantity and form involved in this situation."

A response to this letter comes a month later, on May 24, from Henry Nowak, director of the AEC's Division of Waste and Scrap Management. "First, what is the intent of the phrase 'or otherwise'?" he writes. "Does it mean that the licensed burial ground operators could not handle the material within the safety requirements of their present licenses? Is the judgement expressed in this statement that of the Cotter Corporation or that of the licensed burial ground operators?"

My stomach sinks when I read this letter. The tone is so snarky, so rude. Then in June, Cotter asked for permission to spread the leached barium sulfate across the surface of the site, bury it under four feet of clean soil, and then pave the whole thing over with asphalt. The AEC responded by saying that Cotter would first have to fund a radiological evaluation of the wastes, "including principal radioisotopes and their activities"; a feasibility study, including "a complete description of the proposed method of burial"; and produce a complete geological, hydrological, and geochemical survey of the site, and a study of the possible environmental impact. The letters from Cotter stop after that.

162 *"special exposure cohort"*: Credit belongs to Denise Brock, who is now ombudsman for the National Institute for Occupational Safety and Health (NIOSH), for getting the first

portion of this legislation passed. Brock's own father worked for Mallinckrodt Chemical from 1945 until 1958; during that period Mallinckrodt was processing pitchblende ore from the Belgian Congo and workers were receiving radiation doses in excess of a thousand rem (a unit of radiation dosage—today, the maximum allowable dose is five rem per year). Denise Brock's father was diagnosed with lung cancer, which spread to his brain and liver; he later also developed leukemia and died in 1978. In 2003, Denise Brock formed United Nuclear Weapons Workers, a nonprofit workers' advocacy group. Based on the Energy Employees Occupational Illness Compensation Program Act passed in 2000, which offers compensation to nuclear weapons workers who developed certain illnesses as the result of workplace exposure to radioactive materials, Brock petitioned the government to provide automatic compensation to former Mallinckrodt workers who meet certain criteria—they must have worked at least 250 days and must have been diagnosed with at least one in a list of twenty-two "specified" cancers (two of which are lung cancer and leukemia). In 2004 and 2005, she won that petition to create a special exposure cohort for Mallinckrodt workers, giving them access to tax-free compensation and medical costs and to death benefits if the worker has already died. It has been life-changing for so many families, many of whom now call Denise Brock "a true hero."

166 *Karen Silkwood was run off the road in Oklahoma*: Karen Silkwood worked at a plutonium fabrication site in Okla-

homa, where her job was to make plutonium pellets for fuel rods in nuclear reactors. At the time of her death, she had raised concerns about health and safety in the facility. Because of lax security, workers had been able to steal plutonium from the facility, and because of lax health standards, many of them brought plutonium home unknowingly in the form of contamination on their clothing. Karen had collected documentation proving that she herself had plutonium contamination on her own body and in her home. On November 13, 1974, she was driving to meet a reporter from the *New York Times* and her union representative when she died in a car crash under suspicious circumstances.

168   *14 billion years*: A recent art competition in France sponsored by Andra, the nuclear waste agency there, called on artists and collectives to design a warning that could last a hundred thousand years. Notable submissions included a forest of genetically modified trees that would grow an unnatural blue and a children's song that would perpetuate the warning through shared oral tradition. The prize went to Alexis Pandellé's *Prométhée oublié* (*Forgotten Prometheus*): an enormous scar on the ground suggesting a wound that never heals.

175   *The law he's referring to is*: CERCLA was authorized in 1980 in response to the discovery in the late 1970s of a large number of abandoned, leaking hazardous waste dumps. Under Superfund, the Environmental Protection Agency identifies hazardous sites, takes appropriate action, and sees

that the responsible party pays for the cleanup. The fund was established by what is known as a polluter-pays tax, but that tax expired twenty years ago and has never been reinstated. So for the last twenty years, there has been no fund funding the Superfund.

179   *the infamous Pruitt-Igoe*: The Captain Wendell O. Pruitt Homes and William L. Igoe Apartments, known more commonly as Pruitt-Igoe, were a racially segregated housing project on the Near North Side of St. Louis comprising thirty-three eleven-story towers and 2,870 units. In her 2011 doctoral dissertation, "The Manhattan-Rochester Coalition, Research on the Health Effects of Radioactive Materials, and Tests on Vulnerable Populations without Consent in St. Louis, 1945–1970," Lisa Martino-Taylor reveals that Pruitt-Igoe was chosen as a test site for the spraying of zinc cadmium sulfide; residents were told it was a "smoke screen" that could be used for protection in the case of an enemy attack. Not surprisingly, chronic lung and respiratory problems are associated with exposure to zinc cadmium sulfide, though the army denies any health consequences to the testing program, which ceased in 1994. See "Suit filed over government test-spraying in St. Louis during Cold War" in *St. Louis Post-Dispatch*. See also *The Pruitt-Igoe Myth* (2011), a documentary film directed by Chad Freidrichs.

179   *asking for water for her headless baby*: See *White Light/ Black Rain: The Destruction of Hiroshima and Nagasaki* (2007), a documentary film directed by Steven Okazaki.

182   *We ourselves are a source of radiation*: Humans have evolved a threshold for our own natural radiation and for one another's. Anything beyond that threshold is a risk: medical radiation, ultraviolet radiation, radiation from radio frequencies, radiation from contamination or nuclear bombs. Sufficient radiation exposure can cause changes in individual cells that can result in cancer growth.

The descriptions of the mechanism by which this happens are technical and laced with jargon, but my understanding is that the risk is expressed as a range of radiation exposure that causes sufficient damage to change a cell but not enough to kill it. Decades may pass between exposure and the onset of cancer.

One difficulty for researchers, especially in areas like St. Louis, is that cancer caused by radiation exposure is indistinguishable from cancer from hereditary causes or exposure to other carcinogens. Another difficulty is that it is not completely clear whether the wastes at the landfill present a definite cancer-causing risk. The scientific data don't prove that they will cause cancer, and also don't prove that they will not.

ART IN THE AGE OF APOCALYPSES

186   *art cannot rise to an occasion like this*: There was a time, not so long ago now, when I lost all faith in art. My job at that time had led me to Portland, Oregon, for TBA, a performance art festival, where I found myself one night watching a dance that began with this premise: What if one of the

postmodern choreographers from Judson Dance Theater had gone uptown to perform in the Harlem ball scene? The performance I attended was one of the festival's headlining events; its choreographer was a Guggenheim fellow, a Creative Capital fellow, a darling of contemporary dance. As I watched the performance—with the choreographer playing the Judson role, marching back and forth across the stage while a lesser-known (but in my view far more talented) performer vogues from the back of the stage to the front, over and over, until the voguer stops voguing to read a very long section of Sophocles' *Antigone* into a microphone—I very nearly walked out.

It's possible that the performance made me angry only because I had squandered what could have been a perfectly lovely evening in Portland to see a work I found pretentious and annoying. On paper, it had so much potential, but in practice, the piece by the much-loved and well-sponsored artist was about an obscure aesthetic conversation between minimalism and virtuosity, between pedestrianism and theatricality, with no acknowledgment whatsoever of the power differential between these two moments in movement history. I know of no one at Judson, for example, who was murdered for being a postmodern choreographer.

I did not understand the performance; I felt excluded from it, as if I had barged in and heard the tail end of a conversation not intended for me. More than anything else, I felt embarrassed. It seemed suddenly very stupid that I should have a job that required me to think and talk about art, since I felt, on the whole, very betrayed by the business of it all.

When I returned to campus the following week, I heard news that Dom Pérignon had commissioned Jeff Koons to make a limited-edition series of "Venus" balloon sculptures, each of which would contain a bottle of the luxury beverage, though there was no acknowledgment of the complexities of appropriating prehistoric images of fertility and the female form and selling them for twenty thousand dollars each. In fact, this famous investment-banker-turned-sculptor has adamantly disavowed any critical reading or intention in his work. Weeks later, Koons's similar but much more massively sized *Balloon Dog (Orange)*—a mirrored stainless-steel sculpture in the shape of exactly what it sounds like: an orange balloon dog—sold at a Christie's auction for $58.4 million, a record for any work by a living artist.

Meanwhile, that same month, Renisha McBride was shot in the back of the head on the front doorstep of a house in Dearborn, Michigan, and the National Oceanic and Atmospheric Administration released a report that the world's temperature over land and ocean surfaces had reached the highest levels since recordkeeping began in 1880.

I realize these two events may seem unrelated to the world of art making, but I think that may be precisely why I suddenly lost faith in the world of art making.

As the months of the semester ticked on, my job once again led me out of town for art, this time to New Orleans—more specifically, to St. Bernard Parish, just outside New Orleans, where I attended a performance of *Cry You One*, a work of experimental theater that is "part song, part story, part procession for our lost land." The audience was sorted into groups, each group led by an in-character performer, shuffled onto buses, and driven down the road a bit, where our group disembarked, and was paired off. Most of the people in our group had come with someone—in fact, a surprising portion of our group consisted of an acrobatic troupe in town for the New Orleans Fringe Festival—so pairing was nearly automatic. As the sole random loner, I got paired with one of the acrobats, a short, slender woman with long reddish hair, whose pupils pulsed like two giant saucers, a sign, I recognized, that she was high on Ecstasy.

Our leader—in character as a scientist, Dr. Carol Karl—took us on a brief tour of the wetlands with particular attention to all the ways in which the land had been destroyed: the levees just at the edge of this field prevented flooding but had caused land subsidence (or gradual sinking); then hurricanes had brought seawater inland, making the land unfit for growing crops; then the *Deepwater Horizon* spilled nearly 5 million barrels of oil into the ocean, and now with every storm, toxins blow in to further poison the land.

A disturbance at the center of the field brought each of the smaller groups together into one large group. Fiddles came out, the performers broke character and began singing and dancing, and it became abundantly clear that everyone in the audience was also expected to sing and dance. My partner, Ecstacy, took my hand and waist eagerly and waltzed me around the field, looking very lovingly at me with her pulsing-saucer eyes. I waltzed along with her, hesitantly, awkwardly, though what I really wanted to do was stand off to the side with my hands in my pockets and watch. In general, I do not like to be touched by strangers, and I certainly don't like to sing and dance with them with wild abandon without fair warning. Finally, Ecstasy gave up on me and let me make my way to the edge of the crowd, where I kept more or less conspicuously to myself.

After the singing and dancing concluded, we went back into our groups, where Dr. Karl led us into a small tent, where another performer told a story about how the ongoing environmental crisis continues to decimate her Houma ancestral lands. Then we were ferried across a narrow waterway, during which one member of my group asked if I was sick or something and why did I keep my hands always in my pockets. Back on land, the group was directed to climb to the top of the levee, and I cursed myself while I did so for being so reluctant to sing and dance with all the rest, *and what is wrong with me anyway, all shut-up-inside like this, and for what?* But when I reached the top of the levee, I saw the devastation for myself—a wasteland of dead trees, dead water, the corpse of a marshland for miles and miles in every direction it seemed. And at once, all the closed things inside me broke open. I saw the wasteland and understood myself. And like that, I was a little changed.

The performers took to their fiddles, leading the audience as one large group down the levee in a funeral parade for the land. I held hands with total strangers. I sang and danced like everyone else with wild abandon, with Ecstasy even.

187   "*What are the words you do not yet have?*": See Audre Lorde, "The Transformation of Silence into Language and Action."

187   *a poem is a "small (or large) machine made of words"*: I don't even particularly care that Williams means this different from how I take his meaning. In his Introduction to *The Wedge* (1944), he writes:

> To make two bald statements: There's nothing sentimental about a machine, and: A poem is a small (or large) machine made of words. When I say there's nothing sentimental about a poem I mean that there can be no part, as in any other machine, that is redundant.

188   *Looking is a form of recognition*: See also Lia Purpura's *On Looking*.

190   *There's a story I've heard . . . Rick Lowe tell*: See "Rick Lowe: Heart of the City," by Nicole Audrey Spector in *Guernica*, for a retelling of this story.

192   *Chekov says that art exists to prepare the soul for tenderness*: I'm going to be totally honest here. I've seen this quote attributed to Chekov by a whole lot a people, but I haven't been able to find the source.

193   "*Hope is an orientation of the spirit*": See Václav Havel, *Disturbing the Peace*.

194   "*[Art] means nothing if it simply decorates*": See Adrienne Rich, "Why I Refused the National Medal of the Arts" in *Arts of the Possible*.

THE FLOOD

Unlike every other essay in this book, this one is neither researched nor meticulously sourced. I wrote all of the material here during a single week when Hurricane Harvey dropped fifty-one inches of rain and threatened to drown my city. At the time, my husband was out being a hero by rescuing people from their flooded homes, and I was stuck in the house with the kids and the dog. I wanted to *do something*, so I started writing, which, after all of our emergency gear was packed and repacked fifteen times, was the only thing I could think to do. I posted an update each day on Facebook for my family and friends in other parts of the country about how we were faring, but eventually the posts became something more: short essays maybe, about community and sacrifice, and of course (because it's been on my mind for the past several years) about justice. When I made the posts public, they started going viral, in a way. Mostly I was just trying to convince people that they should care about what was happening here in Houston—to convince even the people who are living in this city and hadn't been affected by the flooding—even though I wasn't sure whether anyone is capable of compassion equal to the magnitude of this disaster. We all have our limits. I'm not sure whether empathy can be taught—it's innate to children, I know, who more often grow up to unlearn it rather than the other way around—but I think I've realized it can't be forced.

In the end, my own family was extraordinarily lucky: our house did not flood, though the water came, at its highest, after we evacuated—about fifteen horizontal feet from the house. Let me be clear: we have done absolutely nothing in our short lives to deserve this tremendous stroke of luck— what some in Houston are now calling "dry privilege"—just as the people who were flooded did nothing to deserve their flooding. In the past, I may have been content to count my blessings, to say, "Well, thank goodness it wasn't us," and then move on. Maybe I might ask someone I knew who had been flooded whether they needed anything. But writing these posts each day while the water rose made me realize that's not enough. Because if the way the city is built isn't "good enough" when it floods my neighborhood, or a third of neighborhoods, it isn't good enough when it floods anyone else's neighborhood either. Not even one.

As of this writing, six months after the storm, I don't know a single person who got flooded out of their house who is back at home yet. And it remains unclear just how much damage the storm caused, since there are very many people for whom this city is home who, because of their immigration status, might be reluctant to ask for help or assistance. For these vulnerable populations, the possibility of "recovery" remains deferred, impeded, fraught.

213   *theory of the Stranger*: See Georg Simmel, "The Stranger," in *The Baffler*, translated from the German by Ramona Mosse; the essay originally appeared in Simmel's *Soziologie*.

MAKE WAY FOR JOY

223   *Hate is "a hideous ecstasy"*: In *1984*, Orwell's classic cautionary tale, party members of Oceania are forced each day to gather together in a large auditorium for the "Two Minutes Hate." A video plays in the auditorium, and within moments the crowd begins rioting. Even Winston, Orwell's conscientious protagonist, joins in: "A hideous ecstasy of fear and vindictiveness, a desire to kill, to torture, to smash faces in with a sledgehammer, seemed to flow through the whole group of people like an electric current, turning one even against one's will into a grimacing, screaming lunatic."

It's uncanny how similar it is to the scene that played out across the United States at political rallies for a certain presidential candidate. Think, for example, of all the seemingly normal people who contort their faces and their hearts, who shout racist slurs, who shove and punch and grind down the single dissenter in their midst. The power to make others suffer is all the power they have. And all the while the man who has now become president goads them on, nodding, smiling, for no one's sake but his own.

Aristotle considered hatred a judgment about the type of person someone is and the types of suffering that person deserves. Hatred is the opposite of friendship, he wrote: if friendship is a state of wishing for the well-being of another for that person's own sake; hatred is a wish for another to be harmed, not necessarily for their sake but for our own.

225 *Running makes a tiny space for joy*: Rebecca Solnit writes, "When exactly do the abuses that have been tolerated for so long become intolerable? When does the fear evaporate and the rage generate action that produces joy?" See *The Encyclopedia of Trouble and Spaciousness*.

225 *"The happiest person in the world"*: Emerson actually wrote, "The happiest man is he who learns from nature the lesson of worship," but that was sexist, so I changed it. See "Nature, Addresses, and Lectures" in *Essays and Lectures*.

ACKNOWLEDGMENTS

There are many people whose advice, counsel, and encouragement were essential to the writing of these essays. My dear friends Casey Fleming, Joshua Rivkin, and Cameron Dezen Hammond, for starters, were generous enough to read portions of this book when it was not yet ready to show the rest of the world. Nick Flynn, Melissa Febos, Amber Dermont, Paul Otremba, and Sarah Sentilles listened to me talk through some of the thinking here, even as it was becoming the thinking here. I am grateful to the Fine Arts Work Center, especially Kelle Groom, for the several opportunities I have had to test this work on an audience, and to Kathryn Conrad and Anna Neill at the University of Kansas for the invitation to articulate my thoughts on the difficulty of speaking about sexual assault at a time when their own institution was under investigation for Title IX violations. I am indebted to my former high school classmate Melissa Flamson for drawing my attention to the story of a burning nuclear landfill in St. Louis; to Kay Drey, Faisal Khan, Ed Smith, Alison Carrick, Curtis Carey, Mary Peterson, Brad Vance, and Ben Washburn, who shared with me their experience, expertise, and professional opinion relating to this slow-motion disaster, and to the Just Moms—Dawn Chapman, Karen Nickel, Robbin Dailey, and Debi Disser—whose tireless advocacy on behalf of their families and their communities should inspire us all to demand more and do more for the community we all share. Ladies, I continue to hold you in my thoughts as you work to right these wrongs.

I am grateful to the editors of *Tin House*, *Dame*, and *Guernica* for providing a home to earlier versions of several of the essays from this book, and more than this, I am grateful that in a cultural moment where nearly every headline portends Armageddon, where fearmongering or thinly veiled propaganda is what increasingly passes for information, these safe harbors continue to offer writers the opportunity to do what seems like increasingly dangerous work these days: thinking about injustice in public, speaking truth to power, and fostering a sense of shared understanding with our fellow human beings.

I am deeply grateful to my agent, Ethan Bassoff, who is quite possibly an entirely perfect reader, advocate, and friend; to Liese Mayer, for seeing the potential of this book to be what it has become; and to Kathy Belden, my editor at Scribner, who has shepherded this writing, and in some cases my thinking before there was writing, with precision, generosity, and grace. I am indebted to you, truly. Thank you also to Rosie Mahorter, Ashley Gilliam, Kara Watson, Brian Belfiglio, and the entire Scribner team for your dedication to bringing this book into the world with me.

Thank you to my running partners, Shiro Zavahir Jaleel-Khan and Kathy Nguyen, for sticking with me (and my tricky hip) for all the very many miles, for talking me through difficult periods in my thinking and my running, and for coming back for me when I felt too tired to go on. Sharing the path with you has taught me many lessons that I will carry for many years to come.

Thank you also to the sisters of my heart, Paola Tello and Kelly Secovnie, for loving me so unconditionally all these many years—for laughing at the humor in my mistakes, for offering wisdom in my confusion, for listening to me talk about the issues central to this book even while I searched for language. I love you so damn much.

Thank you to my husband and partner in life, for always hearing me out, for knowing my process often better than I know it myself, for believing that I am capable of more than I think I actually am, and for supporting me in a thousand different ways while I manifest these as yet unrealized capabilities into being. And finally, thank you, always and forever, to our children, for teaching me each day of our lives what a flawed and beautiful place this world can be.

AN INTERVIEW WITH
LACY M. JOHNSON

Electric Literature

Yvonne Conza: *The Reckonings* opens with an epigraph by Djuna Barnes, *Nightwood*: "The unendurable is the beginning of the curve of joy." What does her epigraph represent to your essay collection?

Lacy M. Johnson: The epigraph reminds me of something someone once told me about injustice, which is that an injustice is anything that gets between a person and their joy. That's a broad definition, to be sure, but being forcefully and perhaps permanently separated from your capacity for joy is an unendurable experience — I know that from my own life — and I think that perhaps justice is the curve over which we bend the world or ourselves in order to make the condition of joy a possibility again.

YC: After your second book, *The Other Side*, was published, many readers asked you: "What do you want to

have happen to him, to the man who raped and kidnapped you?" What was your answer?

LMJ: Yes, this came up a lot at readings of *The Other Side*. People thought I must really want terrible things to happen to him, and I don't. I understand now where that question comes from, because it's the primary way we understand justice in this country—you do something bad, something bad happens to you, and therefore justice—but at the time I found it just so surprising. I didn't want to harm the man who kidnapped and raped me—a man I used to love—and vengeance didn't seem at all like justice to me. So, then I started wondering—if that's not justice, what is? What can be?

Around that time, I had recently completed a year of teaching writing in a pediatric cancer ward. One of the students was deteriorating really quickly and I noticed the ways her doctors and nurses attended to (and did not attend to) her pain. During the year when I watched while she was deteriorating and made to suffer in an attempt by doctors to make her well, the State of Texas executed thirteen men, and I noticed the ways these men are made to suffer by the criminal justice system in an attempt to make society well. Those two observations led me back to that question I kept getting every time I read from *The Other Side*. The question kept gnawing at me. It bothered me. Why are we so preoccupied with punishment? Why do we draw such pleasure—or tell ourselves we draw pleasure—from causing pain? And if I'm seeing this in my own life, in the ways others relate to my trauma, how does this question play out in other situations of injustice?

I write about that juxtaposition—a girl dying of cancer and men being executed—in "On Mercy." It was the first essay I wrote for this collection. That essay, and the way it helped to move my question forward, made me realize that I couldn't possibly answer the question with one essay or two essays, that I would need a whole book for it, and the situations I look at in the twelve essays in *The Reckonings* are ones that all feel very charged to me right now. They're very much about this current moment of, as you say, "tyrannies"—and tyrannies of various kinds. In "What We Pay," for instance, I write about the oil spill in the Gulf of Mexico, because while I was going to protests at BP headquarters and living near the Gulf, I kept asking, "How can vengeance be the right answer here?" And of course it's not—because it's at least partially our own unquenchable thirst for oil that sent the *Deepwater Horizon* into the Gulf in the first place—but then what is? And how do I use this situation to move the question a little bit further, to move my thinking a little bit more in the direction of an answer?

YC: In your book you talk about "the shut place" that you carry. Has that space inside of you changed?

LMJ: The reality is that trauma isn't as tidy as a narrative can be. That shut space is always changing—alternately cracking open or closed tight like a trap. The last essay in *The Reckonings* is called "Make Way for Joy," and it's about the ways I've found to move from pain and rage—"the unendurable"—toward a place of power and strength. I do feel more capable of joy now than I did before writing *The Other Side*, a book which brought its own measure of healing because writing the story of the worst thing that ever happened to me reintegrated that unspeakable moment into the fabric of who I am in a way that took the negative charge out of that moment, or it took the crushing pressure off, in a way—because I had found a way to end the story I thought I would never be able to tell.

Writing *The Reckonings* made me realize that the best way that I can create justice for myself—in the context of that personal trauma—is to create opportunities to experience joy, and to give myself permission and space to experience it. And perhaps that is true for some of these other situations as well—even if it is hard to imagine what that looks like from this point in history. That shut place I carry inside me—a place that trauma made—that's a work in progress, and the truth is I'm not ever going to not carry it. But it doesn't necessarily prevent me from feeling happy a lot in my life. I feel capable of great happiness, in fact, and find that I am able to be more present in the right here and now more often. I don't always feel so compelled toward attending to a different time—the memories of before or the anticipation of after or ahead or behind of wherever I am supposed to be. I feel much more able to be wherever I am, and I think that that's progress. That's all I can ask really: for progress. Justice is a project none of us will ever finish. That's why it's important we do this work from a place of love—not hatred and spite, which is what vengeance asks from us—because love gives us the power we need to keep going, keep fighting, keep striving together along that curve toward joy.

YC: How does your writing emerge?

LMJ: My writing always starts with a question . . . I teach this method of writing essays — to follow a question rather than the force of what you want to say. For me, the idea for an essay begins when something bothers me, when I have a worry. I do research and try to learn more about the thing that is bothering me, and the knowledge works to assuage the worry, to a degree, but the writing begins when the knowledge doesn't assuage the worry and a question forms in that gap, in that part of the worry that can't be assuaged.

With a book like *The Reckonings*, the overarching question is, well, if vengeance isn't justice, what is? Or what can be justice for me? Each essay has a question that is a part of that larger question, or is adjacent to it. What can take the form of justice in an essay like "The Fallout," for instance, where there is a landfill on fire in St. Louis that's full of nuclear waste that was left over from the Manhattan Project, when the injustice isn't even finished happening? How do we reckon with a crime we're still committing? How do we heal ourselves from an addiction to destruction when we can't stop destroying what we fear? We are addicted to war and violence, and we see the consequences that our addiction has on this community—which is just one community in a nation that has been ravaged by our obsession with killing better and faster and more destructively—not to mention how this has played out across the world, and continues to play out in the narrative we tell ourselves about our motives for carrying out this destruction, which is revealed to be false when you look even just barely under the surface.

There's this question about justice that permeates the whole book, and then there's a question for each essay, but I always work from a place of asking questions. And sometimes I think I arrive at an answer, or close to an answer, and sometimes all I can do is move the question a little farther along and move my understanding of the thing that worries me to a different place from where I began.

ABOUT THE AUTHOR

Lacy M. Johnson is the author of the memoir *The Other Side*, which was named a finalist for the National Book Critics Circle Award in autobiography, the Dayton Literary Peace Prize, the Edgar Award in Best Fact Crime, and the CLMP Firecracker Award in nonfiction. Her writing has appeared in the *New York Times, Los Angeles Times, Tin House, Guernica*, and elsewhere. She lives in Houston and teaches creative nonfiction at Rice University.